Teaching and Assessing Writing

*Recent Advances
in Understanding,
Evaluating, and Improving
Student Performance*

Edward M. White

Teaching
and Assessing
Writing

Jossey-Bass Publishers

San Francisco   •   London   •   1988

TEACHING AND ASSESSING WRITING
Recent Advances in Understanding, Evaluating,
and Improving Student Performance
by Edward M. White

Copyright © 1985 by: Jossey-Bass Inc., Publishers
350 Sansome Street
San Francisco, California 94104
&
Jossey-Bass Limited
28 Banner Street
London EC1Y 8QE

Library of Congress Cataloging in Publication Data

White, Edward M. (Edward Michael) (date)
    Teaching and assessing writing.

    (The Jossey-Bass higher education series)
    Bibliography: p. 291
    Includes index.
    1. English language—Rhetoric—Study and teaching.
2. English language—Examinations. I. Title.
II. Series.
PE1404.W48   1985   808′.042′071   84-43036
ISBN 0-87589-641-3 (alk. paper)

Manufactured in the United States of America

The paper in this book meets the guidelines for
permanence and durability of the Committee on
Production Guidelines for Book Longevity of the
Council on Library Resources.

JACKET DESIGN BY WILLI BAUM

FIRST EDITION
First printing: March 1985
Second printing: April 1986
Third printing: August 1988

Code 8510

The Jossey-Bass
Higher Education Series

Consulting Editor
Teaching and Learning

Kenneth E. Eble
University of Utah

Foreword

Teaching people to write is one of the chronic problems of American education, right next to teaching them to think, a closely related but even more knotty problem. Although hundreds of books at any period in time give instruction in writing, few squarely face the question of how we evaluate writing, clearly a vital part of teaching it well. In this respect, Edward White's book stands with Mina Shaughnessy's (1977) *Errors and Expectations* as testimony that there is something new under the sun even in books about writing. Specifically, both books aim at enlarging the reader's view of what is involved in evaluating writing and what that evaluating can best contribute to a person's learning to write.

The mating of teaching and assessing is not an accidental coupling. In practice, *teaching* writing is an eminently satisfying task. It is the grading of papers that makes it so much a burden. Edward White has not solved that conflict, but he has spoken directly to making the assessing of writing—not the mere grading of papers—an integral part of teaching. Whether for a teacher in a composition class or for the director in charge of evaluating the writing skills of large numbers of students, his book is precise and detailed about the best way to use evaluation toward the aims of developing writing skills.

Chief among the ways in which evaluation has become more sophisticated and useful to the teacher is the development of holistic scoring. At first confined to large-scale testing programs, this method of training readers to do multiple and carefully conducted readings of student essays is adaptable to all teaching situations. Beyond the method itself are the contributions such a method makes not just to identifying the elements that go into good writing but to illuminating what is meant by good writing in the large. What emerges is an analysis that reinforces what the student has achieved while still indicating directions for further development of skills.

Outside the classroom, educators are pressed to provide evaluations that can be trusted as specific measures of basic educational achievements. White has been a leader in the formation and conduct of large-scale writing evaluation programs in California and throughout the country. His years of experience provide the combination of theory and practice that makes this book the definitive one on the testing of writing skills in educational programs.

The author writes with a skill uncommon among teachers of writing and rare among those primarily engaged with educational tests and measurement. One of the simpler ways for improving writing in schools and colleges is to increase the numbers of teachers who write well. Edward White has written a book whose style and substance speak both to stimulating other teachers to write and to ways in which a shared enthusiasm and practice can lead to developing teachers' writing skills.

January 1985   Kenneth E. Eble
                                                  Professor of English
                                                  University of Utah

Preface

Public and professional concern over student writing skills and complaints about student writing performance recur regularly in both American educational literature and the press. We can count on peaks of interest every decade or so in why Johnny can't write, documented by some egregious examples of student prose, selected statistics, and solemn faculty opinion; nothing in education is so sure to attract attention as evidence that the younger generation is lacking in this most crucial basic skill—whether or not the concept of writing ability is well defined or responsibly measured.

However, this is not simply one more educational fad. American society expresses deep concern about student writing skills because almost everyone agrees that writing ability relates directly to learning and to thinking. The ability to express oneself is so central to education—and to the democratic political theory behind public education—that such attention ought to be expected, even welcomed. Writing is serious business at every level of education (consider, for example, the national investment in over a million students a year enrolled in college freshman composition courses), and educators ought not to be surprised at continuing public and professional demands that it be well done.

Most of those concerned about student writing, including most educators, assume that assessing writing ability is easier and more reliable than it is. Traditionally, such assessment has been either a haphazard matter of individual teachers grading papers or a supposedly objective compilation of statistics from large-scale multiple-choice tests. Only recently have the inadequacies of such measurement begun to lead to much improved ways of evaluating writing. As teachers of writing have moved more prominently into the area of measurement, the intimate relation between assessing and teaching writing has begun to emerge with startling clarity. Not only has the measurement of writing ability begun to change, but the teaching of writing itself has begun to change at the same time. In fact, issues of assessment affect all aspects of writing instruction, from its basic research through its teaching to the program evaluations that become the report card for the entire enterprise.

This book is designed to present recent advances in the theory and practice of assessing writing ability to all teachers in the schools and universities who use writing in their classes (including present or future English teachers and teachers in other disciplines) and to writing examiners, administrators, and others concerned about the effectiveness of student writing. This design means that the book also must consider recent advances in the several areas that writing assessment involves, such as writing research, theories of reading and responding to writing, program evaluation, and, most prominently, the assignment and grading of student papers as a central aspect of the teaching of writing. While by no means a testing handbook, this volume provides detailed guidance nowhere else available to those involved directly in assigning and evaluating student writing; while not planned as a book about how to teach, it is informed throughout by the pedagogical practice of an experienced teacher of writing. The book asserts as a basic principle that the testing of writing must be a professional concern of all teachers involved in the teaching of writing and that an understanding of the issues behind even large-scale testing will improve every teacher's ability to work in the classroom. Thus, by combining theory and practical applications, this book should be useful in a way that books devoted only to theory or only to pedagogical practice seldom are.

No one should imagine that student writing is the sole preserve of English teachers or that only English faculty should be involved in the measurement of writing ability. More and more teachers in the schools and universities, and in all disciplines, are becoming aware that writing is not only a means of recording what has been learned but also a student's chief means of learning. However, faculty outside the field of English often feel insecure when assigning or grading student writing, imagining that an English degree imparts specialized knowledge about writing that they do not possess; it is not widely known that only rarely do English majors, or even English Ph.D.s, receive instruction in the teaching or measurement of writing. This book is particularly designed to encourage the use of writing across the curriculum by presenting—without resorting to technical language—current knowledge in both the measurement and the teaching of writing; the materials included should assist faculty in all disciplines in assigning and responding to student writing more comfortably and effectively than they have to date.

Despite recent advances in the measurement of writing, much assessment of writing skill, particularly in the elementary and high schools, still takes place by means of norm-referenced multiple-choice testing of usage or mechanics. Many teachers are convinced that such measurement devalues writing itself and is destructive to their best work, but they feel powerless to deal with decisions (made "downtown" or "upstate") on which they are never consulted. Besides, the information about the testing of writing contained in this book has heretofore been confined to fairly small circles and is barely beginning to be known. How, the question arises at every turn, can informed teachers convince those in power to use and develop better types of tests?

As teachers at all levels have begun to discover, with some

astonishment, knowledge in this area is power. While some principals, assistant superintendents for instruction, school boards, chancellors, regents, and the like are impervious to argument, most are not; many of those who employ multiple-choice tests as the only measure of writing ability are properly defensive of their stance but will include actual writing samples if they can be shown that writing sample tests can be properly constructed, reliably scored, and economically handled. As a result, when concerned faculty have marshaled the evidence of need for—and shown themselves ready to take responsibility for—a writing testing program that supports the teaching of writing, they have found much more support than they ever imagined. This book gathers in one place the theories, arguments, and practices that will enable teachers to present a convincing case for such a testing program where it is appropriate.

Background

This book is the product of more than a decade of practical experience and theoretical speculation on the assessment of writing ability and its relation to the teaching of writing. Most of the materials presented here were developed from talks, presentations, and workshops I have given in the years since I was appointed the first director of the California State University (CSU) Freshman English Equivalency Examination in 1972. Much of what appears here in book form for the first time has become generally known and practiced among the dozen or so English faculty and test specialists who have been working intensively in the area of writing and its evaluation for the last decade. It is now time to move this knowledge and experience from the oral tradition and from journal articles into a more accessible and unified form.

My first action upon my appointment was to survey the field in order to build on current knowledge. I was a rather rare bird at the time, an English department head with all the usual credentials (a doctorate in literature and publications about literary figures) but with a deep interest in the teaching of writing. My fellow CSU department heads asked me to administer a writing test not because I was a test specialist (I was not) but in recognition of my slightly disreputable concern for freshman composition. My surveys of other "experts" (I had become one by appointment, not by experience) were most surprising: Virtually no one in the field of English claimed to know much about large-scale measurement of writing, although I was frequently referred from one person to another and back again. My search for literature on the subject was almost as barren. Aside from one book published by the College Board (Godshalk, Swineford, and Coffman, 1966) and a series of unpublished research reports from the Educational Testing Service (ETS), almost nothing useful turned up.

I did happen to have some experience as an essay reader for the Advanced Placement Program (AP), which is administered for the College Board by ETS, and I immediately set out to learn all I could from those in charge of essay testing at ETS. I received gracious and valuable help from the AP team, and I also had the great good fortune to spend time with several ETS specialists in essay testing—Evans Alloway, Paul Diederich, Alan Seder, and Albert Serling—all of whom taught me a great deal about the issues and problems of the field. While this book is not wholly complimentary to ETS, my debt (and virtually every writing tester's debt) to the basic work done by and at ETS is substantial.

It became clear as the English Equivalency Examination program began that the assessment of writing and the teaching of writing were intimately related and that many of the abuses in measurement and teaching resulted from the separation of the two. As our committees entered into essay test development, we found ourselves dealing with basic questions about the goals of writing instruction; as we included more and more faculty in our holistic scoring sessions, we noticed that changes in the teaching of writing were beginning to occur on many of the CSU campuses. The workshops I conducted at the Bay Area Writing Project in Berkeley (and then at many of its satellite projects as it grew to become the National Writing Project) proved that teachers in the grade and high schools also found the connection between measurement and teaching interesting

and important. Increasingly in recent years, faculty have come
to me after attending my workshops at schools and universities,
asking where the materials and ideas of the workshop could be
found in print. This book is my attempt to meet that need in
the larger context of general concern about student writing performance.

Plan of the Book

The first five chapters of the book are devoted to the issues and problems that lie behind the practice of teaching and
assessing writing ability. They discuss the relation of teaching
to assessment in current practice (giving some attention to
teacher hostility toward assessment), the history and meaning
of "basic skills" in reading and writing (emphasizing not just
mechanics but also individualization and independent thought),
and the ways holistic scoring of student writing supports a hu-
manistic attitude toward writing and writers, as well as providing a reliable way to rank essays. In addition, these chapters
examine the different definitions of writing proficiency and the
kinds of tests most suitable for various definitions and purposes,
including placement, proficiency, and equivalency tests. They
also look at the intimate connection between reading and writing. The last of these chapters, in particular, examines some theories of reading, paying special attention to recent literary
theory, and connects these reading theories to ways of responding to student writing and to holistic scoring.

Chapters Six through Ten focus on practical applications
of the principles presented in the first five chapters and include
materials as well as detailed guidelines for conducting writing
tests, from small classroom assignments to national programs.
The first of these chapters describes the development of writing
topics for test and classroom use and the importance of clarity,
validity, reliability, and interest in that development. This chapter is followed by one looking closely at three ways of scoring
writing, particularly holistic scoring, including sample questions
and scoring guides for each. Chapter Eight presents, for the first
time in book form, a detailed description of the organization

and management of a controlled essay reading, discussing such matters as personnel, materials, room arrangements, and scoring rates. This chapter should be valuable to those responsible for directing holistic essay readings, to teachers at all levels who participate in such readings, and to the increasing number of teachers who are using holistic scoring in their classrooms. The next chapter extends the discussion to writing research, which has made important contributions to teaching theory and practice in the last decade. The measurement problems of validity, reliability, and sampling are discussed in the context of the research. Chapter Ten considers program evaluation, describing more and less effective procedures, resources, and plans.

The last three chapters step back to give overviews of classroom, program, and research issues in teaching and assessing writing. Chapter Eleven details ways to avoid pitfalls in writing testing programs, beginning with problems in program planning and concluding with the political pitfalls that often follow the reporting of results. Chapter Twelve looks to the future, proposing a research agenda for this new field, particularly in the evaluation of the writing process and in the needed combination of cognitive research with rhetorical studies of modes of discourse. Chapter Thirteen focuses on the classroom, where the issues and practices discussed in the book can and should be applied.

The reference section that concludes the book is selective rather than comprehensive, designed for the teacher, evaluator, or other reader looking for further information on the issues and practices dealt with in the book.

Acknowledgments

Anyone who seeks, as I do here, to integrate much diverse information into a comprehensive whole is bound to deal with special fields of study in a way that some specialists may find elementary. But it is important to such complex areas of study as statistics (and the other areas whose turf I have invaded) that their contributions to the improvement of writing instruction be recognized and made more common property.

The various specialists with whom I have worked over the last decade will recognize their ideas embedded throughout this book and will, I hope, accept this general acknowledgment of the education I received, generally indirectly, at their hands. Those involved in the teaching and assessing of writing, most of whom will never see specialized articles in journals outside their own fields, need to have access to concepts and practices derived from many other fields. This book will be successful if it helps these readers expand their ability to integrate the many kinds of knowledge that their profession requires but that their preparation has often ignored.

Several chapters and parts of chapters appeared in earlier draft in various publications that have given permission for their use here. Chapters Two and Five appeared in early versions in *College Composition and Communication,* and materials from Chapter Four appeared in *College English,* both of which are published by the National Council of Teachers of English (NCTE). NCTE has also given permission to reprint the analytic scale in Chapter Seven and the mode diagram in Chapter Six, both of which appear in Cooper and Odell (1977). Parts of Chapter Three appeared in *Selections,* published by the Graduate Management Admissions Council. One holistic scoring guide and the primary trait scoring guide in Chapter Seven derive from materials developed by Research in Effective Teaching of Writing, funded by the National Institute of Education through the Foundation of the California State University, Edward M. White, principal investigator. One of the holistic scoring guides in Chapter Seven, the two sample student papers for the scoring guide, and the reliability study in Chapter Nine were first published in the 1973 and 1977 volumes of *Comparison and Contrast: The California State University Freshman English Equivalency Examination,* edited by Edward M. White and published by the California State University. The student writing contained in Chapter Thirteen was originally printed in *The Best of 495* (White, 1983).

I also owe special debts to Albert Serling, who first showed me the complexity of the subject; to Rex Burbank, who taught me much of what I know about holistic scoring practice;

to Linda Polin, whose ideas helped shape Chapters Nine and Ten and who prepared a first draft of Chapter Nine; and to Kenneth Eble, who, as consulting editor for Jossey-Bass Publishers, was a constant source of wisdom and encouragement during the production of the manuscript.

San Bernardino, California   Edward M. White
January 1985

Contents

Foreword   ix

Preface   xi

The Author   xxiii

1. Reconsidering the Links Between Teaching and Assessing Writing   1

2. Development and Uses of Holistic Scoring   18

3. Measuring Writing Ability by Using Proficiency Tests   34

4. Selecting Appropriate Writing Tests   59

5. How Theories of Reading Affect Responses to Student Writing   84

6. Designing Effective Writing Assignments   100

7. Evaluating and Scoring Writing Assignments   120

8. Organizing and Managing Holistic Essay
    Readings   149

9. Understanding and Using Recent Writing Research 170

10. Evaluating Writing Programs and Projects   195

11. Avoiding Pitfalls in the Testing of Writing   216

12. Continuing Issues in Teaching and Assessing
    Writing   240

13. Helping Students Improve Their Writing:
    Some Practical Approaches for the Classroom   251

    References   291

    Index   299

The Author

~~~~~~

Edward M. White is professor and former chair of the Department of English at the California State University, San Bernardino. He received his B.A. degree (1955) from New York University and both the M.A. (1956) and Ph.D. (1960) degrees from Harvard University, focusing on literature.

Since 1970, when White published his first freshman composition textbook, his major research concern has been the teaching of writing. In 1972, he was appointed the first director of the California State University (CSU) Freshman English Equivalency Examination, a position he held through 1983. During those years, he served the nineteen-campus CSU in several additional capacities, coordinating systemwide activities in credit by examination, in the development of an English Placement Test, and in overall administration of its writing skills improvement program.

White has given many workshops on measurement and the improvement of teaching for such institutions as the Bay Area Writing Project, the Lily Endowment, and the National

Council of Teachers of English; he has consulted on test development with the Educational Testing Service, the National Assessment of Educational Progress, the American Association of Medical Colleges, and many universities, community colleges, and school districts. His articles on measurement and teaching have appeared in many journals, including *College English, College Composition and Communication, Basic Studies, College Board Review, Voice,* and *The Chronicle of Higher Education.* His series of monographs describing the English Equivalency Examination (*Comparison and Contrast,* 1973-1981) is available through ERIC.

White has been principal investigator for Research in Effective Teaching of Writing, a project funded by the National Institute of Education, 1980-1985. Initial reports on the project have been entered in ERIC (1983) and published in *WPA,* the journal of the Council of Writing Program Administrators. White and his research team are preparing a volume derived from this project describing the comparative results of different writing programs on faculty and students in different settings.

Teaching and Assessing Writing

~~~~~~

Recent Advances
in Understanding,
Evaluating, and Improving
Student Performance

Reconsidering
the Links Between
Teaching and Assessing
Writing

Most of those who teach writing in America dislike and distrust testing. While this negative attitude stems in part from a general distrust of the use of numbers to measure people, a more important factor is the great gulf that now exists between the measurement and the teaching of writing. Many writing tests currently are imposed from outside the classroom, decided on by those unacquainted with either the students or the course of study, and scored in more or less mysterious ways. The widespread use of multiple-choice mechanics and usage tests trivializes reading and writing from the earliest grades through many university programs. In addition, test results are used routinely to support or suggest incompetence on the part of the students, the teachers, or both. It is no wonder that so many of those teaching in American classrooms, from first grade teachers wondering about the machinery that will bar some children from getting into second grade to college professors seeing their best students attempting to pass graduate record or law school entrance examinations, consider testing to be at best a necessary evil and at worst a destructive intrusion into the learning process. Teachers of writing in particular, charged in part with a concern for the creativity and individuality of students, normally consider testing to be a dirty word and an offensive action.

There is no point in denying that most testing of writing is poorly done, destructive to the goals of teaching, and improperly used. No sensible person could defend current practice, which has set up three hostile camps: the teachers, avoiding and undermining testing programs when they can, in the name of humane teaching; the public, with its general distrust of education, naively believing any number set out in the name of testing as if it revealed an unpleasant suspected truth; and test professionals, often aware of the uncertainty of their findings and unskilled in coping with more than routine number crunching and established item types, trying feebly to inform teachers and the public of technical issues with large political and economic impact. The present situation could hardly be worse.

Closing the Gap Between Teaching and Testing

Since one major tenet of this book is that testing not only can be but should be a vital part of every writing teacher's professional equipment, this opening chapter confronts directly the almost unanimous opposition on the part of teachers to the testing of writing. Thus, I must say at the outset that the assessment concepts and procedures that are vital to the teaching of writing are very different from the confused, inefficient, and inappropriate testing that most writing teachers rightly condemn. When the testing of writing is done properly, it supports teaching both practically and conceptually, involves teachers in test planning and test design, and helps bring recent discoveries about the teaching of writing into the classroom.

It is not hard to see why most testing of writing is done poorly. Most teachers of writing know little or nothing about testing, and most specialists in testing know even less about the teaching and learning of writing. Furthermore, both groups of professionals suspect each other, and they confirm their suspicions by rarely communicating with those in a distant, slightly disreputable field. To be sure, not all of this distrust is unfounded. Writing teachers rightly believe that test specialists

simplify writing and slight what is most important, while testing specialists rightly believe that teacher ignorance of testing
and teacher arrogance about that ignorance lead to unfair treatment of students. Meanwhile, educational administrators and
test directors face demands for test scores, program evaluation,
and general accountability for resources, while the public wants
some hard numbers to show that the schools and universities are
doing their jobs. And so the testing goes on, as it must.

The gulf between teachers and test specialists becomes
most apparent when people of good will try to bridge it. I have
watched test consultants grow red-faced from frustration as
they tried to explain the elementary statistics behind multiple-
choice test construction to a friendly group of writing teachers
who could not or would not understand; the routine and unexamined faith most writing teachers bring to essay testing, despite the poor design and unreliable grading it usually displays,
drives test specialists wild. I have also watched a committee of
distinguished composition faculty patiently (for the first few
hours) try to educate a test consultant about writing; the consultant, typically, had such a narrow, blind commitment to
multiple-choice testing that the committee voted to disband
rather than continue to work with him. The usual result of
these failed attempts at communication is to reinforce the prejudices that militate against the understanding that is so badly
needed. Writing teachers typically show contempt for test specialists, whom they thus brush off as ignorant technicians; test
consultants, instead of learning about the importance and possibilities of essay testing, spend their time and energy trying to
manipulate the (usually mandatory) faculty committees, which
they see as obstructing their task with meaningless and unmeas-
urable complications.

The peculiar irony of this unfortunate situation is that no
one gives more test grades than writing teachers, even as they
articulate their unwillingness to trust or even to learn about the
fairly simple concepts of measurement that will make their job
easier and their teaching more effective. In turn, the distrust
generated by this attitude is returned by administrators as well
as by test professionals, and it sometimes leads to the deliberate

omission of teachers from programs designed to measure writing ability. The best hope for changing this situation rests with improved communication between teachers and test specialists and with greater understanding on all sides of the issues and concepts that underlie both perspectives on student writing.

This book is designed to support—from whatever part of the academy they may come—those who ask students to write in their classes or who become involved with programs that test writing ability at any of three different levels: the classroom, the campus (as in a placement or exit proficiency test), or the large-scale program that is multicampus, statewide, or national in scope. Of course, issues in measurement at these levels overlap. The same kinds of problems that may hamper national testing programs also tend to distort classroom teaching; put positively, better understanding of how to test writing at any level will improve classroom teaching at all levels. Furthermore, a teacher who knows how to use testing for more than mere grading in the classroom (to reduce writing anxiety, foster rewriting, develop positive attitudes toward the writing process, and so on) will be an informed and valuable member of any test committee; and a test specialist or educational administrator who understands the intimate relation of testing to teaching will be in demand at all levels of education.

In recent years, a very small cadre of writing teachers has developed some expertness in testing, and a handful of test professionals has come to understand the complexity of writing and writing measurement. A few school and university administrators have supported advanced testing and evaluation designs for writing programs and, in so doing, have gained an appreciation for the difficulties and rewards involved. Until that group grows larger, however, the testing of writing will continue to manifest the special problems that come from ignorance as well as the general problems that stem from the lack of communication endemic to academic programs in general.

The last decade or so has seen enough changes in both the teaching and the testing of writing to suggest that the dismal picture I have been painting is ripe for change. Indeed, there already are signs that this change is beginning to take place. Such huge educational systems as the California State University, the City University of New York, and the Department of Higher Education of the State of New Jersey have instituted major testing programs in writing by bringing together professional test specialists, evaluators, and teachers. Just as encouraging are the widespread in-service workshops sponsored by the (San Francisco) Bay Area Writing Project—intense summer sessions that bring together teachers, professors, writing researchers, and those trained in testing. Furthermore, recent advances both in research in the teaching of writing and in the measurement of writing have led to new communication at the university research level between teachers and test specialists. More and more professionals are recognizing the need to bridge the gap that has led to the present situation.

Thus, the field of writing is particularly ready for the reconsideration of testing and its relation to the teaching of writing that this book proposes. Writing research (which at long last has developed significant findings for teachers) depends on measurement for validation of its findings, and the advances in testing chronicled in this volume have in fact allowed some of this writing research to occur. The proficiency testing movement, with its ubiquitous demand for certification of literacy at all levels from grade school through graduate school, has created an important cadre of English teachers who have made it their business to become specialists in testing—as a form of professional self-defense. Additional self-defense in measurement has become necessary as we have been asked to justify huge national and institutional expenditures on writing programs; outsiders using uninformed or (as one all-purpose evaluator puts it) "goal-free" evaluation will evaluate writing programs if writing teachers are unwilling or unable to participate in more responsible program evaluations. No sensible person in these academic hard times can object to the request that an expensive program show that it is producing some benefits; the only question to be asked is who is to evaluate writing programs and how.

These issues in measurement now lie at the door of those who teach writing, and by their presence they suggest that writing teachers can no longer afford the luxury of blind opposition to testing. However, it is always easy for teachers committed to the classroom to convince themselves that there are others to handle large professional issues, while their most essential task remains working with their own students. If measurement had no implications for the conduct of writing instruction, the testing issues in this book would remain of interest principally to specialists and concerned administrators, no matter how many exhortations to professional responsibility were included.

It is thus of primary importance that virtually all writing teachers who have become professionally involved in measurement have found their teaching changing profoundly. For example, consider the case of a college faculty member or a high school teacher who (usually unwillingly) finds himself or herself a member of an essay-testing team responsible for a multicampus writing assessment program. Since essay test development requires decisions about the kind of writing to be required, the committee needs to discuss such issues as the rhetorical mode or modes to be examined and what quality of writing might reasonably be expected of particular students under particular conditions; as the team considers many possible writing topics, rejecting most and choosing some for pre-testing, discussion about good and bad topics will occur; as the committee reviews the results of pre-testing and develops procedures for scoring the papers, discussion about reliable and fair grading must occur. Since these issues are of major importance to every writing class, the teacher who fails to see their application in his or her working life must have an extraordinary imperviousness to experiential learning.

When we speak of the opposition to testing on the part of writing teachers, we are not being strictly accurate. Their opposition is not to testing itself but to testing imposed by those outside the classroom, or, less charitably put, to less subjective evaluation than usually goes on. The great achievement of modern essay testing is that it allows the teacher enough subjectivity to deal with each student as an individual while at the same time reducing the partial, arbitrary, and whimsical nature of the grading of writing. In short, those who learn from the best testing procedures and carry those procedures back to their cam-

puses and their classrooms have learned how to tame the beast.
They can regain power over the testing of their students, since
knowledge leads to power, and hence they can use this power
for the benefit of their students and for the attainment of the
best goals of education in reading and writing.

An even more compelling reason for writing teachers to
consider an understanding of evaluation an indispensable part
of their professional development concerns the strange paradox of revision: professional writers revise constantly, while
naive and untrained writers, whose need for revision is much
more severe, almost never revise. Routinely, teachers at all
levels exhort, command, or require revision, but almost always
in vain; the typical student paper is still written the night before
it is due, and the typical student has absolutely no idea of the
quality of the paper before (and often even after) the instructor
has read it. Instructors spend endless hours meticulously marking papers in the belief that grading papers is the same as teaching writing, with irrepressible and unwarranted faith that conventional teacher comments on present papers will affect the
writing of future papers.

When we look at this situation, in all its busy futility, the
pressing need for teacher sophistication in evaluation becomes
inescapable. Even serious students fail to revise, by and large,
because they do not know how to evaluate their writing; since
they see nothing to be changed (until the writing instructor uses
the arcane and incomprehensible grading process), they see no
need for revision, and hence they do not revise. Since the grading process normally remains not only mysterious (it is even
written in quaint symbols) but irrational (one teacher praises
the same things another teacher condemns), most students find
revision futile: Who knows what the teacher really wants this
time? So revision waits until after the teacher has commented,
if revision occurs at all, and then the new work responds only
minimally to teacher corrections, often making things worse
rather than better.

Experience with and understanding of the best procedures in essay testing will allow the writing teacher to teach revision much more effectively. A teacher with awareness of issues

why teach revision

in the creation of writing topics will make assignments with such clarity that the students will really know what is wanted; such a teacher will not hesitate to discuss the purpose and possibilities of these topics in class and will be ready with various "pre-writing" activities to help get students started. When papers or drafts of papers are turned in, such a teacher will prepare, or work with the class to prepare, a scoring guide that describes with some precision the differences between successful and unsuccessful papers; such a scoring guide allows the students to be part of the grading and responding process for one another's papers as well. Finally, the very openness of the grading process, with its positive tone (a typical scoring guide will caution readers to reward students for what is well done rather than merely punish them for what is not well done), encourages revision, since students learn to see the differences between the various qualities of writing and hence can begin to see what can be done to improve their work.

I am not suggesting that a magic formula called evaluation will easily transform the world of writing instruction. Nothing in the teaching of writing is that simple. Rather, I am saying that an understanding of some of the best procedures in the testing of writing not only will be important for those concerned with research and with student or program evaluation but also will be of substantial value for all writing teachers in their classes. It is time for teachers of writing at all levels to put aside their reflexive reaction against testing so that they can replace the inappropriate tests that still dominate the field with better, more supportive, more useful devices. It is time for us to learn from the recent advances in essay testing how to be better teachers of writing. We cannot consider ourselves fully professional until we do.

Defining, Teaching, and Measuring Basic Skills in Writing

Any discussion of the testing of writing needs to begin with a consideration of the subject itself and of ways of teaching and learning that subject. A theory of knowledge of the subject must precede any practice of testing that is to make coherent sense and that is to be useful to those teaching and learning; indeed, when theories of knowledge and of content are not taken into consideration, ill-considered tests can lead to a thoughtless curriculum as teachers wind up teaching to inappropriate tests.

This book is not directed to English teachers alone. Happily, at all levels of education, the teaching of writing at long last is going on across the curriculum, across the disciplines, across the various specializations; the measurement of writing ability calls for even wider participation—by all those teaching writing as well as various administrative and psychometric specialists. Nonetheless, most people connect the teaching of writing with the teaching of English (the discipline specifically devoted to reading and writing), and thus we need to begin our consideration of the writing curriculum and testing with a brief look at the discipline of English. Inappropriate testing has been destructive to the teaching of writing for the last two generations, during which such teaching traditionally has been entrusted to English teachers at all levels. One important reason for this destructive testing emerges from the contradictory purposes of the English curriculum as it has developed in America.

Multiple-choice usage testing has become so predominant as a means of testing writing that it has come to define the entire field of English for most of the population. Such testing often asks students to identify supposedly correct spelling, usage, or grammar out of context or to find errors in testwriter prose—sometimes technical errors on trivial matters that have little to do with communication or even with normal academic writing. But these are the tests that everyone remembers from school days and that serve to define the subject of English in the public mind. Every contemporary English teacher dreads the social moment when a stranger asks, "What do you do?" Those who confess the truth must confront the inevitable response, as the inquirer turns away with a scowl: "English was always my worst subject; I'd better watch what I say." New teachers, excited about English as a creative and even a revolutionary subject with great writers, great subjects, and great ideas, are puzzled or infuriated by such a response. I remember the murderous thoughts that crossed my mind after one of my daughters' boyfriends found out my profession and asked, with genuine perplexity, "What kind of job is that for a grown man?" Why indeed should a grown person spend his or her days pointing out picky errors in other people's language to no useful purpose? Or, even more to the point, how can the grand subjects of reading and writing be rescued from the trivialization they have come to receive, usually in a well-motivated quest for "basic skills"?

It is important to understand the issues that have shaped the English curriculum if we are to make sense of the contradictions and confusions that make the teaching and testing of writing so difficult. Particularly in these days of proficiency testing of basic skills in English, a clear understanding of the contrasting and conflicting goals of English instruction is necessary if we are to define the term *basic skills* with clarity and then proceed to measure these skills responsibly. It is an inescapable fact that English is called upon to accomplish conflicting ends for a society with complex needs: English studies must both socialize and individualize students, despite the innate contradictions between these two goals.

English as a Socializing Discipline. The history of the American public high school helped set its basic tone and mission: to socialize and conventionalize students so that they will fit into a demanding, work-oriented society. The development of English as a discipline has been well chronicled by D. J. Palmer (1965), A. N. Applebee (1974), Richard Ohmann (1976), Alan Hollingsworth (1972)—to whose workshops and speeches the following discussion is particularly indebted—and others. It is a long and complex story, beginning with the dissenting academies in seventeenth-century England; the developing curriculum there showed a continuing concern for rhetorical and grammatical issues and at a late date was finally enriched by the addition of literature as an important study in its own right. Our concern here is not with the history in itself but only with the way that history has shaped current policies and goals.

When the citizens of Boston created a new kind of secondary school in 1821, it was designed to bring "the children of the poor and unfortunate elements of the community" into "the active life," that is, into the trades and into active citizenry but specifically not into the university. After some squabbling about names with the headmaster of the Boston Public Latin Grammar School (founded in 1635 to prepare university students), the new school came to be called the English High School. By 1870, the American high school, based on the Boston model, had appeared in most cities able to support public education. Its goals by that time had changed only slightly: Its mission in large part remained to prepare the children of the dispossessed and middle classes for business and the trades, for comfortable participation in ordinary social intercourse, and for enthusiastic spectatorship at patriotic and (increasingly) sports activities. Presently, the schools also prepare students for universities and make some gestures toward introduction to science, literature, languages, and the arts; that is, they have added some Boston Latin motifs into the Boston English curriculum.

A major part of schooling must be to socialize young people into their culture by teaching them its accepted truths, history, myths, rituals, crafts, and manners. This is not a surprising discovery, since education in all human societies traditionally has fulfilled this mission as its part in the transmission and preservation of culture. Furthermore, it should come as no surprise that English as an American school subject should be asked to play a major part in this socialization process. Manners are crucial to social standing and to social mobility, and linguistic etiquette is the most important of all manners in a highly verbal society.

When we look at the jobs assigned to English in its function as a socializing discipline, we find them affecting writing instruction at all levels. Grade school students first learn to write on the lines from left to right and then proceed to study spelling, vocabulary, and capitalization; the high school adolescent practices accepted punctuation and usage; the college student memorizes footnote style—all in the name of learning English. Do it the *right* way, we tell the student (quite properly, by the way) or you will be penalized. And the "right way" is defined very simply: It is the way it is done.

Think of spelling, for example, the archetypical socializing study, the darling of those who in the name of "standards" want education to focus on rote drill. The fact that Shakespeare spelled his name in an engaging variety of ways did not mean he was a bad speller; there was no such thing as a bad speller until much later when spelling began to matter. When printers began to normalize spelling, for their convenience, and when the written and spoken language diverged to the degree that simple phonetic spelling became impossible, spelling became (as it now is) an important social skill, comparable to knowing how to use knives and forks at table. Spelling is important—and important for English teachers to attend to—because manners are important for social mobility, and good spelling suggests good linguistic upbringing. Spelling is important not because it makes sense, or because it is good mental discipline, or because it has anything at all to do with thinking; spelling is important solely because people will think you are stupid if you fail to spell words the way everyone else spells words.

why teach revision

Spelling, or footnote style, or a dozen or so other matters that are part of the conventions of language, ought not to pose the theoretical problems for teachers that they often do. As long as we recognize that an important part of our job is to socialize students and that it is by no means the most important part of the job, we should be able to go about it with good will and good humor. It is not a sin to spell badly; it is a social indiscretion, rather like wearing torn jeans to the prom.

Of course, there are several problems with this socializing aspect of the English discipline, and I want to look briefly at these problems. There are those who go to extremes on the matter, either ignoring the socializing skills entirely or (more usually) believing that those skills are all that should be taught; both of these extreme attitudes are simply unprofessional, wherever they appear, and are quite indefensible. Again, to consider English solely or principally as a socializing discipline implies a particular political and intellectual attitude toward education. It defines education as did the parent from Orange County who said, "We're paying you to *educate* our kids. Stop messing with their minds"—as rote training without intellectual content. And finally, the socializing skills, in English as in other areas, are not particularly intellectually challenging either to teach or to test, and so they become the easy way out for those prone to formula teaching and mechanical testing.

The socializing skills, then, are an accepted, appropriate, and necessary part of English at all levels. While they are neither the most important nor the only basic skills in the field, they form the code of linguistic behavior that allows more important matters to take place, and hence they need to be taught and tested. They are particularly valuable skills for students who are striving to move beyond the social level of their parents (since codes of behavior are learned at home), and all teachers should make plain the social value of these imitative skills without pretending that they have intellectual content. The particular danger of the socializing nature of English is that it is too often taken to be the major or even the only content of the field. Far too often, this relatively minor part of the discipline is defined as the basic skill of English, valued out of proportion, and tested in a rote fashion that demeans the field, the students, and the teachers.

There is, of course, no very clean break between the socializing skills of writing (or of behavior, for that matter) and substantive skills of expression. Some faults of sentence structure, such as fused sentences or comma splices, seem to be no more than careless breaches of linguistic etiquette; others, such as lack of clear predication or clarity of verb tenses, seem to reflect issues related to the deep structure of the sentence, the thought, or even the mind. The accuracy of vocabulary in expressing ideas is usually no trivial matter, although accidents of dialect or usage may be. As mere socialization shades into real substance, reasonable people will differ on the importance of this or that aspect of writing. But, unfortunately, the overall emphasis on the least significant aspects of writing in most so-called writing tests leaves no doubt that socialization, not writing, is what is being tested.

English as an Individualizing Discipline. While English must be seen in part as a socializing discipline, the major thrust of the modern English curriculum is directly contradictory to socialization. If the principal rule for socialization is to perform in conventional ways, the overriding motivation for good writing (or good reading, for that matter) is to think for oneself. We do not want creative spelling or punctuation, but we do want creative writing and thinking. We do not aim for new responses to the issue of subject-verb agreement, but we demand that students read and respond to literature or to political ideas or to issues in their lives for themselves.

The sharp contrast between these two aspects of English is often submerged in practice; since to be professionally responsible we must encourage both socialization and individualization, English instruction needs to contain and manage the innate contradiction. But we ought to be aware of the different kinds of demands the two aspects of English make on students: Spell and punctuate the way everyone else does, but do not simply tell me what everyone else thinks—you are required to present your own ideas, to have an individual response, to develop your own sense of identity through your reading and writing.

Why teach spelling

The tradition out of which this individualizing discipline emerges is ancient indeed: Classical rhetoric stressed invention, the discovery and elaboration of one's own thoughts, while the creation and reading of literature has always been so personal as to border on the revolutionary. The creation of a poem is a powerful political statement of nonconformity punishable by imprisonment or worse in many parts of the world; the transformation of marks on a page into meaning can only occur within a creative individual mind. The exiling of Ovid or Solzhenitsyn, the imprisonment of Defoe or Timerman, the deaths of Socrates or Mishima, the routine murders of writers by despots, and the underground circulation of writing under oppressive regimes all point to a vital and nonconformist tradition that is absolutely "basic" to the study of reading and writing. English as an American school subject nurtures the individualizing imagination through challenging reading and writing and supports the very foundations of political democracy by demanding independent thought and individual responses to ideas. While the socializing aspect of the discipline reduces behavior to more or less acceptable parts, the individualizing thrust treats people as units, as wholes greater than the sum of their behaviors.

Although it is unprofessional to ignore the conventionalizing nature of parts of the English curriculum, it is far more unprofessional to ignore the individualizing nature of the core of English. Basic skills in English ought never, at any level, to be defined in such a way as to omit or minimize the importance of the individualizing function of the discipline. These skills cannot be reserved for attention in college or even in high school. The writing teachers (and there are many) who deal only with "the naming of parts" in their classes in the belief that what they call grammar must precede thinking, reading, and writing are making a social decision about their function in society, not a pedagogical decision about teaching. The reading and writing of stories and poems, the exercise of the individualizing imagination, can and should be a part of the English curriculum from the first grade.

Both the teaching and the testing of English as an individualizing discipline are difficult and frequently unwelcome. It is easier to ask students to fill in workbooks than to assign writing projects; it is less time consuming (and hence less expensive) to correct rote exercises than it is to respond humanly to human expression. Many parents of schoolchildren value the socializing skills so highly that they question or resent teaching that fosters individualizing activities. It is difficult to ask students to think for themselves without getting into sensitive areas, such as sex, religion, or politics, and even the parents of college students become very uneasy if students are encouraged to question accepted truths in these areas. College students who have problems with writing think they need more of what they call grammar (usually collections of ill-formulated rules for supposedly correct writing) and are unhappy if asked to think for themselves and to write and revise papers. Teachers who encourage too much individuality or allow too much adventurous reading may find themselves known as troublemakers—and not only by timid administrators: Every English department has articulate members who believe in their hearts that departures from the socializing view of the discipline show grave failures in up-holding academic standards.

The individualizing tradition generally holds sway in lib-eral arts programs at the college or university level, particularly where the tradition of teaching literature remains strong. How-ever, when we move to "remedial" writing programs on these campuses, we often find a hard-core socializing program, some-times using the same workbooks or programmed texts that have failed to work previously for the same students. As we move to the technical or business schools and then to the high schools, we find less and less individualizing (though always some) until we wind up in the grade schools, where only a few heroic teachers redeem the dry rote of the work sheets and the usage tests that make up the usual study of English.

Despite this unhappy picture, there are some faculty at all levels who keep insisting that basic skills in English must in-clude reading (not merely decoding) and writing (not merely identifying errors). The basic skills of using the imagination and of comprehending complex meanings, of thinking for oneself and evaluating the thinking of others, of understanding oneself in relation to the world of experience and the world of ideas—these basic skills still assert their claims. The best teachers still respond to these claims, the best pedagogy still envisions stu-dents as whole people and not merely trainable parts, and the best tests engage students at the individual as well as the social level.

But now we must turn to the problem of testing writing ability in the light of these comments on the English curricu-lum. The socializing aspects of writing instruction can be, and usually are, tested by multiple-choice norm-referenced tests; these tests will be discussed in Chapter Four. The more pressing problem is to find some way to measure the individualizing part of the discipline without ignoring appropriate components of the socializing aspect. The answer to that problem is to develop opportunities for students to respond as individuals to topics that require them to think and write; but that in turn poses the problem of how to cope with the writing samples that such tests produce. Over the last decade or so, new practices have provided a practical answer to that problem—an answer that has led not only to new kinds of testing programs but to a reconsideration of the purposes and procedures of teaching writing. The theoretical implications of holistic scoring are of interest not only to English teachers and those concerned with the English curriculum but also to all those who use writing as part of learning and all those concerned with the evaluation of learning.

2

Development and Uses
of Holistic Scoring

To proceed holistically is to see things as units, as complete, as *wholes,* and to do so is to oppose the dominant tendency of our time, the analytic spirit, which breaks things down into constituent parts in order to see how they work. Analytic reductionism assumes that knowledge of the parts will lead to understanding of the whole—a theory that works very well with machinery or other objects but less well with art or life forms. A table leg is much the same whether attached to the table or not; my leg or that of Michelangelo's *David* changes meaning drastically when detached. The holistic approach argues against reductionism and denies that the whole is only the sum of its parts.

The advent of holistic scoring of student papers is one interesting and practical manifestation of this spirit. The measurement of writing as a unit of expression (rather than as a series of isolated skills) seems related to several movements in the field of English, such as process research in composition and poststructural literary criticism, which reject the reductionism implied by product analysis and formalism. Holistic scoring, process research, and literary theory have developed along parallel paths during the last fifteen years, each stressing the rediscovery of the functioning human being behind texts and each rejecting more restricted ways of thinking about texts. Thus holistic scoring, with its emphasis on evaluation and response to student writing as a unit without subscores or separable aspects, presents itself in opposition to multiple-choice testing on the one hand

and analytic approaches to writing on the other. It is the most obvious example in the field of English of the attempt to evoke and evaluate wholes rather than parts, individual thought rather than mere socialized correctness.

It is a little hard to believe that, as recently as the early 1970s, the only systematic work in large-scale essay scoring was being done in just two locations: the National Assessment of Educational Progress (NAEP), at that time in Denver, and ETS, in Princeton, New Jersey. The concept of holistic scoring was almost unknown in the field of English, and the term elicited hostility or wisecracks from the uninformed. In contrast, in the early 1980s, a survey of English departments conducted by a committee of the College Conference on Composition and Communication showed an amazing change: Not only did almost 90 percent of responding English departments state that they used holistic scoring, but nowhere did either the committee chair or the responding parties feel the need to define the term by more than a parenthetical reminder (Purnell, 1982). In one decade, in a notoriously conservative and slow-moving profession, a new concept in testing and (hence) in teaching writing became accepted while no one was watching.

This chapter is designed to chronicle the development of holistic scoring in the measurement of writing ability, to define the term and others associated with it with some care, and to suggest the central reasons for its use. Finally, we need to look at some of the problems and disadvantages of this powerful and generally positive approach to student writing. As with any other complex but practical concept, holistic scoring is frequently misunderstood, misinterpreted, and misused. Since this advance in measurement has had, and continues to have, important uses in writing research, in teaching, and in program evaluation, holistic scoring needs to be better understood and its advantages and disadvantages need to be seen clearly.

History of Holistic Scoring

The early development of what we now call holistic scoring took place wholly under the auspices of the Educational Testing Service, and ETS deserves considerable credit for spon-

soring the research and developing the techniques that have led
to the present state of the art. The problem of developing valid,
reliable, and economical measures of writing ability has been a
particularly difficult and thorny one for ETS, and all those
concerned with the teaching and measurement of writing have
profited from the results of the prolonged internal debate this
problem produced. On one side were those who pointed to the
well-established unreliability of essay scores and who saw the
cost of scoring writing samples as prohibitive; for them, multiple-choice testing, with its established reliability and economy,
was the preferred, sometimes the only, way to measure writing
ability fairly. On the other side were those who argued that a
valid measure of writing needs to include writing. This latter
group gained strength from a College Board study entitled *The
Measurement of Writing Ability* (Godshalk, Swineford, and
Coffman, 1966), which neatly straddled the issue, concluding
that a mass of correlational data showed that the best test of
writing ability would include both multiple-choice and written
portions. The most compelling arguments raised by those hold-
ing this position and by their academic supporters were on educational and holistic grounds. Testing shapes curriculum, they
said, and multiple-choice usage tests were denying the importance of writing in the schools as well as defeating those who
were teaching literature, creativity, and other individualizing
subjects. Writing combines many skills and cognitive activities,
only some of which can be readily measured by machine-
scored tests, and so vital a combination can only be well evaluated as a whole. While the reliability of multiple-choice tests
was (and, indeed, remains) higher than that of more direct
measures, the validity of indirect testing in this field was open
to serious question: Only a few statisticians were fully convinced that such tests in fact measured writing ability.

Despite the persuasive arguments in favor of including
writing on tests of writing ability, multiple-choice testing of
usage (sometimes erroneously called objective testing, as if
machine-scored tests had been created with no human participation) remained the dominant form of testing for some time.
Indeed, it remains dominant in the schools today, though de-
creasingly so in the university. In order for the direct measure-

ment of writing ability to become an accepted component of writing testing, it had to meet the two major criteria of reliability and economy without losing its face validity as a legitimate test of writing skill.

Cost Considerations. While financial considerations generally follow educational policy, anyone involved with measurement needs to be concerned directly with the importance of economy in testing. No matter how valuable we may find some kinds of testing, if they cost too much they will not be used. Thus, it was an important step to demonstrate that the holistic scoring of writing samples could take place quickly enough to be practical: A single score for a piece of writing meant a single decision by a grader, and such decisions could be made with sufficient speed to make direct measurement of writing cost effective. The significance of this fact is not yet well understood. Since the cost of scoring writing samples is always considerably higher than the cost of running answer sheets through a computer, many people conclude that essay testing on the whole is more expensive than multiple-choice testing. However, when we consider the cost of test development, a major hidden cost in all testing, expenses tend to even out. Development of multiple-choice tests, if properly done, is enormously expensive and time consuming. Although essay test development requires considerable committee work, pre-testing, and revision, it is far cheaper and quicker. If, in addition, we consider costs of new forms of a test as well as of the initial administration, a consideration that cannot be avoided in the light of increasingly detailed truth-in-testing legislation, essay testing can be highly cost effective. If we add to the equation the benefits of direct measurement of writing to the teachers, to the curriculum, and to the learning of students (a calculus less than self-evident to many of those controlling educational funding), essay testing becomes economical indeed. (Chapter Eight takes up in detail ways of estimating costs for a holistic essay reading.) The evolution of holistic scoring thus made direct measurement of writing ability an economically feasible alternative to multiple-choice testing even for the accounting office; until its reliability could be demonstrated, however, it could not be widely used.

Reliability of Scoring. Early studies at ETS by Paul Diederich, the principal (almost the only) scholar in the field a generation ago, tended to confirm the unreliability of essay testing as it was then customarily conducted. (He summarizes much of that research in *Measuring Growth in English,* 1974.) When he distributed a quantity of student writing to a large group of readers, with no directions or criteria for scoring, all papers received all possible scores. He went on to categorize the scoring criteria the readers seemed to be using, grouping them into five categories according to what the different readers valued: the scores of readers who seemed to judge papers according to their structure, say, had a low correlation with those of readers whose basic criterion was style. The problem with this general impression scoring was clear: A paper's score depended on the accident of who wound up as reader rather than on its quality, however that quality was defined.

Reliability in testing is a complex subject. No test, of course, is wholly reliable, since student performance will change from test to test for reasons that may have little or nothing to do with the test. Scoring reliability is only one part of this complicated problem, but it is the part most directly controlled by those in charge of the test. Since reliability is in a sense a technical term to describe fairness or simple consistency, good testing practice aims for the highest reliability that can be reached. While economy is important, it means nothing without reliability; unfair and inconsistent scores are meaningless, and meaningless scores, however cheaply obtained, are not worth anything at all. (See Chapter Nine for a detailed discussion of reliability in relation to essay scoring.)

The problem, then, was to develop a method of scoring papers that retained the economy of a single, general impression score, with its underlying view that writing should be evaluated as a whole, and added to it substantial reliability of scoring. At this point, a general confusion of terminology entered the field —a confusion that still remains. The scoring Diederich used in his experiments, without any guides or controls, is sometimes called "general impression" scoring and sometimes "holistic." Many of the objections to and arguments against holistic scoring are, in fact, arguments against the unreliability of the general impression scoring that Diederich tested. I will call that system general impression scoring, reserving the other term for the later and more reliable form; I hope that others who debate these matters will do the same, in the interest of clear discussion.

Two developments from general impression scoring, with very similar outcomes, have led to the present generally accepted form of holistic scoring. At the National Assessment of Educational Progress, committees developed what came to be called "primary trait" scoring, while committees at ETS, particularly those working on the Advanced Placement Program, developed what they and most others now call "holistic" scoring. While the names look very different, and while some proponents argue strongly that one is much better than the other, in fact there is very little difference between them: Primary trait scoring merely defines with greater precision and exclusiveness the criteria to be used in the holistic scoring. Both groups were engaged in developing a series of techniques to increase the reliability of scoring by defining the kinds of skills tapped by different kinds of topics. In fact, both groups retained the single overall score and evolved similar procedures; the subsequent experience of dozens of essay readings has confirmed the good sense and statistical significance of these improvements in reliability. Thus, it is most useful to think of primary trait scoring as a particular kind of holistic scoring, since it uses the same basic assumptions. Analytic scoring, in contrast, has wholly different assumptions. Chapter Seven will consider both of these ways of evaluating writing in considerable detail. Meanwhile, everything in this book that speaks to holistic approaches to measurement and teaching can apply to most forms of primary trait scoring as well.

Holistic scoring is able to achieve acceptably high reliability by adding a series of constraints to the economically efficient practice of general impression scoring. Basic to all these constraints is a carefully developed and precise writing assignment (sometimes called a "prompt"), followed by an attempt to reduce unnecessary variability in the scoring process. Six procedures and practices have been developed for scoring, and where all six are observed with sensitivity and care, high reliability of scoring has been achieved with no appreciable sacrifice of economy. Since these procedures were developed for large-scale tests, I will describe them in that context. But teachers have adapted many of these approaches to writing assessment in creative ways (see Chapter Seven, in particular, for examples of such adaptation). Although later chapters of this book will speak to these procedures and the issues behind them in some detail, we need to outline them here in order to make clear the distinguishing features of holistic scoring.

1. *Controlled Essay Reading.* All those scoring the papers are brought together to read at the same time and place, with the same working hours and breaks. The controlled reading not only eliminates all kinds of extraneous variables from the scoring process, but it establishes a positive social situation which, under the right conditions, becomes an indirect and powerful in-service training workshop. The establishment of a sense of community is important for the success of the reading, since it is that particular "interpretive community" (to adapt a term from the literary critic Stanley Fish) that determines and enforces the standards of measurement.

2. *Scoring Criteria Guide* (sometimes called a "rubric"). This direct statement of descriptors for papers at different points on the scoring scale is developed by those leading the controlled essay reading before the readers gather. After reading many student papers (sometimes many hundreds), these experienced readers will develop a sense of the distinctions between papers on the continuum from the worst to the best. The scoring guide sets down the characteristics (or "traits" in primary trait scoring) that define the points on the scoring scale. Often, the test design committee will prepare a tentative scoring guide that expresses the specifications and intentions of the question, and, since such a plan usually emerges out of pre-testing a topic, this early guide is usually very helpful. But the final scoring guide needs to reflect the reality of the actual test group. The scoring guide allows the writing test to combine the best aspects of norm-referenced testing and criterion-referenced testing, concepts that will be discussed in the next chapter.

3. *Sample Papers* (sometimes called "anchor papers").

While the scoring guide is an abstract description of points on the scale, these papers are examples of these points. Chosen by the leaders of the reading in order to illustrate and make real the scoring guide, these papers are given unmarked to readers for scoring during the training sessions. Not until all readers are in close agreement on the scores of these sample papers and on what characteristics have determined the score can a reliable reading begin. The goal is not only to obtain agreement on the scores of sample papers and on the usefulness of the scoring guide but to help the readers internalize the scoring scale by combining description with example. If this "calibration" of the readers is done with sensitivity and toleration of some difference of view, the readers will agree to agree to common standards for the sake of the test; sufficient time in the training session is essential for reliable scoring and will be more than repaid by readers who score accurately and quickly, needing only occasional reference to the scoring guide or the sample papers after calibration. A careful reading that requires more than half a day to complete will score and discuss additional sample papers after breaks and meals as a way to guard against reader drift away from group standards.

4. *Checks on the Reading in Progress.* Readers are customarily grouped by tables seating six or seven (never more than eight) with an experienced table leader responsible for consistent scoring at the table. The table leader does not originate scores; his or her task is to circulate from reader to reader at the table, checking scores so that all readers will continue scoring at the same level. These repeated checks are intended to reinforce the group standards and help keep individual readers from drifting from original standards. If more than one table of readers is at work, a chief reader or question leader performs the same function for the various table leaders. At a long reading, extra care needs to be taken to guard against reader drift. For example, sometimes a sample paper from early in the reading will be renumbered as a new sample for scoring in order to guard against a scoring drift that might be unfair to papers read late (or early) in the reading. Readers who understand and are sympathetic to the process and who realize that the goal is a

reliable reading that is fair to students will cooperate with these procedures as long as they are carried on with sensitivity and good humor.

5. *Multiple Independent Scoring.* In this procedure, two readers from two different tables in the reading score each essay independently. A one-point difference between the two scores is allowable; papers with a two-point difference or more are read a third time in order to resolve the discrepancy. An excellent reading on a six-point scale will have 5 percent or fewer discrepant scores; an average reading will have 7 to 10 percent of its scores more than one point apart. Unless there is more than one reading for each essay, there is no way to evaluate the reliability of the reading or of individual readers.

6. *Evaluation and Record Keeping.* Since a reliable reading requires reliable readers, a continuing program will keep records of the scoring done by readers, giving particular attention to their consistency in observing the established criteria. The most reliable scorers form the cadre around which future essay readings may be built.

This summary of the procedures that have led to acceptable reliability for holistic scoring is designed for those with a general interest in the subject. Chapter Eight is addressed to those who have responsibility for the management of such a reading and provides a much more detailed description of the practices that have evolved over the last decade or so. Our concern here remains with the way in which holistic scoring has developed ways of coping with both the financial and the reliability problems that seemed to defeat earlier attempts to test writing directly.

There is some uncertainty at this time as to just how reliable controlled essay readings may be. Unfortunately, statisticians have reached no agreement about ways to measure comparative reliability of readings, and there are many different ways of computing reading reliability. Reports of reliabilities in the .90 range occur from time to time (for example, in the opening chapter of Cooper and Odell, 1977), but it is rarely clear how these numbers are derived. The statistical report published each year by the California State University English

Equivalency Examination includes a statistical consultant's narrative of the methodology and shows just how the reliability statistics have been developed. The report on the 1981 test concludes that "the actual reliability of the essay test therefore lies between the lower limit of .68 and the upper limit of .89"; in practice, this means that any two readers of the test, working independently on a six-point scale, agreed (or differed by no more than one point) approximately 95 percent of the time (White, 1981). As more testing programs begin to use statistical consultants, we may begin to move toward a more consistent way of comparing the accuracy and consistency of essay readings. In general, it appears that carefully controlled essay readings do yield reasonably reliable scores, although a close reading of the data reported by many such readings suggests that overstatement of reliability is common.

Limitations of Holistic Scoring

The present state of the art, then, shows substantial progress over the last decade. Holistic scorings have become routine across the nation, and many of them exhibit the six procedures that yield the most reliable results. The results generally have satisfied reasonable demands for both economy and reliability and have led the way to restoring the role of writing in testing and, since we test that which we hold to be important, in the curriculum. The development of holistic scoring of writing tests has helped the profession resist the forces of pseudo-objectivism (as in workbooks or multiple-choice tests) and analytic reductionism (with its emphasis on the supposedly immutable laws of usage and grammar) in writing classrooms and testing rooms. Those who have been involved in these matters have considerable cause for self-congratulation.

However, we are perhaps a little too prone to self-congratulation, considering the misuses and abuses that have been committed in the name of holistic scoring. It is important to remind ourselves of what such scoring cannot be expected to do and to temper our enthusiasm and that of our colleagues. We need to realize that holistic scoring is only a means of rank ordering papers according to the criteria established in the scoring guide. While efficient, economical, and reliable rank ordering is a great deal more than we had in the past, it is still only rank ordering. That is, a holistic score is like a percentile rating: It has meaning only in reference to the group that was tested and the test criteria embodied in the scoring guide for that particular test. This means, on the one hand, that the usefulness of holistic scores is limited and, on the other, that we cannot regard a holistic score as an absolute value. While these implications appear obvious since they derive from the limits of rank ordering, they are not at all well understood.

The first and most important limitation of the holistic score is that it gives no meaningful diagnostic information beyond the comparative ranking it represents. Even if we assume the score to be reliable, we cannot tell from it much that we might want to know about the student. For example, a low score might represent an inability to control sentence structure, a major spelling incapacity, a total misreading of the question, or a misguided attempt to be whimsical or creative. A high score might mean either a correct but boring response or a genuinely creative piece of prose. All we have is a single score where we might wish to have a profile. Despite enthusiasm for the value of an approach to writing that treats the writing as a whole and the writer as a thinking individual, we must recognize that a holistic score is of limited usefulness because it offers only a ranking. And although many tests require only a ranking, many others need to (or pretend to) offer much more.

The second implication of the limited value of the holistic score emerges from its connection to its particular test group: It cannot represent an absolute value in itself. This means that every time a holistic scoring is completed, those responsible for reporting scores need to make a fresh decision about where cutting levels should be. Suppose that last year a score of seven or above on a college placement test was needed by an entering student to be qualified for a regular freshman composition class. This year the question may be harder or easier or the freshman class may be stronger or weaker in writing skills, so the score of seven is likely to represent a different level of achievement even if the scoring guide remains the same. Should the cutoff score be six or eight? It is an unfortunate fact that most users of holistic scores act as if the ranking has some absolute meaning when it does not. No two essay questions make exactly the same demands on students; no two groups of students have exactly the same range of writing abilities. The additional step of deciding the meaning of a particular test's ranking of students cannot be avoided by those responsible for reporting and using holistic scores. Those who set scoring criteria and passing scores before looking at student performance assume that essay testing can become wholly criterion referenced (an issue dealt with in Chapter Eleven) and that questions and student populations can be kept stable.

The third important limitation of holistic scores is one common to all test scores: Reliabilities are customarily overestimated and the inescapable inaccuracy of scores tends to be ignored. All tests yield only approximations of ability levels, and even the most highly developed multiple-choice tests (which have virtually perfect scoring reliability) report a wide band of possible error. For example, despite the efforts of ETS and the College Board to point out that the standard error of measurement of the verbal portion of the Scholastic Aptitude Test (SAT) is thirty points in each direction and that scores on the SAT should be seen as a band rather than a point, almost everyone ignores the caution. Ten points more or less on the SAT can mean the difference between admission or rejection at far too many colleges. In a similar way, those who use holistic scores tend to ignore the fact that most papers, if rescored by the same readers at the same reading, might well receive at least slightly different scores. (See Chapter Nine for a detailed discussion of this issue.)

The inability of holistic scores to give diagnostic information has led to a not very successful development of analytic scoring, an attempt to gain a series of separate scores for separate subskills from each student writing sample. In theory, analytic scoring should provide the diagnostic information that holistic scoring fails to provide and in the process yield a desirable increase in information from the writing sample. In practice, three major problems have so far demonstrated the limitations of analytic scoring: (1) There is as yet no agreement (except among the uninformed) about what, if any, separable subskills exist in writing. (2) It is extremely difficult to obtain reliable analytic scores, since there is so little professional consensus about subskills. (3) Analytic scoring tends to be quite complicated for readers, which leads to slow scoring, which in turn leads to high cost. Since analytic scoring solves neither the reliability nor the cost problem, it is not a likely candidate to replace holistic scoring. Analytic theory also assumes that writing can be seen and evaluated as a sum of its parts and so stands in opposition to the assumptions behind holistic scoring; in ways parallel to multiple-choice testing, analytic scoring imagines a model of writing that is neatly sequential and comfortably segmented. As with machine-scored tests, analytic essay scoring offers some valuable adjunct measures of some kinds of skills but not a useful or valid measurement of writing. Its promise of producing diagnostic information has not yet been demonstrated successfully with large numbers of papers.

The Value of Holistic Measurement of Writing

Thus we are left with holistic scoring, with all its limitations, as the most successful method of scoring writing in quantity that is now available. This method of scoring has made the direct testing of writing practical and reliable; it indirectly and effectively brings together English teachers to consider and discuss the goals of writing instruction; and it embodies a concept of writing that is responsible in the widest sense. Nonetheless, we need to be fully aware of the limitations of holistic scoring if we are to use it responsibly and protect the direct testing of writing from those who would undermine it in the name of efficiency. Those who misunderstand or misuse holistic scores, however well motivated, are not supporting the teaching of writing or the testing of writing, since they open the whole procedure to justified attack.

The most common abuse of the holistic scoring process occurs when the leaders of an essay reading are not well informed about the need for reader agreement with the procedure. These leaders, the table leaders and chief readers, have a heavy responsibility: Their task is to ensure a reliable essay reading while at the same time respecting the professionalism, good will, and individuality of the readers who are grading the papers. The best of these leaders are fine teachers so able to work collegially with readers that group standards emerge from informed and willing assent. When readers feel comfortable with the question, the scoring guide, the process, and the people in charge, the grading of endless papers becomes a purposeful, even pleasant endeavor despite the inevitable tedium of the work. Readers will be eager to return to well-run essay readings, and they will take away from the experience much that is valuable to their teaching. After many hours of scoring papers to intelligent criteria, seeing student writing holistically, it is not easy to return to the idiosyncratic, arbitrary, and mechanical response to student work that is standard practice for many of those teaching writing classes. The best of these readings lead the participants to reconsider their teaching practices, but only indirectly, through the social interaction of colleagues working together to achieve a common goal. Indeed, the best holistic scoring sessions have a summer-camp vacation tone to them, sometimes including joyful after-hours memories not easy to come by in our mature years.

But when the readers feel intimidated or coerced by insensitive leaders or harrassed by a bad working environment, the whole situation becomes destructive to personal and professional relations. The worst of these readings allow the leaders to exercise an uncomfortable kind of bureaucratic power instead of academic leadership, and such readings set up an adversary relationship between exploited readers and their employers. Anyone who has been part of such a sad experience will be reluctant to repeat it and is likely to blame holistic grading itself for the corrupt version of it that took place. Like many aspects of human experience (to which we normally respond holistically), the difference between a fine and a terrible essay reading is made up of a series of minor yet symbolic acts and omissions that add up to a major difference in tone and result. Chapter Eight deals with these matters in considerable detail.

The great claim of holistic scoring of student papers is

not that it has finally achieved perfection in testing; clearly this measurement is still in its infancy. We do not know enough about how readers make their judgments, and skeptical scholars with dark suspicions about penmanship and sheer length continue to challenge the assumption that readers are making responsible holistic judgments of writing ability. The value of scoring guides, much more frequently used on the West than the East coast, is still being hotly debated. There are many differences of opinion about the most efficient way to conduct a reading. The devising of the writing topic, the prompt that elicits the student response, is a particularly thorny theoretical and practical problem. Even the basic statistical procedures by which holistic readings may be compared and evaluated are still uncertain. In short, the research on this form of measurement has far to go, and we will be hearing from writing teachers, statisticians, psychologists, and various other kinds of specialists for at least another decade. Chapters Nine and Twelve even speculate about other measurement schemes that may emerge, based more on process or communication models than on the text analysis framework behind the reading of essays.

Holistic scoring, however, is important for reasons beyond measurement, for reasons that return us to the nature of writing and to the importance of the study of writing itself. It is in our writing that we see ourselves thinking, and we ask our students to write so that they can think more clearly, learn more quickly, and develop more fully. Writing, like reading, is an exercise for the whole mind, including its most creative, individual, and imaginative faculties. The rapid growth of holistic scoring in grading reflects this view of reading and writing as activities not describable through an inventory of their parts, and such scoring serves as a direct expression of that view: By maintaining that writing must be seen as a whole and that the evaluating of writing cannot be split into a sequence of objective activities, holistic scoring reinforces the vision of reading and writing as intensely individual activities involving the full self.

Holistic approaches to writing—or to other forms of human expression and activity—are an important response by humanism to analytic reductionism. The holistic attitude says that the human spirit and its most significant form of expression must be seen and understood not in part but as a whole, face to face as it were, almost sacramentally. As holistic measurement procedures have gained increasing credibility and widespread use, those who approach writing as a central human endeavor, as our chief means of learning and our most weighty medium of expression, have gained new support in testing— and hence in teaching—writing as an individualizing activity.

3

Measuring Writing Ability by Using Proficiency Tests

Writing proficiency is one of those slippery terms that hides an even more slippery concept. Some overachieving tots pass proficiency tests on alphabet blocks to win certificates at kindergarten graduation ceremonies; second graders in my home town must be able to identify punctuation marks and write their names in order to make it into third grade; high school graduates must be able to fill in a job application and write a paragraph of three complete sentences before the school board will give them a diploma; certain graduate students at my university are required to write an effective essay in forty-five minutes before they advance to candidacy for the degree. While it is hard to imagine a single description that would apply to all these various tests, they are all comfortably known as "proficiencies," and everyone seems to accept them in both theory and practice as authenticating writing ability.

In many instances, the term *proficiency* seems merely to replace the workaday term *skill*—on the well-established bureaucratic principle that long words for simple concepts seem more dignified than short words; proficiencies are usually closely defined and carefully tested, as skills used to be. But there is an additional sense of adequacy, sufficiency for a particular purpose, in the concept of proficiency that makes the long word larger in every way. If someone is *proficient,* he or she is demonstrably capable. The fact that some of those who pass their "proficiencies" are *not* particularly capable, in fact are at best minimally functional at a few skills, sometimes makes the terminology of proficiency testing seem pretentious.

The problem thus turns out to be familiar: the analytic assumption that a set of clearly defined skills can add up to writing proficiency. The problem is not an easy one, however, when we put proficiency testing, as we should, in a classroom context. While we can test writing holistically at any level, we cannot teach it holistically. Chapter Seven speaks to this problem in relation to scoring guides for tests and suggests that primary trait scoring offers a way to bring holistic procedures for testing to bear on a focused and sequential curriculum. But the fact that we cannot teach everything at once need not lead to a definition of writing proficiency made up of bits and pieces of a curriculum; a limited notion of writing proficiency, articulated as it usually is in a set of definitions of skills and guides for teaching that teachers must follow, can become a means of defining writing as merely a set of socializing skills. While we must accept the necessity of teaching spelling or footnote form in our curricula, we must resist the tendency to think of accurate spelling or clear footnotes (or any set of subskills) as writing proficiency itself.

In recent years, many of the large-scale proficiency tests have begun adopting holistic definitions of writing. The National Teachers Examination, administered by ETS, has at long last added an actual writing portion; many of the new teacher certification tests (now required in thirty states) call for writing to ascertain writing proficiency; the admission testing programs for law and medical schools are experimenting with writing tests based on holistic principles. A survey of state writing assessment programs for the public schools published in 1979 showed that most states were using or contemplating using writing samples as at least part of their assessment; the number is surely higher now (Spandel and Stiggins, 1980). Even the massive General Education Development (GED) Program of the American Council on Education, the GED high school equivalency examination, has begun active research in holistic scoring of writing.

But these welcome developments seem not to have reached many school districts, where commercial multiple-choice tests, such as the Comprehensive Test of Basic Skills, or teacher-constructed tests of spelling and punctuation still seem to be the rule. The power of such tests over the curriculum is so great—and so negative—that writing is still a minor activity in the schools. The grim statistics compiled by Arthur Applebee in his recent survey of writing in the secondary schools show that recent developments and ideas about the measurement and teaching of writing have as yet had little effect on writing instruction (Applebee, 1981). In addition, teachers will teach to their understanding of what proficiency tests measure; the pressures to perform well by seeing one's students perform well on such tests are simply too great to resist. Thus, those defining proficiencies both through documents and through tests have a heavy obligation to ensure that the definitions support the teaching of writing. Such definitions need to guard particularly against the tendency of tests and curricula to trivialize writing, sometimes even with the best of intentions.

Even tests that call for student writing will sometimes be defined in such a way as to emphasize form over substance and hence not support writing instruction. For example, I mentioned a proficiency test that asked for a complete paragraph but then defined a paragraph as consisting of three complete sentences. The deeper concept of paragraph cohesion did not enter into the definition (sentences ought to relate to each other and to a central idea). The even more substantial concept that the paragraph ought to have something to say to an audience, something of some significance to somebody, also was not present. As a result, the teachers did not teach paragraph development or writing but rather the identification of sentence elements; instead of leading teachers to abandon a mechanically oriented workbook and to replace it with real writing instruction, the new proficiency requirement confirmed the importance of the workbook and returned teachers to it.

A similar substitution of form for substance in proficiency requirements has led to the apparent immortality of the five-paragraph theme. This structure, with three paragraphs of details sandwiched between an opening paragraph ("I intend to show that . . .") and a closing paragraph ("In this essay I have shown that . . ."), is sometimes given as a culminating writing proficiency for high school graduates. It is possible, indeed routine, to fill in the form with sentences empty of either meaning or connection, two concepts not commonly appearing on statements defining writing proficiency.

Since colleges, schools, and school districts vary so widely in their curricula, students, and faculty, it is not possible to suggest here the kinds of proficiencies appropriate at various levels. Indeed, the sensible law requiring proficiency testing for high school graduation in California specifically demands that each school district develop, define, and administer its own proficiency tests. But there can be no question that the process by which proficiency definitions and tests come about must follow a model of consultation and support for writing instruction if they are to be useful to the students and teachers who must cope with them.

Proficiency Testing at the University Level

The extension of writing proficiency testing to the university level represents a relatively new phenomenon on the American educational scene. Subject matter comprehensive examinations are, of course, both traditional and common at the graduate as well as the undergraduate level. But only within the last generation has a special, usually upper-division, writing proficiency certification begun to be added to course requirements for the college degree—no doubt as a reflection of general discomfort with university educational standards.

To those outside the university community, it might seem odd that the bachelor's degree should need the support of additional certification in writing skill; if a college degree does not in itself certify a high level of literacy, one might well wonder if it means anything at all. Nonetheless, in recent years, such solid members of the university community as the City University of New York, the University System of Georgia, and the California State University have felt it necessary to protect the quality of their degrees by a writing certification requirement. Though our principal concern here is not the cause of such action, a moment's speculation about the meaning of this requirement will illustrate just how pervasive these matters have become. Two particular aspects of university admissions procedures have a great deal to do with this new requirement: (1) the expansion of college opportunities to previously excluded groups and (2) the introduction of large community college programs for the first two years of study for the bachelor's degree.

The advent of open admissions to the City University of New York in 1970 was only the most prominent example of the expansion of college opportunity over the last two decades (Lederman, Ryzewic, and Ribaudo, 1983). The social forces behind this development are too well known to merit repeating here, although the degree or permanence of institutional change these forces have brought about is by no means clear. A substantial number of students who had either not experienced or not accepted English as a socializing discipline began to appear in college classrooms, even at the most selective institutions. Faculties were faced with increased numbers of students for whom the conventions of academic written prose were a mystery and for whom the traditional freshman English course seemed quite inappropriate.

Responses varied. Some institutions, well aware that inexperience with the conventions of prose did not necessarily mean inability to learn, made few changes in curriculum. Others, aware that the same inexperience presented a serious handicap to students writing papers for a traditional faculty, instituted a wide range of remedial courses and support services. Meanwhile, a general decline in student verbal ability, indicated most dramatically by a precipitous decline in SAT scores, added a considerable group of conventionally trained students without skill in academic writing to the new populations. For these reasons and many others, it became much more difficult to enforce traditional academic standards in freshman English courses.

At the same time, more and more students were beginning their university work at community colleges and transferring to four-year institutions with certifications of completion of all general education requirements, including writing proficiency. Although the two-year colleges tended to take seriously

their responsibilities for writing instruction and general education certification, many of their composition classes were occu-
pied by large numbers of students who were not likely to proceed to four-year institutions. It became difficult for these
community colleges to maintain standards, and the four-year
institutions receiving their transfer students with writing requirements fulfilled became increasingly uncomfortable with
such certification.

While these forces and others were diminishing the actual
standards and the credibility of freshman-level writing certification, the universities were experiencing an increasing fragmen-
tation of their curricula. Fewer students were majoring in the
humanities and other liberal arts disciplines, and increasing
numbers were pursuing majors they felt would lead more directly to jobs in business and technology. Except at a few highly selective institutions, the traditional faculty consensus that
writing well was important in all fields became less and less dependable. Faculty assigning term papers or essay exams found
increasing numbers of advanced students for whom such work
was new and surprising. And employers began to complain more
loudly than ever that degree recipients could not write as
needed on the job.

Thus, the new writing proficiency requirements at the
university level represent a widespread belief that it is now possible to complete course requirements for a bachelor's degree
without being able to write at an acceptable level; the new certification requirements also assume, with somewhat less justification, that it is both possible and desirable to define a level of
writing proficiency that is appropriate for all college graduates
and that it is practical to certify such an achievement. Various
institutions have been seeking to implement policy on this requirement over the last decade, and it is instructive to review
the procedures that are in use. As always, the assessment problems have turned out to be much greater than they were imagined to be, and every method of implementation has shown
both strengths and weaknesses.

Multicampus Testing. The principal advantage of a large-
scale proficiency test is its overall efficiency. Substantial re-

sources can be brought to test development, administration, scoring, and analysis; participating campuses can realize the benefits of the test without incurring much cost. Such long-standing programs as the New York State Regents Examinations for high school subjects have demonstrated the advantages of establishing statewide standards of proficiency in various fields. Yet large-scale proficiency testing in writing is fraught with special problems as part of an overall proficiency design. The statewide examination in Georgia, for example, has aroused substantial faculty opposition among those who find it insensitive and inappropriate for their particular campus or students. Since any definition of writing proficiency must be developed through discussion and consensus and since campus standards for writing are a major component of campus educational quality, it may be that proficiency testing in writing ought not to be done on too large a scale.

The nineteen-campus California State University established a systemwide *placement* test for entering freshmen in 1977, but it did not do the same for its graduation proficiency requirement. The economies of scale that were obviously beneficial for the placement test seemed much less sure for the proficiency requirement, for two main reasons: (1) It was not clear that the best way to certify writing proficiency was through a test, nor was it at all clear what kind of test would certify writing proficiency over a wide range of campuses, majors, and professional programs. (2) While it was relatively easy to define specifications for a placement test for freshman composition, it was difficult to contemplate a single writing proficiency standard for English majors at San Francisco State, accounting majors at Northridge, animal science majors at Pomona, and forestry majors at Humboldt.

Of all writing tests, the proficiency test is the most political, the hardest to agree on, the most dependent on instructional agreement. While the large-scale test gains uniformity of standards and certain economies, it loses the nearness to instruction which alone gives the concept of college writing proficiency a meaningful context. Probably the best method of demonstrating writing proficiency is through the completion of a demanding course requiring a substantial amount of writing and rewriting, as long as some sort of coordination and testing beyond the classroom confirms consistency of standards. A writing proficiency program ought to encourage such a method of certification; a series of writing samples will provide more reliable measurement than any one test can, and careful response and instruction during the course will lead to improved writing overall. A test is generally an unsatisfactory alternative to instruction. The farther a test moves from instruction, the more problems it accumulates, and large-scale writing proficiency testing is no exception.

These pedagogical as well as psychometric principles developed into a compelling argument against a large-scale proficiency test in California. If writing proficiency (that is, the thing itself rather than the test) is the program goal, responsibility for certifying that proficiency should be placed within the college curriculum, not outside it. That is, the test in itself cannot improve student writing; at best it can only lead to a strengthened writing instruction program. If the test is entirely separated from the curriculum, it might not even do that, since such separation seems to turn the test into a hurdle to be gotten over rather than an important part of learning. So the California decision was to resist statewide certification and remand the requirement to the nineteen separate campuses in the state university system. As these campuses have wrestled with the problem, they have provided laboratory cases of the variety of ways to implement such a requirement on a single campus.

Campus Testing Programs. An individual campus faced with the implementation of a writing certification requirement is likely to turn first to a single test. Particularly when the campus is large and complex, a test offers many advantages: a single standard, sometimes imagined to be "objective," an addition to the quality control of the campus without the effort of reviewing or changing the curriculum, and a simple funding apparatus —a test fee. Everything looks deceptively simple. But the test is the beginning of problems, not the end of them. Even if all the cautions in this book (particularly in Chapter Eleven) are followed, the test becomes a major enterprise in itself. Special at-

tention must be given to continuous test development, to student advisement both before and after testing, and to test security and cheating. Fly-by-night outfits are likely to appear in
town the weekend before the test with expensive materials and
cram courses in test taking. Students who have failed the test
several times become increasingly desperate and, with only the
test between them and their degrees, may tend toward increasingly desperate measures. Meanwhile, pressures to lower the
standards of the test or to provide special exemptions for an
increasing number of special cases become almost irresistible,
and the test starts to look more like an entrance-level minimum
competence exam than an exit-level test of writing proficiency.

At the same time, students who do not pass the test after
one or two attempts and who seriously want to improve their
writing will make continued requests for the establishment of a
course to teach them the skills they lack. The result of such requests has been a new and appalling course, now evolving wherever the passing of a special proficiency test is required for college graduation: the *upper-division* remedial English course.
These courses are never called remedial in their title, since no one
is willing to admit that the institution enrolls juniors and seniors
without writing proficiency; hence, they are given a wonderful
variety of pseudonyms: intensive English, grammar review, proficiency test preparation, and the like. With the exception of a
few heroic and responsible faculty, the teachers of these courses
are generally those with the least experience, status, and knowledge.

Some faculty claim that a single proficiency test, despite
its problems, is still the most effective way to raise literacy standards on their campuses. As large numbers of students with particular majors fail the test, the faculty in that field must recognize its responsibility to teach writing in its courses, and only
the test can convey that message. But it is extremely difficult to
include substantive matters on such a proficiency test, and the
standards for scoring tend to become very low; after all, the test
is an absolute barrier to the degree for a very wide variety of
students, and it is politically impossible to fail too large a percentage of graduating seniors. In addition, some inept students,
unwilling or unable to take additional writing courses, may

wind up taking the test repeatedly, hoping that some miraculous event will allow them to pass. When one is involved in scoring such examinations, numbers of essays turn up written by students taking the test for the ninth or tenth time. Not only is there an air of desperation in the exams of such students, but their recurrent papers serve to lower disproportionately the overall quality of test performance.

These examinations violate an essential general principle of testing: No single test is sufficiently reliable to be depended upon, by itself, for a major decision about students. A second proposition, which this book argues as forcefully as it can, is almost as important: When testing becomes separated from teaching, both teaching and testing suffer. And when passing a test begins to seem unrelated to learning, we ask our students to become cynical about learning itself.

Course Certification. Some faculty committees and administrators find the foregoing arguments so compelling that they decide to omit proficiency examinations entirely and depend wholly on certification by the teachers of courses. Students who pass particular courses will be presumed to be proficient writers, and there is an end to it. But that procedure is no more an end to problems than is a test. Again, a new series of difficulties present themselves. Some campuses will decide to remand certification of writing proficiency to the department of the student's major. History majors should write well enough to please historians, engineers to satisfy the engineering faculty, and so on. But that decision tends to work out very badly, since many of these faculty know little about the teaching and measurement of writing and since some of them may be less than adequate writers themselves. Thus, results tend to be very uneven: Some departments become very demanding, requiring a disciplinary writing course with high standards, while others become cynical and designate a course that may have no more than a single essay examination, if that. I have even seen a course in musical composition designated by one satirical music department and a course in computer programming proposed by a naive math department as satisfying writing proficiency requirements.

In an attempt to make such course designations more

consistent and fair to students, some campuses establish guidelines for writing proficiency courses and even assign faculty committees and administrators to enforce the guidelines. Thus, departments may only be allowed to designate courses that require, say, five separate writing assignments adding up to 5,000 words and that require some attention to revision in the course syllabus. The most effective of such programs require a common examination of some kind, a mid-term or final across all sections, in order to bring the faculty together to agree on a consistent set of standards.

When such common requirements are in fact enforced—and they seem to work only on relatively small campuses—the certification program can both ensure standards and support teaching. However, the coordination effort called for is strenuous and even extraordinary, involving as it does agreement among a wide variety of faculty on matters generally held to be private: course curriculum and grading standards for departmental offerings. But the effort pays off handsomely. Not only does the writing certification program become an embedded part of the education in each major, but a de facto faculty development program in the teaching and measurement of writing ability is likely to emerge.

Unfortunately, with no common test or strong coordinator to hold together such a program, the centrifugal forces usually become too strong to resist. Without constant attention, the program will relax into a series of departmental courses that may or may not involve writing, taught by new faculty members in various departments with little or no training or interest in the teaching or measurement of writing.

Some campuses with experience in this area no longer expect the academic departments to certify writing proficiency. All students must pass an English department writing course or a course administered by the English department. While such a procedure reduces the problems of administration and inconsistency, it tends to confirm the destructive myth that only the English faculty need be concerned about student writing. In addition, it puts an immense strain on English department staffing, which usually must accommodate freshman composition as well, and it diminishes the emphasis on the study of literature that most English departments wish to maintain. The proficiency course becomes a burden to be borne by unwilling literature teachers, the English department alone becomes responsible for denying degrees to students approved by everyone else, and the rest of the faculty (whose lack of concern for student writing has spurred the demand for proficiency certification) is left free to continue business as usual.

Test with Course Option. In an attempt to preserve the benefits of a campuswide test without including all its disadvantages, some campuses will allow those who fail the campus test to receive certification by passing a particular course. Under this procedure, a student will be certified as proficient despite a failing score on the test if he or she receives a passing grade in, say, English Z, Intensive English. The advantages of this procedure are clear. Most students presumably will pass the test and receive certification. Only the weakest students will need an upper-division writing course, so the staffing burden for such a course is no longer overwhelming. If the test is responsibly run and the course well staffed, the quality of the college degree is protected without asking every department to review its curriculum.

However, this procedure, unlike the one that follows, winds up combining the worst aspects of both test and course certification. Since the test is the primary means of certification, all the pressures on the test will urge a higher passing rate and lower standards; the test generally will be seen as a minimum proficiency skills test to be failed only by dumbbells. Thus, all the problems of the single campus test procedure will remain, with the single important exception that adequate writers who do not test well will now have a more appropriate route to the degree.

Meanwhile, it is hard to exaggerate the negative effects on the course that must be taken by those who fail the test. The resentment felt by the teacher assigned to teach the upper-division remedial class is usually matched or overmatched by the resentment of the students forced to take it. No one expects it to be a substantive class; some simulacrum of minimum competence is bound to be the goal. The (usually young and inexperienced) teacher is solely responsible for upholding university literacy standards under great pressure from students who have managed to get by despite poor writing ability.

Thus, the test with course option tends to be a depressing method of certifying student writing proficiency. Both the test and the course behind the test tend to be public embarrassments, euphemistically titled and attended with reluctance by everyone involved. One major university now lists between sixty and seventy-five sections of an upper-division remedial writing course each term and hires a trained corps of graduate students to teach this pedagogical oddity each year. Those involved argue that the course is well taught and essential, particularly for the large numbers of able students for whom English is a second language. Nonetheless, the test is exceedingly elementary and the course hardly above the high school level despite its upper-division designation. One wonders whether the proficiency program in fact protects university standards or, rather, protects those faculty throughout the university who neglect their own responsibilities toward their students' writing.

Effective Certification Through General Faculty Involvement. Since student writing proficiency is a result of consistent attention by the general faculty to student writing, and since the call for certification outside the curriculum reflects dissatisfaction with faculty standards, any serious certification program must involve the faculty as a whole. Therefore, a university's general education requirements, which express in specific terms what the faculty values for all its students, are the appropriate and natural location for a required upper-division writing course, to be taught by faculty throughout the institution.

Most of the other methods of certification avoid the painful and political process of involving the faculty in fundamental curriculum change. Yet a felt need for a certification program —the assumption from which we are proceeding here—ought to be seen as a demand for such change. This is why testing programs extraneous to the curriculum have so many problems: They too often treat symptoms and actively avoid dealing with root issues. It is in fact no advantage to institute a certification program that does not involve many faculty; while such a program is relatively easy to put in place, it is also easy to dismantle when attention or budgets turn elsewhere. Since no real changes are involved, the program tends to be more cosmetic than actual, despite the energy expended by those committed to it.

The best way to certify student writing proficiency at the college level is to require of all students a passing grade in a significant general education writing course at the upper-division level, a course with clear, common, and public standards. If such a course becomes an accepted requirement, no one will consider it to be remedial and all the pressures on the course will urge substance and quality.

What appears to be the major disadvantage of this procedure turns out to be a substantial advantage: The faculty must be willing to include the certification course at the upper-division level as part of the required general education program. Woodrow Wilson is said to have complained that it is easier to move a cemetery than a university faculty, yet without such movement a writing proficiency program is bound to be rather an empty gesture. If the faculty as a whole is willing to assume responsibility for student writing and to demonstrate that responsibility by adding and teaching an upper-division general education requirement, the pressure for proficiency certification outside the curriculum is bound to disappear in time. The greatest success a writing proficiency program can achieve is to become unnecessary; if most faculty decide to require writing in their classes and demand high-quality work, so large a proportion of students will pass any certification program that the need for it will wither away. (I administered such a program in the 1960s and presided happily over its abolition.)

Once a writing proficiency course becomes part of the required curriculum, many of the problems we have been describing become manageable. Staffing demands need not fall only on the English department but can be spread throughout the institution, with all the advantages of widespread concern for student writing. Coordination of the program remains necessary and difficult, but there is within each institution a tradition of coordination, common course requirements, and common examinations for multisection general education courses upon which to draw. Most important, those teaching and those taking the course will have no incentive to debase it; it will in fact seem more like a senior honors seminar than a remedial writing course, and students as well as faculty will bring inventiveness and interest to it.

Experience has shown that a common examination is absolutely necessary if the centrifugal forces that are always at work on advanced courses are to be resisted. If the staff teaching the proficiency course each term must meet to plan, discuss, select, and grade a common examination for all students taking their classes, there will be a built-in corrective to the tendency to specialize the disciplinary content of the sections or to diminish the importance of writing. A recent study has shown, in addition, that bringing a staff of writing faculty together to develop and score a test is the single most effective way to organize a faculty development program (White and Polin, 1983): Since everyone needs to be involved and to discuss the purposes of the class, teachers learn more about the teaching of writing indirectly by working together on a test than they do directly in any number of retreats, lectures, and seminars.

Some students write so well that they are able to test out of the required course by demonstrating a high level of proficiency on a difficult written examination. Such an examination can be unabashedly demanding, requiring, for example, analytic skill and substantial ability to organize, demonstrate, and connect ideas; since the standard means of certification is a course, the pressures to depreciate the test will not be difficult to resist. As long as the course is seen as the basic certification device, the challenge test can be appropriately demanding, designed for those special students who clearly do not need the course. Perhaps those who pass can form a special honors seminar or in some other way build on their demonstrated writing ability. Failing the test is no disgrace, since relatively few pass and most do not even attempt it. Most important, the challenge test now sinks in importance and prominence to a properly subordinate place to instruction. While the test will, of course, call for several kinds of writing and show careful concern for validity and reliability, it need not carry the entire burden for institutional standards.

This procedure for certification, involving the introduction of a new general education requirement at the upper division and requiring assent from most of the faculty and participation by many of them, requires more than most universities are willing to give. As this book goes to press, I am completing my third year as coordinator of such a program, so I know that it is possible and practical, but no one should imagine it to be easy. Establishment of the program is likely to take some years of committee work, debate, and compromise, while maintenance calls for substantial resources and attention. Most of the university administrators and faculty concerned about the writing ability of their graduates do not want to confront the issue if it calls for so much trouble, and so they will prefer to complain (often about English teachers or the high schools) or to think that a test will make the problem go away. Some administrators and department chairs will find it much wiser and more convenient not to ask why students can complete some courses of study without competence in writing. Others will genuinely see writing as an outmoded or minor matter compared with the real business (whatever they take it to be) of the university. Still others will feel that certification of writing proficiency should be in the hands of the freshman English staff or the admissions office. Some may even feel that writing ability is a faddish concern, even now being replaced by worries about mathematics and science training. For these reasons and many more, the stop-gap and halfway measures I have been describing on many campuses seem to be a more reasonable response to pressures for certification of writing ability than the thorough reform I am recommending.

It is idle to imagine that the need for institutional certification of student writing proficiency will disappear in the near future. Indeed, there is every reason to expect that the expansion of opportunity to less privileged populations and the renewed vigor of the community colleges will continue to provide most colleges in the United States with unconventionally trained upper-division students; there also seem to be no signs that the specializing majors in the college curriculum will ask their advanced students to return to the core of the liberal arts. Thus, it is probable that demands for the certification of student writing proficiency outside the curriculum will continue and increase. Those responsible for such programs would do well to build on the experience summarized in this chapter. In this area, as in most others, the close linking of testing to teaching allows the most constructive solution to educational problems, which are never as simple as they appear to be. The basic problem of inadequate student writing skill is so profound that only thorough solutions involving the entire faculty are likely to have much impact; the superficial and easy answers seem in general to create as many difficulties as they solve.

Proficiency Testing for Admission to Professional Schools

In recent years, the national admission testing programs for law, medical, and management schools have all shown interest in essay testing. The Law School Admissions Test (LSAT) has experimented with actual written portions; the Medical College Admissions Test (MCAT) is pilot testing an essay portion as this book goes to press; the Graduate Management Admissions Council is so interested in the possibility of including a written portion that it invited me to write an article on the value of essay testing for its new journal, *Selections* (White, 1984). Despite the elaborate multiple-choice tests whose scores traditionally play a substantial part in deciding who enters these lucrative professions, the admissions committees to these professional schools have articulated an additional need for the particular kind of information that student writing provides. The subscores, the partial scores, and even the combined scores are not enough: A sensitive admissions committee also is looking to the admissions test for some indication of the total human being and of how he or she thinks—that is, a holistic writing score.

As we speculate about the kind of writing proficiency such admissions committees ought to value, we wind up in very complex territory indeed. We are asking about the kind of thinking we should expect of those who will become the next generation of attorneys, physicians, and managers—that is, not only those most financially rewarded by our society but those who largely run it. We would certainly want such people to manifest a high order of skill at understanding, analyzing, and then synthesizing complex ideas; we would also look for clear and well-organized thought that develops ideas coherently. In addition, at this level we might look for the ability to communicate concepts convincingly to an audience, using appropriate evidence and sensitivity. The very best of these students will demonstrate all of this with some signs of originality and personal style.

With such goals in mind, and I have by no means exhausted the possible list, it is no surprise that the admissions committees have turned to essay testing. The existing multiple-choice portions of their tests seem to approach only a few of these goals, focusing as they do on knowledge, problem solving, and verbal and quantitative aptitude. Some of the subtests do seem to measure aspects of reasoning, but most of the criteria summarized in the last paragraph can best be measured by asking students to write.

If we look for a moment at graduate schools of management, for example, we find a particular need for students who can put details together meaningfully in relation to an audience. Both of these matters—the ability to synthesize and the ability to imagine and relate to an audience—are particularly important in the area of management, with its growing concern for integrative ability and its highly social nature demanding skilled communication. Analytic skills are surely valuable, and admissions committees need to measure these skills, but executives need to have some aptitude for envisioning wholes as well as parts, for adding together the concepts, charts, numbers, projections—all the data and arguments that present themselves—to shape a decision that is greater than the sum of the parts. Furthermore, not even the most solid and creative decisions can be acted upon until they are communicated clearly and effectively to the various audiences whose assent is required. Admissions committees to schools of management want to see a mind at work, most particularly to see how that mind conceives, builds, and supports conclusions and how those conclusions are put into words.

Test development committees at this level are faced with the difficult problems of devising questions that will measure such complicated matters and of scoring them with the necessary reliability and sensitivity. Happily, we now know enough about the growth of mental ability and the measurement of writing ability to allow such problems to be dealt with.

The contribution of writing testing to the admissions process at the graduate and professional level must be seen as moving past simple notions of correctness or even of clarity to the very functions of the mind itself. I do not mean to suggest that a few sentences of writing reveal all that one needs to know about an applicant; all the cautions about misuse of testing in this book apply with particular force to admissions tests, since decisions based on them are of utmost importance and usually are beyond appeal. Nonetheless, as the following sample test indicates, a writing test can supply extremely valuable information about the applicant's thought process as part of an overall assessment.

The following question and set of answers demonstrate the way developmental concepts can show up on an advanced writing test. The supposed student responses, illustrating important differences in methods of thought, are entirely typical of the range of writing normally to be found on American college and university campuses and to be expected on a writing test for admission to a professional school. The point of the illustration is not only that the last few responses are better written in a general sense or more sophisticated than the first few listed but that they are better written because they reflect different ways of thinking that can be seen and scored reliably on a writing test. People who do not know how to develop ideas by means other than repeating them or by listing more or less related items are not likely to come up with convincing ideas about anything and probably need more education before entering graduate or professional programs. The first three student samples suggest that they may have been written by students thinking at that level. The better responses show not only the ability to make arguments and connections but also the ability to move through several different levels of abstraction in the course of discussion. These writers are demonstrating one of the most important writing and thinking skills; such students are likely to be those most ready to undertake graduate and professional training.

Let us imagine a business-oriented writing test designed to discover the candidates' abilities to develop and support an idea. Let us also suppose that a test committee gives the applicants material that provides relevant background information to be analyzed and asks them to write on the following topic: *To what degree are Japanese management practices suitable for American industry?*

The committee immediately will find that many students imagine they are developing an idea when they are only restating it:

"Japanese management practices would never work in this country since they are native to a different culture. The American way of life is simply opposed to the kind of life-style typical of Japan. Furthermore, in Japan, people relate to each other differently."

Other weak writers will recognize that their assertions need to be supported, but the support will be inappropriate, vague, and unconvincing:

"If American managers would only learn from Japanese practice, American industry would be transformed. With management and labor working together, all of our problems will be solved. All it takes is good will and Christian tolerance."

These two examples are very short for two reasons: (1) Such writers often have difficulty saying very much, since they do not know how to expand and develop ideas. (2) A few such writers do write at very great length but wind up filling space by repetition, a boring exercise that we need not repeat here.

More capable students will begin to supply arguments and evidence to support what they say but are likely to find some difficulty in relating particulars to generalities—one of the most

complex of mental operations. Such students will list examples
or give reasons, but they will simplify complex issues and fail
to relate their examples or reasons to each other or to their central point:

"American managers are unsuited for cooperative management styles by their inbred patterns of life. In the first place,
most of them are male. Secondly, they tend not to believe in
Oriental philosophies. Moreover, their pastimes tend to be competitive ones. They share the American simplifying pattern of
seeing those who are different as antagonists. For these reasons,
and for many others, it is futile to think that a Japanese management style would work in America."

A still more sophisticated thinker will connect the supporting evidence, although the evidence may remain skimpy or
the arguments simplistic:

"American managers are culturally unsuited for the cooperative style that has distinguished Japanese business practice in
recent years. For example, most of them are male, and hence
insensitive, competitive, and opposed to learning from outsiders. In addition, American religions are generally individualistic,
as opposed to the quiet cooperativeness of Oriental philosophy,
and so religious training supports the competitive male orientation. It is inconceivable that men so used to ordering the world
for their private benefit, and to resisting outsiders as threats,
could listen to their workers and put the good of the enterprise
ahead of their own advancement."

The best writers will see the complexity of the issue and
respond to it with a corresponding complexity of their own,
with several levels of abstraction and with a clear sense of coherence. While not all long papers are good papers, the sheer pressure of ideas often drives the best thinkers to produce a longer
argument:

"Those who argue that Japanese methods of management
should be imported into American business need to take account of the cultural differences national management styles
express. It may be that a less adversarial or hierarchical style
would improve labor relations, increase productivity, and solve
the balance of payments problem; but I am a bit skeptical. Cer-

tainly, we have much to learn from the Japanese. In particular, we should look closely at their methods of developing employee commitment to corporate goals, their general involvement in quality control, and their flexible pattern of communications among all levels of workers. But it makes no sense to throw away American methods that have served us so well for so long without a good long look at what we might lose as well as what we might gain; we can no more simply adopt another culture's way of management than we can serve sushi at McDonald's. The very concept is one more example of bad management thinking, the desire to adopt ready-made, even foreign solutions for half-understood problems instead of working from problems to their best solutions."

While it is possible to praise—or even attack—the best writing in a general way, those grading the test would want to be precise about the differences among papers receiving different scores. Before grading could begin, a scoring guide would need to describe carefully the kinds of arguments typical at the various score levels. For example, the last paper shows a particular ability to move from interesting and complex abstractions (management styles express cultural differences; problems need to generate solutions, not the reverse) to the use of concrete detail to support the abstractions (sushi at McDonald's). Even where the language must be abstract, as in the list of three practices to be looked at closely, the terms are always clear, never disappearing into generalized clichés. The author has a firm voice—firm enough to get away with "I am a bit skeptical"—and an obvious sense of audience.

The point of looking with such care at the most advanced kind of writing proficiency test is that the testing of writing at this level can accomplish even very complicated measurement goals. Such testing seeks to find out how the mind functions in response to particular kinds of demands and thus has a special place in any admissions process. Furthermore, the sensitive use of this kind of testing is bound to support the most substantial aspects of education: Nothing quite sharpens students' desire to learn to write well as the knowledge that a writing test lies between them and the professional school they plan to enter.

Nonetheless, in common with all writing proficiency tests, writing portions on graduate and professional admissions tests might easily lead to a narrowing of the writing experience of those preparing to apply. While it is both practical and reasonable to ask applicants to professional schools to demonstrate organizing, analyzing, and synthesizing skills, test development committees need to guard against questions that will disadvantage applicants with personal traits or casts of mind that might be in short supply because of sheer unconventionality. The creation and revision of the right kind of writing proficiency test for a particular professional field is a difficult job, calling for high levels of sensitivity as well as knowledge. No one should imagine it can be done quickly or easily.

Proficiency Testing and Cognitive Development

As we look at the differences in the writing topics that students can handle at different stages of growth, we gain some clues as to the kinds of questions appropriate for different kinds of proficiency tests. By the age of nine, most children can handle narrative sequences and concrete associations; they tend to succeed in writing tales or descriptions and can write remarkable short poems, as long as the reader is willing to supply the abstractions and conclusions not yet available to the writer. We sometimes encounter adult writers caught in this phase; some college students, for example, turn all questions, even the most analytic ones, into personal narratives.

As children develop, they begin to learn how to handle abstract operations of the mind, such as giving relevant evidence for arguments or synthesizing ideas. But many complex and increasingly sophisticated steps must be taken before the writing that reflects (or even generates) the thinking becomes mature. What Jean Piaget (1955, 1962) called "egocentricity" and writing researcher Linda Flower (1979) calls "writer-based prose" needs to yield to some sense of an outside audience; the student needs to understand that arguments convincing to the self are not necessarily convincing, or even apparent, to others.

Methods of argumentation also move through growth

stages that have been well studied. Some students feel that passionate repetition of a belief is all that is required, while others appeal to supposed authorities of human or divine origin as if a quotation or a fact were the same as a proof. The ability to connect conclusions to evidence and to relate conclusions and evidence clearly to a concept develops late indeed, and for many this ability never develops at all.

Despite such insights, the development of writing ability is not at all well charted at this point, despite considerable effort by educational researchers. James Britton (1975), for example, has argued that what he calls "expressive writing"—a bridge for children from oral speech to the written page—is crucial for later development into "transactional" writing that conveys information and, for the most able, into "poetic" writing. Yet the "Betterburg" experiment (see Chapter Nine) has shown that, when called for, second graders can produce competent transactional prose, and poet Kenneth Koch (1970) has had remarkable success at eliciting literary writing from very young children. No one has yet been able to make direct links between the growth stages charted by the cognitive psychologists and the stages in the development of writing ability. Even such modest and common sense generalizations as I have just given must allow for exceptions and for our own ignorance of how complex skills are learned.

The implications for proficiency testing of this uncertainty about the growth of writing ability are clear. We must be very careful to validate our tests, to make sure that our definitions of proficiency are realistic and fair. School-level proficiency testing calls for consistent and widespread consultation with teachers, who are more likely to know what is appropriate for their students than any number of abstract studies may indicate. University-level writing proficiency is by no means a static or universal concept; it must be worked out painfully in the political-academic arena of each institution. As in the schools, the definition of writing proficiency and the means of measurement have a profound effect on teaching and so must be developed with careful attention to classroom and curricular implications. Proficiency testing for entrance into graduate and professional schools affects not only admission policy and procedure but undergraduate education as well. Those responsible for considering the addition of a writing portion to the MCAT, for example, are aware that some 46,000 students a year may begin substituting a writing course for a science course as they look forward to the admission test. Compared with such practical matters, our slight knowledge of writing as a growth process should play only a small role in defining what we mean by writing proficiency.

Finally, we must keep in mind that writing proficiency is a question, not an answer—a problem for definition, not a solution to a problem. We move most effectively toward the answers we need when we see the term in a context that it simultaneously reflects and changes.

4

Selecting Appropriate
Writing Tests

The crucial decision of what test to use often is made far too early in large testing programs. Classroom practice is instructive in this respect: Faculty normally are busy constructing their final exams just a few days before they are to be given. The reason for this is, in part, simple human procrastination, but it is a sound pedagogical practice nonetheless. The final exam, if it is to be valid, needs to cover the material of the course, and coverage or emphasis cannot be determined too far ahead of time; if the exam is to be fair to the students, it needs to deal with the actual (not the proposed) material of the course. In addition, the final should be appropriate for this term's group of students, which may not be the same as last term's. In short, those choosing an examination need to be sure that it meets clear test specifications and is right for the students involved as well as for the material to be covered.

Unfortunately, in large-scale testing programs this process usually works backward. The testing instrument is often chosen first, not after the preliminary work is done, and decisions about its relation to instruction, its usefulness for the particular student population, or the meaning of its results all follow and depend on the particular test that has been chosen. In many cases, the test is selected for peculiar reasons—political, commercial, or merely personal, for example—and the entire testing program is distorted as a result.

It is for this reason that the odd complaint of "teaching

to the test" has become a cliché in American education, a descriptor for distorted, even partially dishonest instruction. The objection is inherently paradoxical, since virtually every classroom teacher teaches to his or her own tests all the time and sees that as sensible and appropriate. Indeed, evaluation is so naturally a part of learning ("How'm I doing, teacher?") that no reasonable person questions the procedure. But when the testing seems, or in fact is, distant from or irrelevant to what is being taught and learned, teaching to the test suddenly becomes an issue. And when, as is often the case in school district testing programs, the test is not appropriate for the student population, teachers need to choose between helping students learn and helping students pass tests. Sometimes, of course, school administrators believe that mandating an inappropriate test (such as one normed on a wholly different population, using a wholly different curriculum) helps raise academic standards and motivate better performance. Such a procedure is a negative and damaging way to suggest curriculum reform. The major problem in test selection is to begin by choosing the test before developing the test goals, specifications, and uses.

Test Purposes

Many classroom tests do have a clear and well-understood goal: to find out if students have learned the material taught in the class. But as we move beyond the single-classroom test, goals become varied and complex. Many teachers are far less clear about the purpose and sequence of their out-of-class writing assignments than they are about in-class tests. And when we move beyond the individual classroom to tests of larger groups, a clear consensus on purpose becomes harder and harder to achieve. Yet it is crucial to understand the purpose of a test before choosing a testing device. One way to see the importance of this point is to notice the differences among three familiar kinds of writing tests: proficiency, placement, and equivalency examinations.

Proficiency Testing. Proficiency tests, as we saw in the previous chapter, supposedly measure student performance on well-defined and clearly understood "proficiencies." It is easy for the uninformed to imagine that a concept so widely used—with such institutional and legal authority—as *writing proficiency* must have some commonly accepted meaning. However, the term has such a variety of definitions, from the merest handwriting or spelling measure to a thesis requirement, that any test to measure writing proficiency must begin by carefully defining its terms. To ignore this task or to assume that the job has been done by someone else (because someone else has produced something called a "proficiency test") is to make the most elemental and common error in testing.

Since, in one sense, a test is a means of gathering information, a sensible program will consider exactly what kind of information is to be gathered and why. Unfortunately, most testing programs proceed backward: They begin with a test and only later inquire into what the test is in fact discovering. A common error is to begin by selecting (or even constructing) an inexpensive multiple-choice test, frequently one based on an outmoded or casual understanding of linguistics or writing or grammar. Another error is to construct an essay test of questionable validity to be scored with questionable reliability, using classroom materials on hand. After a few test administrations, when it is found that the test seems to be measuring social or economic or racial proficiencies rather than writing skills, someone gets around to asking for a serious definition of what the test is really testing.

A less common and more interesting problem for proficiency testing emerges from the common misconception that English teachers, since they teach writing, of necessity know what writing proficiency is and how to test it. While an important truth is buried in this assumption (and while it is destructive to ignore the experience of writing teachers), we cannot proceed as though English teachers agree on the meaning of writing proficiency and how to test it. Until the vexing issue of definition has been resolved, it is futile to launch into a testing program of any sort.

The previous chapter dealt with the complicated problem of what constitutes writing proficiency under a wide variety of circumstances. The important point here is that the issue must be considered and resolved before—not after—a testing program is implemented. Since the definition reflects the goals and standards of the institution, many campus groups should participate in defining proficiency. Without a widely accepted definition, inappropriate and flawed testing will result, and test scores will be received with some skepticism.

Placement Testing. Unlike proficiency testing, testing for placement provides goals that are much easier to determine. A placement test has the narrow aim of fitting students into a known curriculum, and hence it calls for the active participation of the faculty who are teaching in that curriculum. Although it is extremely difficult to gain agreement about definitions for proficiencies, it is relatively easy to define what is required for placement. For example, those teaching "remedial English" and "freshman English" at a particular college will be able to say what distinguishes the student who is ready to move on into the regular curriculum. Perhaps we might hear that the significant issue is sentence construction, the ability to master the complex elements that lead to full, complete, variable, and correct sentences in English. Or perhaps the dividing line is nearer to mechanics (such as mastery of the tense structure) or to paragraphing (such as understanding ways of connecting sentences or ideas). A placement test, in short, does not need to define or examine proficiencies but only those skills that help identify appropriate courses for students of varying ability. Furthermore, a placement test can allow for more refined placement of students by instructors after instruction has begun, if necessary, and therefore need not be as costly or elaborate as a proficiency test, whose scores may lead to irrevocable decisions. Thus a placement test, with its quite different goals, is different in many ways from a proficiency test, and that difference should be understood right from the start.

Equivalency Testing. Equivalency testing is a form of proficiency testing, since it is designed to offer credit by examination to students who have learned independently that which a class is designed to teach. The very specificity of such testing makes the consideration of goals absolutely necessary. Two national programs sponsored by the College Board and administered by the Educational Testing Service are designed to offer credit by examination in college freshman English: the Advanced Placement Program and the College Level Examination Program. In addition, some institutions offer their own tests for the same purpose: for example, the California State University English Equivalency Examination. The goal in these cases is to define (and then examine) the most important skills and knowledge taught in freshman English; while reaching that goal is fraught with problems, at least the issue is clear. Certainly, the key people making decisions about an equivalency testing program need to be the faculty teaching the course in question, and the fairness of the test needs to be demonstrated by norming it on students completing the class.

Although equivalency testing offers major advantages to all parties (the best students take more advanced work and more of it, and the faculty find more homogenous classes), many faculty are initially threatened by the concept that students can learn outside the classroom what professors teach in class. Faculty are also deeply concerned that the equivalency test will both trivialize their subject and debase academic standards. Thus a testing program that awards unit credit needs to accommodate and alleviate these deep-seated faculty suspicions by involving faculty at all stages in the program.

Norm-Referenced Versus Criterion-Referenced Tests

Norm-referenced testing, the standard method of mental measurement since the model was developed by and for aptitude testing of World War I draftees, has a superficial appeal for the testing of writing. It suggests such virtues as objectivity, comparability, and statistical complexity. However, such testing has some serious problems, particularly for the unwary.

Since norm referencing is derived from the aptitude testing model, it assumes a "normal" distribution of the skills it measures, which means in practice that it is designed to produce a bell curve. Thus, if you score at the tenth percentile on mechanical ability, 90 percent of the population has greater mechanical aptitude than you, and you should be kept away from valuable equipment. In order to produce a bell curve, the test design requires a preponderance of questions that about half the test population will answer correctly, with a few very easy questions (to produce the left-hand slope of the curve) and a few very hard questions (for the right-hand slope). If the curve becomes distorted, as it may if too many students answer too many questions correctly or incorrectly, the test is revised to reestablish the normal curve. This means that norm-referenced test questions tend inevitably toward the aptitude testing model and away from questions susceptible to learning. Furthermore, the population used to determine the points on the bell curve is crucial, since the curve (against which all other test takers will be compared) is determined by the ability and (sometimes even more significantly) the aptitude and upbringing of the norming population.

Since norm referencing assumes a normal distribution of the skills it measures, it is disrupted by education; even short-term training can alter some score distributions and skew the bell curve. So such tests attempt to discount the effects of short-term learning in order to preserve the purity of the model. That situation is particularly unfortunate for writing testing, since writing "aptitude" will often reflect the economic, social, or ethnic conditions of the home at the time the student was learning the language; whatever discounts school learning in the measurement of writing ability tends to benefit the already advantaged.

Although I am not suggesting that norm referencing is either evil or necessarily inappropriate in all cases, I am pointing out the potential problems for those who would measure writing ability by a norm-referenced test. The norming population must be a primary concern: A test normed on Eastern prep school students will probably distort the results when used on a less-advantaged group of students, whatever their writing ability, if the test contains the usual number of questions calling for cultural advantages and an ear for the privileged dialect. As I will demonstrate later in this chapter, students from minority cultures seem to score particularly poorly on such tests, despite relatively normal distributions on writing sample tests.

Even if the norming group seems an appropriate one, a careful review of the test is particularly necessary in order to check for the aptitude test item or the social class item that often appears on norm-referenced writing tests. Here, for example, is a sample question adapted from a popular test designed to measure college-level competence in English composition:

> English-speaking musicians use professionally large numbers of words from which one of the following languages?
> a. German
> b. French
> c. Spanish
> d. Latin
> e. Italian

The testmakers obviously are looking in this question for a scrap of information about the ways in which English uses foreign words—in this case the Italian vocabulary for some aspects of musical notation. Some students may, in fact, pick up such information in a composition course, although it seems unlikely; but the student most able to darken the proper space on an answer sheet is probably the one whose parents wanted to and could afford to give him or her classical music lessons as a child. Those not so privileged (including, no doubt, some professional musicians) are not likely to know the answer, regardless of their writing ability. And someone who knew *too* much—say a specialist in medieval music—might even give the "wrong" answer, Latin.

It would be easy to select other unfair items from norm-referenced tests (or any other kind), particularly those items that are culture linked, such as the one above, or that are based on dialect or usage differences that have no bearing on writing ability. The particular issue here is not that such unfair items exist but that norm referencing encourages such items because they "work" for certain convenient norming populations. (Essay testing has its share and more of such questions, but they tend to be so difficult to score consistently that they are rarely repeated; essay readers are much more opinionated and vocal than are the computers that score multiple-choice answer sheets.)

It is sometimes hard for those who are not specialists in testing to realize how narrowly and precisely conceived are the most professional norm-referenced tests. I once asked an ETS test specialist about a particular item on the Scholastic Aptitude Test. "It's really a stupid question," I said to him, in some exasperation. He cheerfully agreed. "Sure is. But those who succeed in the first year of college get it right, and those who don't get it wrong. And that's what the test is all about." He was right, in a narrow sense, since ETS consistently tries to make those who use—and misuse—the SAT understand that its sole purpose is to predict first-year college success. But no amount of information seems to keep people from imagining the SAT to be a general intelligence test or (even worse) a proficiency test for the nation's high schools.

The basic problems with using norm-referenced tests to measure writing ability, then, are located both in their construction and in their norming populations. If the test in fact measures what a test committee is seeking to find out and if the norming population is indeed appropriate, then there is good reason to celebrate: Someone else has borne the burden of test development with the same goals. If, however, existing tests do not meet test specifications or are not appropriate for the population, it is time to consider adapting criterion-referenced testing, that is, testing according to standards defined without reference to a student population.

Criterion-referenced testing is different in its development and in its results from norm referencing: Since it is based on test criteria rather than on a norm population, criterion-referenced testing does not seek to obtain a normal curve. On the contrary, the specific nature of such testing leads to questions directed to the material of a course of instruction or a body of knowledge. Those who have not learned the material will turn out very poor responses, while those who have mastered the material will do extremely well; a skewed curve does not mean a badly constructed test but rather a test group that either knows the material or does not. The particular advantage of criterion-referenced testing is obvious: The questions can be developed directly out of stated test criteria and for the specific purposes of the particular test or testing program. The disadvantage of such testing is equally obvious: Since it is highly unlikely that a criterion-referenced test for a specific purpose will be available commercially, test development is usually necessary, and the statistical comfort of national normative data will not be available. In test construction, the danger comes from the use of unrealistic or unfair criteria or from criteria that may be fair for one population but not another.

Since essay testing is able to combine the advantages of both norm and criterion referencing, usually emphasizing the criteria, many institutions and state programs have moved into such testing in recent years; almost without exception, they have found the effort to be well worth it, since the establishment of essay testing programs yields not only useful and credible scores but also major benefits in faculty development and curricular change. Where such testing has generated faculty resistance (as in Georgia), the objections have centered on the perceived rigidity of the criteria, which, without the moderating influence of norm referencing, may work to the disadvantage of some elements of the population.

While the debate between criterion and norm referencing of writing tests often develops into an argument between the advocates of essay and multiple-choice testing, the two issues are not altogether the same. It is perfectly possible to develop criterion-referenced multiple-choice tests, and, unfortunately, it is becoming more and more common to adopt an essay test with its norms and statistics from some other program. Both criterion and norm referencing have their value, of course, as well as their problems; difficulties arise for those who fail to be clear conceptually about which kind of test they are giving or the degree to which they are combining both kinds. The question almost never comes up in class, where tests are routinely criterion referenced, or in relation to the very large-scale tests, where norm referencing is standard. But the issue is ever-present in writing tests of moderate size.

Holistic scoring nicely blends both criterion and norm referencing: The scoring guide sets out the criteria for scoring, while the ranking of papers against each other in accordance with sample papers tends toward the normative. Making the decision about the meaning of the holistic ranking that takes place after the scoring is completed, on the one hand, allows those in charge to moderate the impersonality of the criteria by the humanity of the actual performance; on the other hand, it allows them to adjust the populism of the score distribution according to the professionalism of the criteria. In this area, as in so many others, the flexibility and integrative nature of the holistic approach give those who use it well great opportunities to blend the testing with the teaching of writing.

Multiple-Choice Versus Essay Testing of Writing

Although the issues of norm and criterion referencing are not identical to the problems raised by multiple-choice testing of writing, the issues are close enough for the latter tired but pressing matter to enter here. The issue of multiple-choice versus essay testing of writing has become a bit dated since the development of relatively reliable and cost-effective holistic scoring procedures. Insofar as a test seeks to measure actual writing ability, the issue can be more generally defined as a conflict between direct and indirect measures. Traditionally and logically, an indirect measure is preferred only when it shows clear advantages over the direct measure. Until recently, advocates of indirect (usually multiple-choice) measurement of writing ability could point to the high cost and low reliability of scoring writing samples as compared with the low cost and high efficiency of multiple-choice answer sheets. Now the argument has shifted: The high development costs of multiple-choice testing, the constant security and revision expenses of multiple-choice tests under truth-in-testing laws, the lower validity of such tests, and the damage to curriculum such tests cause by devaluing actual writing—all these suggest the weaknesses of multiple-choice measurement in the field of writing.

A number of studies have sought to relate the scores students receive on multiple-choice tests with those the same students receive on a writing sample. The correlations vary somewhat, as one would expect from the great number of variables involved (different kinds of students, multiple-choice tests, essay questions, scoring systems, and so on), but they tend to hover about the .5 range. The number, as usual, raises more questions than it answers. The correlation is roughly the same as that between adult female height and weight in America. That is, you can guess a woman's height from her weight with about the same accuracy that you can guess a student's essay test score from his or her multiple-choice score. Is that level of accuracy good enough? Partisans of multiple-choice testing will argue that the correlation is good enough for many decisions, such as a placement test, and good enough to support the inclusion of a significant number of multiple-choice items on any writing test. Those opposed, many of them writing teachers, find such correlations too low, particularly in light of evidence that the correlation drops markedly for the disadvantaged. Statisticians will remind us that a rough guide to the "overlap" of any two measures is the square of the correlation; this suggests that only about 25 percent of what is tested on most multiple-choice "writing" tests is also tested in a writing sample.

Nonetheless, particularly in the elementary and high schools, norm-referenced testing of usage or mechanics is still the standard way to test writing skill. Those who argue for the economy and reliability of multiple-choice tests do not yet know that their arguments are outdated. The question remains: How can informed teachers facilitate the development and use of better types of tests? One intent of this book is to help those teachers marshal the evidence—through theories, arguments, and practices—to present a convincing case for a writing testing program.

Ideally, the time to make such a case is in the planning stage of a new program or in the evaluation stage of a continuing one; that is when a clear understanding of the issues surrounding criterion and norm referencing, multiple-choice and essay questions, placement and proficiency testing will help shape a testing program. Knowledge, in this area as in most, tends to destroy dogmatism and lead to a moderate and cooperative stance. Perhaps the advocates of a norm-referenced multiple-choice test will be content to use it to examine reading ability, while writing can be tested by a set of writing samples scored holistically to carefully established criteria. Perhaps even some aspects of the writing curriculum are in fact best tested by a multiple-choice measure, while a writing sample or two might provide a validity check (at least at first). Many of those defending multiple-choice tests of writing are properly defensive of their stance and will be ready to include writing if they can be shown that writing samples can be properly constructed, reliably scored, and economically handled.

At present, arguments about these matters tend to be uninformed, emotional, and badly timed. Passions and name calling flower; the advocates of writing samples argue for the virtues of the past, of culture, of humanism, and the patrons of the machine-scored test stand for a modern age of technology. But the solution to the issue is often quite undramatic once test specifications and other planning matters have been attended to. Different kinds of skills are most effectively measured by different kinds of tests. Writing as a whole is best dealt with by writing-sample testing; reading (which correlates highly with writing), sentence construction skills, ability to discern logical relationships, and the like seem best dealt with by multiple-choice testing. Where highly refined measurement is needed (as in the awarding of college credit or in certification for graduation), the most responsible test will combine both kinds of measures; where less refined measurement is required (as in placement testing, where testing errors can be readily rectified by teachers), one or the other kind of test might suffice, depending on local curricula, personnel, and facilities. Nonetheless, whenever a writing test is put into the context of the entire instructional program, only very powerful arguments can prevail against the obvious value of including writing itself as at least part of the test.

These debates probably can never be wholly avoided, but their ill effects can be substantially mitigated by delaying the selection of a testing instrument until after careful program planning is under way. With a statement of goals, criteria, and uses, and with a clear connection between the instructional program and the test, it becomes possible to consider the testing instrument within a context that encourages logical and purposeful discussion.

Bias in Writing Tests

In recent years, the courts have become involved in the testing of writing, most particularly in determining the fairness of such testing for various ethnic groups. In Florida, a high school proficiency testing program had to be revised after a court found that it was testing for skills that had not been taught to substantial numbers of minority children. In Michigan, a similar legal quarrel developed over the issue of "black English"; there, the court immersed itself in technical linguistic arguments over the legitimacy of that particular dialect for testing purposes.

It is not only these (and other) legal questions that ought to lead anyone testing writing to consider possible bias; the entire history of mental measurement is marked by the questionable use of questionable data in the service of the prejudices of the time. Stephen J. Gould's *The Mismeasure of Man* (1981) should be required reading for anyone involved in testing others, on whatever scale; in it he documents a particularly inglorious history of distorted test results, and he suggests, with what may be hyperbole, that it is the nature of science itself to distort facts in the interest of what it imagines to be the truth.

In this light, it is particularly interesting to review the comparative claims of essay and multiple-choice testing to fairness in the testing of ethnic minorities. The problem is complex, dealing as it does with the ambiguous and vexing definition of bias. Every test is, by definition, biased against those who do not know what is called for; the problem is to ensure that no unintended or illegal or immoral bias takes place. Those who believe that multiple-choice tests are objective are likely to assume that such tests are, on the face of it, more fair to minorities than are essay or other kinds of tests, since no humans (with intended or unintended prejudice) are part of the scoring. Evidence is beginning to accumulate, however, that casts doubt on that assumption.

The following study illustrates some of the problems of conducting research in this area, particularly the very large numbers of students and tests required to produce sufficient minority student data for statistical purposes. The conclusions, which suggest that essay testing is substantially more fair than multiple-choice testing to racial and ethnic minorities, are consistent with the view of writing and writing testing taken throughout this book.

Overview of the Study. Over 10,000 students entering the California State University in Fall 1977 took two tests, both designed for placement into either remedial or regular freshman composition programs. Almost 70 percent of the students in that group identified themselves ethnically, allowing for meaningful statistical analysis of test results by ethnicity. The study compared three different test score distributions—from a holistically scored essay, a multiple-choice usage test, and a measure that combined the essay with certain other multiple-choice portions—in order to ascertain whether ethnicity had any effect on these score distributions by the same individuals on different kinds of writing tests. Results were gathered and five sets of graphs (Figures 1 through 5) were prepared under the direction of Leon L. Thomas, then associate dean of Institutional Research for the CSU. The findings showed that those identifying themselves as white showed relatively little change from test to test while those identifying themselves as a member of one of three racial minorities had sharply differing scores. Further, those who identified themselves as black had a radically different and lower score distribution from the multiple-choice usage than they did from the holistically scored essay test.

The Tests. The students in the sample took both the Test of Standard Written English (TSWE), offered by the College Board as part of the Scholastic Aptitude Test, and the English Placement Test (EPT), offered by the California State University with the consultant support of the Educational Testing Service. While both tests have the same purpose, they are different in a number of important respects.

The TSWE is described by the College Board in its informational brochure for students as follows: "The questions on the Test of Standard Written English evaluate your ability to recognize standard written English, the language of most college textbooks and the English you will probably be expected to use in the papers you write for most college courses. The TSWE tests some basic principles of grammar and usage, such as agreement of subject and verb and of pronoun and antecedent, and it also deals with more complicated writing problems, such as whether or not the comparisons made in a sentence are logical. The test begins with 25 usage questions, then has 15 sentence correction questions, and ends with 10 more usage questions."

The test consists of fifty questions, which are to be answered in thirty minutes. The questions are of the familiar error-hunting type, as in the sample question provided by the College Board:

He spoke <u>bluntly</u> and <u>angrily</u> to <u>we spectators</u>. <u>No error</u>
       A   B   C   D   E

The assumption is, of course, that students who can locate such errors in test designer prose will not make similar errors in their own writing, or, to be more fair to the correlational concept of indirect measurement, that students who can accurately find such errors are likely to be better writers than those who cannot.

The EPT is a much longer test (two and one half hours) and consists of four parts: an essay section calling for forty-five minutes of student writing, a multiple-choice reading comprehension test taking thirty-five minutes, and two additional multiple-choice parts called "sentence construction" and "logic and organization." It is designed to be more diagnostic than the TSWE, although the description in the EPT student brochure shows a very similar purpose: "The English Placement Test has two purposes. The first is to provide an indication of your general skill in reading and in written communication, and the second, based on an analysis of the specific skills measured, is to provide a brief description of your strengths and weaknesses."

The multiple-choice portions of the EPT, which are not

our concern here, tend to avoid error hunting as they measure
their more precise specifications, and there is no isolated usage
test at all. The essay is generally based on personal experience
and calls for organized description with a limited amount of
abstraction. The following sample essay question is distributed
to students applying for the examination:

> Write an essay describing an occasion on
> which you privately or openly resisted a viewpoint
> that had become popular with your friends and ac-
> quaintances or one on which you felt that actions
> taken by them were wrong. 1) Describe the situa-
> tion, 2) explain why you disagreed with the group,
> and 3) tell how you handled the situation.

The scoring guide for the essay is, in general, very similar
to Holistic Scoring Guide No. 1, printed in Chapter Seven. The
essay scoring was reported and is used here as a sum of the two
ratings given by two separate readers on a six-point scale; the
best score is two scores of six, or a total of twelve.

The two tests are similar enough in intention—to identify
students who require extra work in writing before entering freshman composition courses—and different enough in concept and
construction to allow for the study of ethnic differences on the
different portions of the tests. It is important to note that the
differences on the tests have nothing to do with "standards" or
with the value of teaching students appropriate usage for formal
writing situations. Both of the tests in the study agree on the
need for high standards and appropriate usage. The EPT, without a usage section, is careful to point out to students preparing
for the test that usage in context is an important component of
the essay score: "Of course, the rating your essay receives from
the faculty members who score it will, to some extent, also be
dependent on how well you spell and punctuate and how carefully you follow such conventions of standard written English
as subject-verb agreement."

The Student Sample. The student sample is unusually
well-suited to the purpose of the study. A very large number of
students must participate in order to provide significant minor-

ity-majority comparisons—one of the reasons such studies are rare. The California State University, with its nineteen campuses in a variety of urban, suburban, and rural settings, its centralized data banks, and its huge number of students (approaching one third of a million), is one of the few institutions that provide the opportunity for such a study. The students who took both the EPT and the TSWE in preparation for admission in Fall 1977 were in every way representative of the entire first-time freshman population that year: Entrants were then (as now) restricted to those in the top third of the high school graduating class, with the exception of a small percentage of special admissions under such programs as the Educational Opportunities Program.

Of the 10,719 students in the sample, 7,300 identified themselves ethnically, principally in the following four categories: 5,246 white, 585 black, 449 Mexican-American, 617 Asian-American. These numbers approximate the proportion of these minorities in the CSU entering class and are large enough for meaningful statistical analysis of test results by ethnicity.

Test Results. Figures 1 through 5 present an unusual opportunity to compare the performance of different ethnic groups on a multiple-choice usage test (TSWE) and on an essay test that includes usage in a writing context (EPT essay). The graph designated A in each figure gives the score distribution for the particular group on the EPT as a whole, the long four-part test including the essay as one fourth of the total score; the graph marked B is for the TSWE, and the graph marked C is for the EPT essay score. The means, standard deviations, and number of students in each group are listed below each graph.

Both tests are intended to make the most careful distinctions at the low end of the test scale. Students above the mean are to be considered ready for college-level work, and the tests give no further information of use to that group. The most useful measurement is designed to take place in the scoring range at which the decision about possible remedial placement is likely to occur. Ordinarily, this means a distribution that is skewed left, that is, stretched out and tailed off in the lower range. The three graphs in Figure 1, showing the performance

Figure 1. All Participants.

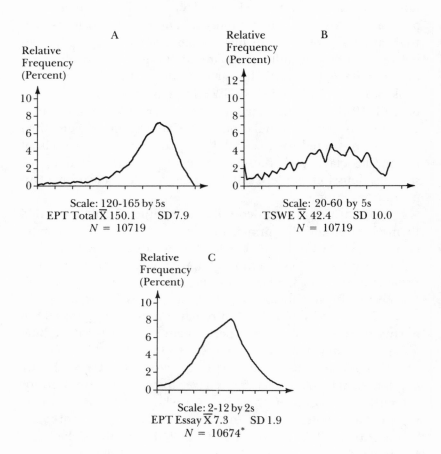

*Essay score distributions do not include a few students who did not attempt the essay, although they completed the multiple-choice portions of the EPT as well as the TSWE.

Source: White and Thomas, 1981, p. 279.

of the total group on (A) the EPT, (B) the TSWE, and (C) the EPT essay, all show this characteristic in varying degrees.

The essay portion of the EPT (graph C in Figure 1) shows a relatively more "normal" distribution than does the EPT total score (graph A), as is characteristic of many holistically scored tests; since its holistic scoring uses a combination of norm and

criterion referencing, developing its criteria in part from the papers in the sample, its score distributions will tend more toward
a bell curve than will those of strictly criterion-referenced tests.
There is, nonetheless, a noticeable left skew from the essay test,
although not as much as in the EPT total. The TSWE scale
(graph B) is considerably flatter than either of the EPT scales,
with curious concentrations of scores at the bottom and top
ends of the scale, but it is also skewed left.

Since the white students composed almost 72 percent of
the 7,300 students who identified themselves by ethnicity, it is
not surprising that the score patterns of these students are very
close to those achieved by the total group (see Figure 2). Mean
scores tend to be higher, and we notice fewer low scores overall.
The TSWE shows approximately 4 percent of white students receiving the highest possible score. While the EPT scales do not
show as marked a shift upward, the shift still may be observed.

So far, there are no surprises in these graphs. The short
multiple-choice usage test seems to correlate reasonably well
with the writing sample, although the longer test seems rather
better for the purpose of distinguishing among the weak students. Those who identify themselves ethnically as white seem
to do better on the test than non-whites, reflecting an aspect of
American society confirmed by virtually all testing programs.
The patterns of scores on all the charts are roughly similar. But
when we turn to the score distributions of those who identified
themselves as black, we discover some radical differences of pattern and range of distribution.

The dramatic set of graphs in Figure 3 shows the very different score distributions black students received on the TSWE
and the EPT. The multiple-choice usage test not only groups
over 11 percent of the black students at the lowest possible
score, but it distributes black students in a pattern of performance wholly different from that shown by the same test for
the majority (compare graph B for Figures 1 and 2). It might be
argued that such a distribution reflects the writing ability of this
group had those same students—precisely the same individuals—
not performed otherwise on the EPT. While these students have
a lower EPT total mean score than the white students, they are

Figure 2. White Participants.

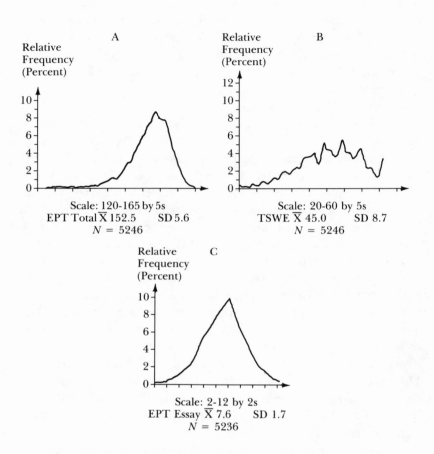

Scale: 120-165 by 5s
EPT Total X̄ 152.5   SD 5.6
N = 5246

Scale: 20-60 by 5s
TSWE X̄ 45.0   SD 8.7
N = 5246

Scale: 2-12 by 2s
EPT Essay X̄ 7.6   SD 1.7
N = 5236

Source: White and Thomas, 1981, p. 279.

distributed along the whole range of scores, and their pattern reflects the left-skewedness that is desirable for placement testing.

After these graphs were initially published (White and Thomas, 1981), some of those responsible for the TSWE argued that graph B of Figure 3 appears as it does because the test was too hard for this group of students; a revision of the test with easier questions would spread the bottom group out to the left

Figure 3. Black Participants.

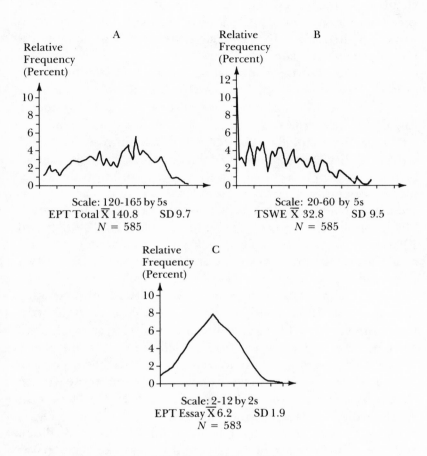

Scale: 120-165 by 5s
EPT Total $\overline{X}$ 140.8   SD 9.7
$N = 585$

Scale: 20-60 by 5s
TSWE $\overline{X}$ 32.8   SD 9.5
$N = 585$

Scale: 2-12 by 2s
EPT Essay $\overline{X}$ 6.2   SD 1.9
$N = 583$

Source: White and Thomas, 1981, p. 280.

in a pattern similar to the other patterns. This may be so, and I understand that the test has since been revised. The issue, however, is not whether that particular test is now better or worse than some others but rather the degree to which multiple-choice usage tests in general distribute minority students differently than do direct measures of writing. The 1977 form and scoring of the TSWE—a highly professional test constructed by ETS and administered by the College Board to over a million students—clearly allow us to examine that issue, whatever the claimed virtues of revisions of that particular test. Indeed, the very high correlation of the TSWE scores with SAT scores suggests that the issue before us relates to certain aspects of multiple-choice tests in general.

Perhaps the most interesting comparison is between the performance of these students on the TSWE and their performance on the EPT essay test. We need to be cautious, since a single personal experience essay, even if scored with considerable reliability, should not be considered a definitive measure of writing ability. Such an essay does, however, serve as a direct measure of the characteristic indirectly measured by the multiple-choice test and must be considered a validity check for it. We have already seen that white students demonstrate a considerable similarity in score distributions on the TSWE usage and EPT essay writing tests. For black students, the dramatic dissimilarity casts some real doubt on the validity of usage testing as an indicator of writing ability.

Of course, it is possible that the faculty members grading the essay tests for our 1977 sample were insensitive to the writing errors made by black students and, in effect, showed a bias toward these students when they graded the papers. But this is unlikely for several reasons: Readers would have had no way to distinguish the papers written by minorities from those written by the rest of the students (while deciding over 21,000 scores), strict quality control measures (as described in Chapter Eight) have led to high inter-rater reliability for EPT essay readings, and the criteria for scoring papers do stress such matters as grammar, syntax, and diction.

The most likely explanation for the different patterns of performance shown in graphs B and C of Figure 3 has to do with the significance of a multiple-choice usage test for determining the writing ability of black students. It is altogether likely that the *type* of question that usually appears on usage tests and that dominates the TSWE particularly penalizes nonsignificant features of minority dialects. It is also possible that the ability to identify errors in testmaker prose relates more strongly to the dialect learned as a young child (that is, the dialect spoken in the home and on the playground) than to a learned ability to write in prose acceptable to college professors as essay readers.

The College Board, of course, has a particular stake in demonstrating that its tests do not show racial bias and has published a number of reports dealing with such questions. Despite its general affiliation with the social values of the prestigious Eastern private schools, the College Board has obvious good intentions in this regard and some real concern for the issue. It is well to be cautious about its reports, however, particularly in relation to the minority populations used in them. Research Bulletin RB-77-15, *Group Comparisons for the TSWE* (Breland, 1977a), for example, provides data on 9,144 students; however, not all minority groups are well represented in these data, as only 8 of those students identified themselves as Mexican-American.

Figures 4 and 5 show the patterns of performance for two additional ethnic/racial groups. Once again, we see that for these minority groups there is an important difference in pattern of score distribution between the EPT, particularly the essay portion, and the TSWE. For these two groups of students, we may presume a certain amount of second-language interference rather than the dialect interference typical of the black group. The multiple-choice usage test once again rendered a much more negative judgment of these students' use of English than did the evaluators of their writing.

Conclusions. This study is by no means conclusive. But it does suggest a series of propositions and warnings. Particularly important is that it shows that the TSWE, a conventional multiple-choice usage test, does not distribute the scores of minority students the way trained and accurate evaluators of writing samples do. It may be that multiple-choice usage tests in general and even, perhaps, many kinds of multiple-choice tests share this disparity. Those who use such tests (or indeed any kind of test) should be aware of possible differences in measurement (unrelated to the subject supposedly being tested) for minority students.

The first major study of the correlation between essay

Figure 4. Mexican-American Participants.

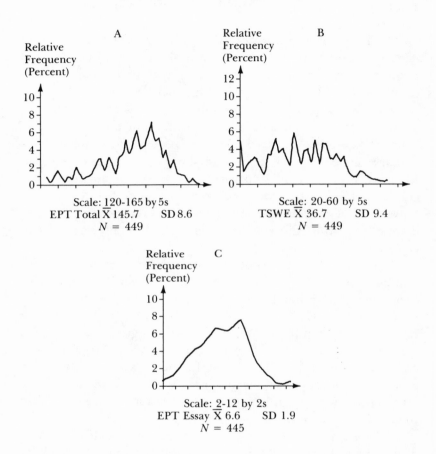

Source: White and Thomas, 1981, p. 281.

and multiple-choice usage tests, published by the College Board, argued for the inclusion of both test types: "The combination of objective items (which measure accurately some skills involved in writing) with an essay (which measures directly, if somewhat less accurately, the writing itself) proved to be more valid than either type of item alone" (Godshalk, Swineford, and Coffman, 1966, p. vi). The study of CSU entering freshmen tends to support that statement by suggesting that the validity

Figure 5. Asian-American Participants.

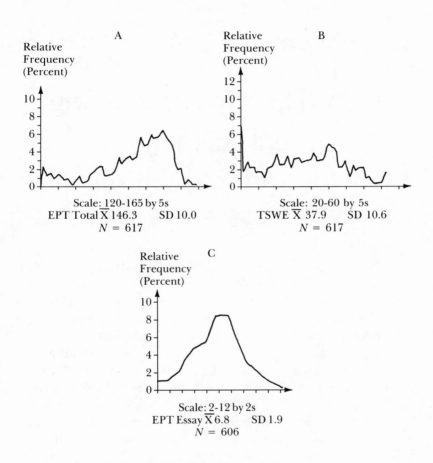

Scale: 120-165 by 5s
EPT Total X̄ 146.3   SD 10.0
N = 617

Scale: 20-60 by 5s
TSWE X̄ 37.9   SD 10.6
N = 617

Scale: 2-12 by 2s
EPT Essay X̄ 6.8   SD 1.9
N = 606

Source: White and Thomas, 1981, p. 281.

of multiple-choice tests may well vary according to the ethnic background of the student. A carefully devised and properly scored essay test seems not to contain that same problem of validity for minorities, and those seeking more fair treatment for minorities in testing would do well to argue for expanded use of essay testing.

5

How Theories of Reading
Affect Responses
to Student Writing

English teachers at all levels are principally trained to be sophisticated readers; it is generally assumed that trained readers will make effective teachers of writing. Most of those reading this book, including most of those who are English teachers, probably have received little or no formal training in either the teaching of composition or testing. If the book reaches the wide audience for which it is intended, many readers will be from outside the field of English altogether. Whatever these readers' specialties, the teaching and testing of writing need to form an important part of their pedagogical equipment, since writing is a crucial means of learning in all fields. That means that it is important to reflect on the nature of reading as well as writing, since reading and writing are linked in ways similar to the bond apparent in the most effective marriages: obvious intimacy without a wholly clear or sharply defined relationship. My concern in this chapter is to connect two prominent theories of reading to recent concepts about responding to student writing in composition instruction and, eventually, to the holistic theory of testing.

It has become clear in recent years that the way we conceive of reading has a profound effect on the way we understand and respond to what we read. For example, if we believe that meaning resides essentially in the text we have before us, as do most of those trained to teach literature, we will perceive our job as readers as gaining access to that (largely external) meaning. If, however, we believe that meaning is a function of our own (basically internal) creativity in relation to black marks on a white page, we will consider our job as readers to be quite different—nearer to being a producer than to being a more or less active recipient. This distinction, which may not seem to be a difference to some readers and which may seem artificially exaggerated to others, has loomed very large among those concerned with critical theory in recent years. Our concern here is to clarify such differences in critical theory, since they must and do affect the ways in which we measure and respond to student writing.

The Formalistic Theory of Reading

Before we turn to the issues raised by the most recent literary theorists, it is important to remind ourselves of some of the certainties about reading on which we used to rely and which recent theories have put in question. Much of the formal criticism developed in the 1930s and 1940s rested on the supposition that the reader's task was essentially to submit himself or herself to the text in order to discern the meaning that resided there quite independently of either the reader or the author (who, after producing the text, was just one more reader). A good location of that idea is Mark Schorer's influential essay, "Technique as Discovery," first published in the *Hudson Review* in 1948:

> Modern criticism has shown us that to speak of content as such is not to speak of art at all, but of experience; and that it is only when we speak of the *achieved* content, the form of the work of art, that we speak as critics. The difference between content, or experience, and achieved content, or art, is technique.
> When we speak of technique, then, we speak of nearly everything. For technique is the means

by which the writer's experience, which is his subject matter, compels him to attend to it; technique
is the only means he has of discovering, exploring,
developing his subject, of conveying its meaning,
and, finally, of evaluating it. And surely it follows
that certain techniques are sharper tools than others, and will discover more; that the writer capable
of the most exacting technical scrutiny of his subject matter will produce works with thickness and
resonance, works which reverberate with maximum
meaning [p. 67].

Schorer is arguing for strict attention to the form of a
piece of writing as the way to understand its meaning. Although
he is writing about literature, the same approach would hold for
any sort of reading: Every writer shapes experience or knowledge by technique, and not only is that technique what gives
the work meaning but it is so embedded in the very construction of the writing that it virtually constitutes the writing. The
practical effect of that theory leads to an intense concentra-
tion on the text, which "reverberates" with its meaning on its
own; the work *itself* has content, thickness, and resonance, independent of author and reader. Our task as readers is to understand so much about technique that we can obtain entry into
the achieved content of the work and hence come to understand the "maximum meaning" it has to offer.

If you are an English teacher, you will recognize this approach to reading as what was called "the new criticism" during its period of greatest influence, from the early 1930s to the
late 1950s. It seized the imagination of two generations of
teachers and critics, revolutionized the approach to literature,
and led to an extraordinary production of articles, books, and
editions illuminating literature. It still seems to be the dominant approach to reading in the high schools, where its relatively antiseptic approach to literature, often applied in mechanical fashion, has played some part in the alienation of
students from reading for pleasure.

While much has been written about the implications of
this theory of reading for the study of literature, few have con-

sidered its profound and far-reaching effects on the teaching and measurement of writing. On the positive side, it urged readers of student writing to attend to the texts that the student produced rather than to the student's social class, appearance, or moral predisposition. Since the theory argued that language and thought were in fact the same thing, the teacher could face with a certain valuable skepticism the student who claimed, "I know what I mean, but I just don't know how to say it": "If you don't know how to say it," one could self-righteously reply, "then you don't know what you mean!" Most important, the theory focused both student and teacher attention on the craftsmanship of prose, what Schorer calls "technique," and the way that that craftsmanship conveys meaning. In so doing, this theory provided a useful if limited framework for the teaching of writing, since craftsmanship is always teachable, if not always learnable, in a way that inspiration, say, is not.

However, the belief that meaning resided in the text itself caused a series of theoretical and practical problems for writing teachers, particularly in relation to evaluation. Even though every sensible teacher knew that we must respond differently to a student text than to a finished piece of literature, the theory gave no good basis for such a different response—much needed by our best students—and suggested few practical ways of coping with the weakest of our students. Most damaging of all, the theory urged us to consider student writing as a product to be analyzed, as if every student composition were a failed Shakespeare sonnet.

This concern with writing as a product led to a heightened concern for and preoccupation with editing and the appearance of the student text. The very weakest of our students, whose products were particularly unsightly, were declared "remedial"—that is, verbally diseased—and sent to do therapeutic exercises in grammatical workbooks (which kept them busy and gave us the illusion that they were learning something). Our expectations (that is, our reading theory) had to change before we could begin understanding how to teach such students, as Mina Shaughnessy has convincingly demonstrated (1977).

Some of the more extreme partisans of recent writing theories argue too loudly that "writing is a process, not a product" and hence confuse the issue. Writing is, as every sensible person knows, a product (in most cases) as well as a process. Every student turning in a paper to be graded, every scholar producing a paper for delivery or publication or promotion, every employee sending off a memo knows perfectly well that writing is an important and measurable product. We make ourselves foolish if we ignore that aspect of writing. Our students rightly expect us to evaluate their writing products, and they need such evaluation in order to improve. But the theory of reading, and hence of writing, that defines writing as *only* or even *principally* a product distorts the teaching of writing. It turns the writing teacher into only a judge of texts and limits teacher intervention (and hence value) to the end of the writing process, where such intervention is not likely to do very much good for the essay in hand. It also provides some justification for multiple-choice usage testing of writing ability and suggests that the measurement of writing samples (necessarily concerned with writing products, and usually first-draft products at that) ought to be analytic rather than holistic, since analytic measurement is much more attuned to surface correctness.

It thus strikes me as no accident that three movements in the teaching of reading and writing began to take place at about the same time: (1) Proponents of writing as process began articulating their views and pursuing their research. (2) Measurement of writing by holistic evaluation of actual writing began to gain prominence and acceptance. (3) Poststructural theorists began arguing that reading was a process, a creative interaction between reader and text. While the three movements were quite independent, operating in entirely different circles, each in its own way was a rebellion against formalism and against the traditional analytic ways of thinking about reading and writing. The formalistic focus on the text as product, to the virtual exclusion of all else, had come to be as constricting for the teaching and measurement of writing as it was for the reading of literature.

Poststructural Theories of Reading

An early sign of the change in the teaching of reading and writing appeared when rhetoric, the ancient discipline concerned with much more than form (most particularly with invention and audience response), began to reassert its claims and a group of modern rhetoricians began stressing the importance of relating forms of invention to the concept of audience. Edward Corbett's *Classical Rhetoric for the Modern Student* came out in 1965, the same year that W. Ross Winterowd published *Rhetoric and Writing*; five years later, Young, Becker, and Pike published their influential *Rhetoric: Discovery and Change* (1970). During this period, Richard Young, Janet Emig, and many others began to focus the attention of composition teachers on the sequential and recursive stages of the writing process and on the many possible locations of useful teacher intervention. Research into the writing process has been flourishing on many fronts in recent years, from the detailed charts and elaborate equipment of Linda Flower and Sondra Perl to the theoretical and practical work on how schoolchildren learn writing that is being done by such diverse investigators as James Britton (whose work reflects the approaches of Piaget and other learning theorists) and Steven Krashen (whose work reflects current concepts in linguistics and foreign language learning).

At the same time this burst of activity in the field of composition was going on, poststructural literary theory was taking root in many of the graduate schools; for example, Jacques Derrida's *Of Grammatology* first appeared in 1967. The 1970s saw major articles and books by Wolfgang Iser (*The Implied Reader*, 1974), and Stanley Fish, whose *Is There a Text in This Class?* (1980) compiles his major articles from the previous decade. In addition, of course, we have an outpouring of books and articles from a catalogue of reader-response and deconstructionist critics and a covey of new journals, such as *Diacritics* and *New Literary Criticism*.

None of the issues raised by poststructural criticism is easy or without elaborate complexity. In many ways, the differences among poststructural critics are large, and arguments about those differences have created a lively, if minor, new industry: David Bleich and Norman Holland argue about varieties of subjectivism, and Iser and Fish by no means speak with the same voice as they debate the ways readers interact with texts. Indeed, Fish himself speaks with different voices, arguing at length with himself (1980), as is typical of critics for whom texts have lost their traditional moorings. We speak of Derrida at our peril, and we must be sure which manifestation of Roland Barthes or even of Hillis Miller (early or late) we are quoting if we are to be true to the context of their remarks.

Nonetheless, it remains possible to speak of these theorists as a group in certain restricted contexts. They unite in their opposition to the belief that meaning resides in a text, and it is this opposition in particular that has substantial implications for the teaching and evaluation of writing.

Like most traditionally trained readers, I initially found this position hard to understand; I was incredulous that serious critics could allow meaning to escape the control of either the text or the critics. I recall posing a question to Norman Holland during a session on psychological criticism at a Modern Language Association convention (I ventured that I had told a student she had "misread" a play), only to be told by this normally gentle man that I was "unforgivably arrogant." While Holland is more extreme than most reader-response critics, he was emphasizing his belief that every reader creates a text; his *Five Readers Reading* (1975) comes perilously close to presenting a text as a Rorschach blot, open to whatever the reader may discern. Another school of theorists, the "deconstructionists," has its roots (and language, unfortunately) in French philosophy rather than in psychology; they disavow psychological subjectivism but nonetheless argue that, at best, the text offers only a guide to the reader, as if it were a musical score that must be performed or (to use a favorite term) "played" in order to become meaningful.

A convenient and inclusive summary of many of the attitudes expressed in these new theories was published in the Fall 1982 issue of *Critical Texts*. Vincent Leitch captures the destabilization of the text, the peculiar language of the writers, and the relocation of the reader from the outside of the reading process (where the job was to discern the meaning in the text) to the center of the process (where we join with or even replace the author as creator of meaning):

> In the era of post-structuralism, literature becomes textuality and tradition turns into intertextuality. Authors die so that readers may come into prominence. Selves, whether of critic, poet or reader, appear as language constructions—texts. What are texts? Strings of differential traces. Sequences of floating signifiers. Sets of infiltrated signs, dragging along numerous intertextual elements. Sites for the free play of grammar, rhetoric and illusory reference, as Paul de Man puts it. What about the "meaning" or "truth" of the text? The random flights of signifiers across the textual surface, the dissemination of meaning, offers "truth" under one condition: that the chaotic processes of textuality be willfully regulated, controlled or stopped. Truth comes forth in the reifications of reading. It is not an entity or property of the text. No text utters its truth; the truth lies elsewhere— in a reading. Constitutionally, reading is misreading. Post-structuralism wishes to deregulate controlled dissemination and celebrate misreading [p. 3].

As I said earlier, I am not attempting to deal with the author's peculiar use of language or his concepts in relation to literary criticism—which are surely as wide of "truth" as he claims all texts to be. I am concerned with the implications of this theory of reading for the evaluation and teaching of writing. There is an undoubted faddism in this year's—or is it last year's?—jargon. As I write, the language in fashion is derived from a combination of Saussurian linguistics and French philosophy. A little while ago, a combination of Lévi-Strauss anthropology and Jungian mythology was all the rage, and, not so long before that, Freudian and Marxist terminology were absolutely required. We might say that new insights require new language, or, if we are wicked or jealous, that in literary criticism as in clothing new name brands create an artificial demand for a standard product. But we ought not to let the shifting fashions in terminology disguise from us the radically new conception of reading that is contained in virtually all critical theory emerging over the last two decades.

Thus, the context into which we need to put poststructural criticism and the passage I have just cited is that of a resistance movement to the narrow analytic reading theory of the formalistic "new" critics of the past. The text loses its privileged status as an object of study or reverence and becomes "strings of differential traces" with which the reader can play. The reader can only misread, because there is no meaning or truth in the text itself, which is, to borrow the phrase, a process, not a product. The process of reading itself becomes an object of study, and the examination of the reader's movement through the text in part substitutes for what used to be considered the meaning of the text. The author's intentions, the reader's individual associations with words, the reading situation, and all kinds of other matters outlawed by formal criticism can now be considered as part of the total meaning a reader creates from the text.

In short, these theories of reading have brought a new liberation—some would call it anarchy—into the reading process and placed on the reader a much heavier responsibility to actually create meanings that may or may not be present on the page for other readers. The writer is not relieved of responsibility by this process but rather now must assume a new responsibility: to create the kind of reader he or she needs for the text being produced. The teacher is also not free to abandon texts to naive readers, although we are forbidden to declare that some misreadings are wrong. Our obligation is to help our students see what other, highly sophisticated readers have made of the text so that they can enrich the text with various readings.

When we return to the task of reading and evaluating student writing in this new context, we find that this revolution in the concept of reading has an eerily familiar air to it. Where have we been accustomed to seeing writing that is, to adopt

Leitch's terminology, a "chaotic process of textuality" that only makes sense to a peculiarly sensitive reader, one who must "misread" in order to understand? Where, as teachers of writing, do we regularly see texts that can at best charitably be called "sequences of floating signifiers"? Whatever one can say about literary texts in this regard (and I do not mean to trivialize the elaborate concepts to which Leitch alludes), we can surely agree that this is a most apt description of the first-draft work most of us write and that our students normally hand to us for grading. I do not say this in mockery. The simple fact is that the definition of textuality and the reader's role in developing the meaning of a text that we find in recent theories of reading happens to describe much of our experience of responding with professional care to the writing our students produce for us. Part of the problem of evaluating student writing comes out of our deep understanding that we need to consider the process of writing as well as the product before us and that much of what the student is trying to say did not get very clearly into the words on the page.

It is important to distinguish the kind of misreading that Leitch describes from the misreading inherent in the New Criticism, where all meaning was assumed to lie in the text. If we are limited to what the student puts on the paper, we tend to be literalists, putting aside our intuitions of what the student *meant* to say or our predictions of what the student *could* say if he or she followed the best insights now buried in the present text. This formalistic misreading of student writing, which pretends to be objective, demands that the student believe that *our* concept of what was written is what is "really" there. By comparing the student text with what Nancy Sommers (whose work I will discuss shortly) calls our "ideal text," we appropriate the student's writing, deny the creative impulse that must drive writing, and turn revision into editing to please the teacher's concept of the paper. This supposed objectivity makes us not only less effective teachers but less insightful evaluators, since we are likely to be content with the equivalent objectivity claimed by usage testing or analytic scoring.

Once we accept the necessity of "misreading" as the poststructuralists use the term, we tend to be less sure of the objectivity of our reading and more ready to grant to the student possible intentions or insights not yet entirely present on the page. Even more important for our teaching, we can respond to early drafts with questions rather than with judgment (or invective!), since our aim is to urge the student back into "the chaotic process of textuality" (that is, the flux of ideas behind the writing) where revision occurs. As evaluators, we will tend to read holistically, looking for what is done well even if it is implicit, rather than analytically, looking for what our model tells us is error.

The recent theories of reading differ most sharply from the old New Criticism in their underlying assumption that meaning is not necessarily identical with expression. This assumption allows us to spend time, as we should in our writing classes, on both invention and revision. We know from our practice as teachers and as writers that the act of invention, the discovery of what we have to say, goes on throughout the writing process; we learn as we write, and successive drafts bring us closer and closer not to some predetermined coding of the known but to an understanding of the previously unknown. As teachers of writing, we seek in the texts our students produce that sense of original vision, that unique perception of new combinations of experiences and ideas that Derrida punningly calls "différance." Our creative misreading of the drafts we receive, our perception of possibilities as well as product, our awareness that we see on the page only a "trace" of a mind in action, then allow us to ask our students to pursue and refine these traces in revision.

This theory of reading brings reading and writing together as parallel acts, both consisting of the making of meaning: The writer seeks to make meaning out of experience, while the reader seeks to make meaning out of a text. Writers, as several critics have reminded us (Iser, 1974; Ong, 1975; Meyers, 1982), create readers as well as texts; the writer needs to keep in mind the "implied reader" designed by the text and to see this reader as an active partner in creation. Bad prose or ineffective writing often asks us to be people—or readers—that we refuse to accept.

Thus, the best composition teachers help their students improve their writing by making them conscious of readers and of the ways readers interact with their texts.

It is for these reasons, I think, that the most effective teachers of writing are traditionally those who are the most human and the most demanding of their students. Whatever their curriculum, they establish themselves or other defined audiences as live and sympathetic readers willing to participate in the quest for meaning that is writing. The research that Nancy Sommers and others have recently published on teacher response to writing tends to confirm these impressions. They point out that the writing class, to be effective, needs to decenter authority, to model the fact that every writer needs to be—and in fact is—an authority on what he or she is writing. Readers can recognize that authority in the writer without necessarily granting it to the text at hand, and therefore they can urge revision without taking ownership of the paper from the writer. (Surely, the most irritating question a writing teacher can hear from students about their revisions is, "Is that what you wanted?" Revisions should take them closer to what *they* want.)

Sommers caustically deplores the confusion she has found in her study of routine paper marking by college writing teachers. These markings almost universally treat the student text as simultaneously a finished product with editing faults and an unfinished part of the writing and thinking process. It is as if our confusion about evaluation is somehow bound up with a confusion about the nature of the student text, an odd form of literature created for the sole purpose of being criticized. Sommers finds that writing teachers tend to say the same things about student writing even though the texts in front of them change, as do the writers. "There seems to be among teachers an accepted, albeit unwritten canon for commenting on student texts. This uniform code of commands, requests, and pleadings demonstrates that the teacher holds a licence for vagueness while the student is commanded to be specific" (Sommers, 1982, pp. 152-153).

Sommers has demonstrated that there is a widespread

problem in responding to student writing. I earlier alluded to this problem as a measurement issue, which it surely is, and suggested that some understanding of the process and materials of systematic measurement of writing would go a long way toward improving the situation. But I think we also need to see the problem as a reading issue. As teachers of writing, now beginning to apply process theories of writing, deal with these process theories of reading, they will begin to find themselves becoming much more useful and constructive commentators on student papers. They will see their endless hours of work on these papers as taking part in the writing process rather than simply "grading" products, and they will be more ready to invite other readers and different judgments (perhaps from other students) to become part of this process. And when they must function as more or less simple evaluators, as in the grading of a test, they will be more ready to join in a community of readers to share judgment, as is the case in the typical holistic essay reading.

Holistic Scoring and the Interpretive Community

I have been suggesting that one reason composition teachers have not been—and need not be—taken aback by the new theories of reading posed by poststructuralism is that, despite the elaborate jargon, the new ideas tend to support the practice that many of us have been using intuitively. We have been reading student papers creatively, as part of the writing process, and considering ourselves more than simple graders of products in our classrooms. Sheer humanity and good sense have kept us responsive to much more about our students than just the texts they produce. And we have found ways, such as holistic scoring, to express that fuller vision of our students and their writing.

Those who have been developing the critical theories of reading I have been discussing have also needed to face the pedagogical implications of their theories. Just as holistic methods of testing allow us to consider writing as more than just the sum of its parts, so Stanley Fish's (1980) concept of "the interpretive community" rescues his theory of reading from the anarchy of pure subjectivism and the severe limitations of naive readers. I am linking these two concepts here not merely because a holistic essay reading exemplifies Fish's idea in a number of interesting ways but because together they show how some poststructuralist theories and the best composition practice support each other.

Fish defines an interpretive community as made up of those whose common agreement about how to read texts becomes an agreement about how they will in fact "write" for themselves those texts: "Interpretive communities are made up of those who share interpretive strategies not for reading (in the conventional sense) but for writing texts, for constituting their properties and assigning their intentions. In other words, these strategies exist prior to the act of reading and therefore determine the shape of what is read rather than, as is usually assumed, the other way around" (1980, p. 171). As Fish develops this concept, it serves a number of purposes. "This, then, is the explanation both for the stability of interpretation among different readers (they belong to the same community) and for the regularity with which a single reader will employ different interpretive strategies and thus make different texts (he belongs to different communities)" (p. 171). Fish also argues that literature may be defined as whatever a particular interpretive community decides is literature.

This useful concept helps us, for example, return to the problem posed so sharply by Nancy Sommers' research. Most composition instructors seem to have a coherent set of powerful assumptions and strategies for approaching (Fish would say writing) student texts. We not only get what we look for, according to this theory, but we actually create what we look for when we read student papers; the grim sameness in most of the teacher commentary Sommers and her fellow researchers have collected suggests that many of us are caught in a pattern of response of our own making that we then blame on our students. One way to think of what this book is trying to do—and what many of the process-oriented programs for writing teachers are trying to do—is to shake up an out-of-date interpretive community, to revise what we ask for—and thus what we get—from student writing.

Part of the value of a holistic scoring session stems from

exactly this effect on the participants. Such a reading depends on the establishment of a temporary, artificial interpretive community, a group of faculty who agree to agree on scoring standards for that particular test. The various techniques outlined in Chapter Two and detailed in Chapter Eight are all designed to create such a community so that the readers will agree on group standards, internalize them, and achieve very high rates of scoring reliability. These ad hoc and temporary communities of readers determine the meaning and value of the texts they grade in ways that evoke or even embody (in a simplified form) Fish's construct and, in their workaday way, demonstrate the validity of his idea.

Many readers leave a well-conducted holistic reading buoyed by the professional and human communications that have taken place, and some are able to shift into a new interpretive community for student papers as a result. As they see high levels of agreement among their colleagues, looking for what is well done in writing conceived as an expressive whole, they gain confidence in their own abilities to respond fairly to student writing (and to students) and to discuss openly the evaluation procedures they use. This confidence, in turn, can lead to more open evaluation techniques in their classrooms, with strong implications for the encouragement of revision. Participation in the test-scoring interpretive community thus can radiate into a participation in the wider community of professional teachers of writing; this enhanced sense of community, in a lonely and solitary profession, tends to be one of the most beneficial by-products of holistic readings.

The nature of the community in a holistic scoring session is thus more important than it sometimes seems to be, particularly to cost-cutting administrators. If an unpleasant environment, tyrannical leaders of the reading, or insufficient time inhibit the development of a true community of assent to both the process and the scoring criteria guide, the reading simply breaks down—because the needed community breaks down. This is yet another reason that scoring guides need to be developed by teams of experienced and sensitive readers only after reading through a large sample of student writing to the question in hand; such guides are devices for developing an interpretive community and hence ought never to be imported from other questions or other groups. Furthermore, this concept of community helps us see why the most effective chief readers never simply impose standards on a group or, if they must make decisions about standards, they do so only after full and substantial discussion. The readers must "own" scoring standards before they can work together as a reliable team by bringing similar expectations to the papers they grade.

I am drawing a rough analogy here between the interpretive community of essay readers, drawn together for a holistic scoring, and the interpretive community of, say, sophisticated readers of Shakespeare, in Fish's construct. Fish is concerned wholly with the reading of literary texts, while we are looking at the evaluation of student texts. There are obvious and important differences between the two applications of the interpretive community, despite the clear similarities. But it is a nice irony that reading theories developed among theoretical literary critics should have such a strong objective correlative among practical teachers trying to assess writing. It is essential to be aware of these theories, since we are always putting some theory of reading into practice in our work; as John Maynard Keynes is rumored to have said, anyone who thinks he is functioning without an underlying theory is simply in the grip of a theory he does not understand. The concept of the interpretive community allows us to integrate poststructural reading theory into our teaching and measurement practice. The principal benefit accrues to the students of writing teachers who understand that reading, no less than writing, is a process of the creative imagination, not a mere product to be analyzed.

6

Designing Effective Writing Assignments

Faculty devising writing topics almost invariably underestimate the difficulty even good students have with the usual essay test question or other writing assignment. Most faculty tend to be unaware of the many unstated criteria they assume the students will understand, and (since faculty tend to be those who did well on tests in school) most teachers see no need to provide clearer directions to those students who cannot guess what the question actually demands. Unfortunately, these faculty blame the poor writing that often appears on term papers or in test booklets on the deficiencies of their students, never even considering that a better question might have led to better writing. I do not mean to imply that a good assignment will transform weak students into fine writers. But it does seem clear that many students will fail to write as well as they can when confronted with vague and confusing topics or topics that are ill suited to their age, capacity, or background.

The purpose of this chapter is to summarize for teachers and examiners of writing ability the most useful experience and findings about writing topics from large-scale testing programs. Since more effective assignments will lead to more effective writing, faculty willing to plan their assignments with some of these points in mind are likely to find the teaching of writing more satisfactory. Those responsible for developing tests or testing programs should profit from the experience of essay test development that has taken place over the last two decades in

100

constructing tests that will be more valid because they will allow all writers to do their best.

It is instructive to begin considering the design of writing topics from the viewpoint of the student confronted with the usual forty-five-minute impromptu test of writing skill. Writing to set topics requires a particular set of skills on the part of the student, even a student who understands the material to be tested: comprehending the question in all its parts (particularly the underlying assumptions), understanding the mode of discourse called for, conceiving and organizing the response, fitting the response into a given time span, and, not least by any means, tailoring the response to the primary audience—teachers grading writing. Finally, the student who is writing the test needs to edit the work to remove the spelling errors and other scribal mistakes that appear in almost every writer's first drafts. If the student has learned the codes of test taking well enough to cope with all these matters, many of them unstated on most tests, then writing can get under way (in itself a serious problem for many) and the task can be completed. The student who can get through these matters with considerable dispatch will write to the topic as well as he or she can and use the time allowed to the best advantage. If these matters remain a mystery, either because the student has little experience with essay testing or because the question is unclear about what is called for, writing will be muddled, error ridden, inappropriate, or just plain bad in any of a dozen other ways. Furthermore, the test is likely to be invalid, since it will not necessarily measure writing ability.

Similar problems confront the student writing an out-of-class essay, term paper, or research paper. The specific restrictions of time and space that contribute to test anxiety may not be present, but all the issues I have just listed remain, sometimes in an exaggerated form. Writing anxiety is a special form of test anxiety that has been much studied in recent years (Rose, 1983; Smith, 1984), and it has become clear that uncertainty over both the assignment and the grading criteria is a major component of that disabling syndrome. A carefully designed writing topic will help students write their best and find that writing more rewarding, whatever the nature of the assignment.

We should note, however, that some kinds of topics that would never appear on a large-scale writing test may well be perfectly appropriate in class. The strict demand for validity—that is, that the responses to the question accurately reflect the writing ability of the students—may actually conflict with a teacher's need to stretch the abilities of some students. As students reach for new skills, they often will struggle or even fail on early drafts.

In my freshman composition classes, I often use a question that turned out to be invalid for a testing program but that, when carefully used, is quite appropriate for instruction. One college-level test development committee on which I served had devised a comparison-contrast test using two statements about the education of women. One of the statements argued that women should receive higher education specifically tailored for them; the other argued that higher education for women should be modeled on that traditionally offered to the best-qualified men. The committee thought the question would provide a valid test of student analytic ability, since the two statements were similar in many interesting ways yet quite different; in addition (and here is where the committee made its mistake), the topic was on an emotional subject about which there had been much talk, and so one presumably could build on a general fund of informed opinion.

Happily, the committee carefully pre-tested this topic on a wide range of college freshmen and discovered just how invalid it was—and thus chose not to include the topic on the actual test. (It is more usual to make such grim discoveries only after a test has been given, as grading gets under way.) When we read the pre-test essays, we were at first stunned to realize how bad many of them were, how they avoided the analytic task and turned instead into generalized and unsupported statements of belief on "women's place" (very often, to our chagrin, in the home). The essays from students known by their teachers to be excellent writers were often just as bad as those from the weakest writers. Since the responses did not correspond to the writing ability of the students, the question was abandoned and replaced by one that was more valid for testing purposes.

Afterward, however, several of us on the committee decided to use the question on the education of women in our classes. The pre-testing had shown that many college freshmen, even very able writers, are unable to write an analytic essay on a subject that excites their emotions. Under testing conditions, these students ignore analytic demands for passages with which they disagree or simply ignore such passages and substitute unsupported opinion, even unexamined stock phrases, for developed argument. Whereas testing seeks to evaluate fairly such a skill level, education sets out to alter that situation. So we use the assignment in class, knowing full well that many students will perform badly on their first drafts, and then we use the results to help students learn how to deal with such topics. Good students, when they see an example of the topic well handled, will see quickly that they went astray and learn from the experience to produce much improved second drafts. Since a major goal of composition instruction is to help students learn how to write to more complicated and more demanding topics than they are accustomed to handling, we should not allow the validity standards of writing tests to keep us from challenging our students with new tasks. But we do need to reassure them that their first drafts are learning exercises, not valid measures of ability—a useful lesson for all writers.

The luxury of using invalid topics does not extend to tests that seek to measure accurately student writing ability. The committee would have been unprofessional to have used the topic on women's education in a college freshman composition placement test, since good freshman writers perform badly on it. The question in fact embodies a very demanding set of test criteria: It measures experience with complex analysis, a high-level ability to synthesize the ideas of others into one's own writing on short notice, and the maturity and sophistication to handle calmly controversial subject matter. These are valuable skills and appropriate criteria for advanced students; on the beginning freshman level, however (not to speak of the high school students who are often asked such questions on tests), the criteria are unrealistic and hence unfair.

As we proceed to summarize the experience of essay test

developers, it is well to keep in mind that the difference between topics for testing and topics for teaching is a real and important one. But it is also important to guard against using this difference as an excuse for giving students unclear or inappropriate writing topics in class, since our teaching certainly ought to demand as much care as our testing.

Freedom and Choice in Test Questions

Some faculty, particularly those without much experience in test design, argue that writing topics are a bad idea to begin with: To set a topic is to limit student imagination and restrict student freedom to write on whatever is of most importance to the writer. Since the best writing, these advocates of liberty insist, is produced from internal motivation, not external demand, a single set topic cannot possibly meet the internal needs of all those who are writing. Besides, choosing a topic is itself so important a task for a writer that that very choice should be part of the assignment.

I think these arguments are quite mistaken. The supposed freedom of such assignments turns out to be the freedom for the student to guess what is really required. As every student knows, there is always a hidden assignment behind a request to write whatever one wants to write and a concealed set of grading criteria behind the hidden assignment. Writing is an unnatural act and few of us, even professional writers, work for the unrewarded pleasure of it. The demand to write, in school no less than on the job, is almost always an external demand and an exacting one; few of us find our poetic impulses stirred by difficult required tasks, no matter how we might relish them under other circumstances.

I think the urge to avoid designing a clear writing topic usually stems from much less elevated motives than a passion for liberty and poetry. At best, it reveals an unrealistic attempt to remove school from the reality of a world in which writing is a regular unromantic tool of thought and action, a world in which performance is demanded on time and evaluated rigorously. At worst, it shows an unprofessional lack of attention to the purpose of the writing assignment, the distinctions among different kinds of writing, or the appropriate sequence of tasks designed to teach or evaluate a difficult skill.

Freedom is an equivocal virtue. We want freedom to travel but not freedom from train and airline schedules that make travel convenient and manageable. Certain limitations make freedom possible, as Robert Frost suggested when he, in conversation, said that writing poetry without rhyme is like playing tennis without a net. We do not liberate a beginning chess player by allowing him or her to move the pieces any which way, nor does an editor support the creative journalist who files a sonnet on spring when the assigned political speech turns out to be uninspired. The student who is set free from a clear writing assignment must construct one before beginning to write. The energy used in that construction, usually requiring considerable guesswork about the teacher's implicit demands and concealed criteria, is a great waste of effort that would more profitably be spent in writing well to a clear topic. We liberate our students to write well by constructing for them appropriate and unambiguous tasks, with clear and understandable goals. Such assignments free students from the enervating, distracting, and often futile labor of guessing what we want, why we want it, and how we will respond.

A less obvious version of this longing for liberty has to do with giving students a choice of topics on a test in the mistaken belief that students will be more free to write well if they are allowed to choose the topic. This practice is very common in classroom tests, where teachers genuinely imagine that students will benefit from choosing among several possible questions. However, almost no large-scale testing programs offer this kind of choice, because it is much more fair to the students to offer choice within the format of a single topic.

The difference between offering a choice of questions and offering choice within a single question is important. The common practice of asking students to, say, choose one question from A, B, or C usually leads to an invalid test. Question A is harder than B, which, in turn, is harder than C; different questions are never of exactly the same order of difficulty. And often the hardest questions are the most interesting or most challenging and therefore the most attractive to the best students. So numbers of the best students, who might have performed very well on question C, attempt question A and do less well than they ought. Many of the weaker students avoid question A, gravitate to question C, and do better than they ought; other weak students, unaware of the difficulties of A or B, select them and do even worse than they ought. Normally, the professor grades this three-question test as if it were a one-question test (since every student writes only one question) and grades all responses together according to the same standards. The benefit to the students is hypothetical, not real; there is no evidence to show that students ordinarily will choose the question on which they will do best. The disadvantage, however, is very clear: The results of the examination will not reflect accurately the students' skill or knowledge, since they are responding to different questions testing different aspects of the material.

Large-scale test developers have learned how to offer the advantages of choice to students within the same question. If we ask students to, say, "describe an object you value and say why you value it," all students will respond to the same demand. While some will choose more appropriate objects than others and hence give themselves easier jobs to do, the choice of object is itself part of the test for all students. The question would become worse if expanded: "describe an object, or objects, or person you value and explain the reasons for that valuation." Since experience has shown that the question becomes much harder to handle with more than one subject, the option to choose multiple objects becomes a trap for the unwary. Experience has also shown that people are much more difficult to describe and evaluate than are objects, although they do not appear to be so to most students. Adding the option for students to write about their beloved grandparents, which few will do in other than general or clichéd ways, does those writing the test no favor.

Classroom tests, then, ought to reflect this same concern for giving all students the same question. I used to ask students completing my course in the eighteenth-century English novel to choose among three questions on three of the novels: *Moll Flanders, Tom Jones,* and *Tristram Shandy.* Only recently have I realized how unfair that choice of questions was to my class. The most interesting novel to the best students is often the last of the three; this is a quite difficult book, and discussing it demands great skill of a writer. I should not have been surprised that my good students often wrote poor examinations. Those selecting the *Moll Flanders* question almost always received a higher grade than those choosing the others. I now ask a single question on a larger topic (focusing specifically on the relationship of the characters in the novels to their worlds, for example, or on the relationship between the rise of the novel and notions of money) and require frequent references to the novels in the response. The students are just as free to demonstrate what they know—more free, in fact—and the test is much more fair.

Every teacher will, of course, use occasional open assignments whose purpose will be to teach invention, the discovery of topics as well as the development of them. And those teaching poetry or fiction will surely be less directive than those asking for research papers or giving final examinations in American history. We need always to be on guard against any one set pattern of assignments. But every teacher who asks students to write ought to be as clear as the goal of the assignment allows about just what the students are supposed to do in response. When the assignment gives several or many options, this clarity becomes very hard to maintain. An important test, in particular, should ask every student to respond to the same question so that everyone starts at the same point and has the same distance to go.

Notions of freedom in testing, as in life, require considerable thought and experience in order to work in practice as they do in theory. Students taking a test or writing a term paper are not free in most senses of the word; they are required to write and will be evaluated on the relative success they achieve. Under such circumstances, the most meaningful kind of freedom is simple fairness, and in testing that comes down to validity and reliability. When we develop writing topics that lead to clear and valid tests, and when we score these tests responsibly and reliably, we are freeing our students from the arbitrary and whimsical testing and grading that now diminish education at all levels. By so doing, we are striking a great blow for our students' right to learn in a free environment.

Topic Development

By now, the model for essay test development for large-scale examinations has become well established. This model is worth describing in some detail for several reasons: (1) Those undertaking direction of such a test should be aware of current practice. (2) Those adapting the model for less exacting testing programs will want to be alert to potential problems from stages they need to omit or compress. (3) Classroom teachers will find that they can (over time) include many of these procedures as part of their usual course and test planning.

Selection and Preliminary Tasks of the Test Committee. The test development committee need not be made up of test specialists, but it must be composed of teachers who know about writing and who are familiar with the kind of students to be tested. This committee has a heavy responsibility: If it does not come up with good questions, no amount of work in scoring or follow-up administration can salvage the test. Good questions are absolutely crucial, and the committee requires the people, conditions, and time to do the job.

The first task for this committee must be either the creation or review of the test criteria—the statement that embodies what the test is attempting to discover. A common mistake made by test committees is to move directly into a consideration of writing topics before coming to agreement on the purpose of the test; no wonder that under such circumstances agreement on topics becomes impossible. If those on the committee achieve consensus on both the aspects of writing to be measured and the kinds of questions most likely to elicit that information, they have done the necessary groundwork for the building of a test.

Sometimes, particularly in the public schools, a test committee is put in the awkward position of developing a test to criteria that are not well informed. An assistant superintendent, say, or a committee of citizens might have listed matters they feel to be important (usually scribal or mechanical), while a committee of teachers may be more concerned with invention, organization, creativity, or other thinking skills. It is idle to imagine that test questions can be developed until these issues are resolved. Numbers of such committees have shown high political skill in working with outside pressure groups, convincing them that mechanical skills can be included as part of a set of criteria that supports rather than undermines the writing curriculum. When these matters of criteria and purpose have been settled, and not before, the committee can turn its attention to particular writing topics.

Faculty come to test design committees assuming that their classroom experience in testing will readily carry over into a large-scale testing program. Sometimes that is the case, but more typically the difference in the situation demands a new approach. Questions that work well in a course setting normally will not work well on a large-scale test: When the classroom context is withdrawn, with all its understood definitions and expectations, these questions must be entirely rewritten and will usually wind up on the heap of rejected possibilities. An even more discouraging finding has emerged from much experience: Many questions that seem immediately attractive to a group of English teachers are very likely to fail to work properly on a large-scale test.

For example, the first time I was responsible for developing an essay test, I proceeded under the naive assumption that I could convene a group of excellent writing teachers, each bringing two of his or her best classroom essay topics, and that we could select our question from the riches before us. As we circulated the proposed topics (including two of my own, of which I was very proud), barely audible groans surfaced. After full discussion, every single question was rejected, and we reformed into test committees to salvage what we could. The second year, in the belief that the first year's experience was atypical since it was so contrary to logical expectation, I tried the same procedure—with exactly the same result. We did not fall into the same error again.

The faculty who form test development committees, then, not only must be excellent writing teachers but need to be flexible committee workers who can comfortably abandon favorite ideas that do not work in a new context. They need to recognize that a good question for a test is usually (like all good writing) the result of steady and patient revision.

Characteristics of a Good Writing Topic. Test development committees have learned to require these characteristics of questions they approve:

> *Clarity.* Students will not waste time trying to figure out what is called for but will be able to get right down to work.
>
> *Validity.* Good students will receive high scores and weak students will receive low scores. There will be a good range of scores without too large a concentration in the middle.
>
> *Reliability.* Scoring of pre-test papers shows considerable agreement by readers, and a scoring guide can be readily constructed to describe score differences.
>
> *Interest.* The question offers sufficient intrinsic interest so that students will write with some genuine concern and those scoring will not go mad (and hence become inaccurate) with boredom.

Each of these four characteristics contains many possible problems. The concept of clarity, for example, often (but not always) includes brevity: Time wasted in reading the question cannot be used in responding to the question; long questions tend to contain ambiguous directions and distracting side alleys. But students do need the essential directions. It might well be worth the extra space to replace "Compare and contrast" with "In what ways are the following passages alike? In what ways are they different?" If generally good students are producing personal narratives instead of an expected analytic essay (a common enough result of an unclear question), the directions need to be revised. Questions based on a text, usually excerpted, often pose problems of clarity, since the test committee knows a context that the students do not; isolated passages from familiar writers turn out to have quite different meanings on a test than they do in their customary locations. Clarity problems appear in new and surprising shapes with every new question, and there is no way to mention here all the possible ways in which essay questions become unclear. An experienced test committee simply accepts the fact that there will be problems of clarity in its questions and looks to the pre-test to discover and correct these problems.

Validity problems become apparent as soon as the test committee begins reading a series of pre-tests. Some questions seem to produce responses that all sound alike; almost all scores wind up in the middle range. These are sometimes questions that elicit clichés ("Should the drinking age be the same as the draft registration age?" "What is the value of a good education?") or simple narratives ("Tell about your summer vacation"). But even clear and original questions do not produce a valid spread of scores if they are too hard or too easy for the test group. Some questions give an unfair advantage to students with a particular kind of knowledge or experience; urban test development committees, for example, sometimes have a hard time imagining rural contexts ("Describe what you see when you walk around your block"). The ideal question will allow the weak students to write comfortably enough at their level while it challenges the best students to produce their best work. One sure sign of a good writing topic is that it produces a good range of scores.

Reliability problems are usually the result of vagueness in the question, but they also can come about when the question (intentionally or not) invites the students to take political, religious, or social positions. How can readers grade fairly a frankly racist or sexist essay or one that seems to argue for idiotic solutions to the problems of the country or the universe? Clarification of the directions to the students may avoid such problems; sometimes a question will even suggest a structure for the response in order to help keep students on the track ("Describe ... use examples ... then discuss"). If numbers of on-topic papers are ungradable, or if the test committee remains unable to reach agreement on the scores of pre-test papers and hence on the characteristics of such papers for a scoring guide, it is time to move to a different question.

An interesting writing topic that works well is a rare find. Most test committees for large-scale testing programs, knowing that no reader will find the four-hundredth essay on *anything* interesting, will happily settle for a tolerable topic, as long as it is clear and yields reliable and valid results. Some questions that seem very interesting to the committee will evoke stultifying responses, in fact, and some apparently dull questions seem to tap into the creativity that students are often afraid to display on tests. As in other areas, it is the pre-test process that reveals the success of the proposed topic.

Pre-Testing. With these principles in mind, the test development committee will consider the test specifications, the goals of the testing program, and the students to be tested and come up with a series of questions for pre-testing. This initial step needs to occur several months before the actual test questions are chosen so that the committee will have ample time to revise its selections or abandon them and start over should none of them work (as will happen from time to time).

The pre-testing population need not be large—fifty to one hundred students often will suffice—but it needs to be carefully chosen. Those taking the pre-test cannot be students who will take the real test but should be representative of them, with the same background, ethnic and cultural diversity, and range of abilities. Students at neighboring colleges or school districts will usually serve nicely, and neighboring faculty normally will pre-test questions for colleagues as a routine professional courtesy.

Careful reading of the pre-tests usually reveals that most of the proposed questions do not work, according to the principles I have just listed: The test does not distinguish the best writers from the average ones, most students find little to say or produce only clichés, most scores group in the middle, clear scoring criteria do not emerge, and so on. But, if the questions have been carefully designed, one or two of them will stand out from the rest, often to the wonder of the committee that reluctantly included them. These are the questions to be revised and clarified for further pre-testing and eventually to be used in the test itself.

The fact that test questions themselves must be tested is not well understood and leads to many problems in testing. Many years ago, I designed a comprehensive examination for graduating English majors at a selective private college; as a new faculty member, I had a particular stake in producing an inventive, interesting, and responsible four-hour examination. The English department approved the test, for it was indeed inventive and interesting; it never occurred to me that it should be pre-tested. Grading of the test was most careful, with teams of faculty spending days reading and discussing the anonymous papers produced by generally excellent students. Results were astonishing: Five students from the graduating class failed the test (a high number for this institution). We were more astonished still when we uncovered the student names on the tests and discovered that the five were the top five students in the department, including the editors of the literary magazine and the college paper, and that all five had already been accepted into first-rate graduate schools. We hustled all of them through graduation, somehow, and went off wondering how such good students could do so badly on their comprehensive examinations. The better question, however, was what was wrong with the test, whose invalidity had been so thoroughly demonstrated? We had not been trained to ask the latter question, and it did not occur to me to ask it until years had gone by.

One type of question often favored by English teachers usually will turn out to be wholly invalid in a large-scale test, and the committee will want to keep a sharp eye out for such questions during initial development and pre-testing. I am speaking here of questions on familiar topics, to which a great fund of stock responses are at hand. George Orwell, in his familiar essay "Politics and the English Language," speaks of the ever-present temptation to accept concepts and phrases floating in the air as substitutes for those words and ideas that should be chosen for the expression of one's particular meaning. Examples of questions that invariably call forth stock responses are those having to do with education or with emotional questions of the day, which usually require substantial pre-writing exercises in class before students (particularly the best students) will move beyond the recitation of clichés. Experienced test development committees avoid such questions as systematically as they do those allowing the pious to record their religious experiences; hardened and irreverent committee members will take care to "Jesus-proof" their questions. The experience of test developers is too extensive to be denied: Few good students will write essays on such topics that reflect their actual writing ability.

Large-scale test committees rarely are satisfied after the first pre-test. Of a dozen or so questions, perhaps two will have emerged as good possibilities, and these two will have been rewritten, sometimes extensively. A second pre-test is necessary, to be followed by a second evaluation of the results for clarity, validity, reliability, and interest. With good luck and skill, the test question will emerge from that evaluation with only minor revisions; a scoring guide draft should also be prepared by the committee at the same time. With bad luck, despite skill and experience, even these questions will not work, and the committee will have two choices: Begin the process again, if there is enough time, or, with a sense of impending doom, choose the least bad possibility and try to salvage it somehow. Wise test administrators allow time for the first choice.

Classroom Implications. When we reflect on this model of essay test development in relation to classroom teaching, we are likely to assume at first that we cannot approach the same rigor in our courses. Few of us can convene committees to work on our tests, and we do not have the resources or the time to do pre-testing in the same way.

But in fact we as classroom teachers have one resource that no test committee can command: We have years in which to develop and refine our assignments—indeed, an entire teaching career. We have, in addition, an enviable control over our test criteria, since we have (or should have) a clear sense of the goals of our courses; we know, and sometimes articulate on a syllabus, what we expect our students to accomplish. Furthermore, we can and do pre-test an assignment every time we give one, and most of our students are not reticent about problems they perceive in clarity or validity or interest. If we listen to them and revise our writing assignments and tests in the light of their comments and our own evaluation of results, over time we ought to develop these teaching tools to a perfection that any test committee should envy. Indeed, on closer examination, teaching faculty have better conditions for test development than any professionally supported test committee could ever obtain.

Why, then, are so many of our tests unclear, invalid, unreliable, even uninteresting? Why are so many of our term paper assignments so lacking in precision that unscrupulous vendors may provide by mail standard responses to them at so much a page? As long as testing remains a peripheral concern to us, an afterthought to our curricula, we will neglect the opportunities for test development that we so richly possess. As long as term papers and other writing assignments are seen principally as ritual products for the student to bring to us as offerings for grading, we will fail to use and develop this major tool for learning. Happily, the recent widespread concern for writing in all disciplines is coinciding with increasing participation and interest in large-scale writing test development. Thus, the knowledge of test development that this chapter summarizes is slowly spreading through the academic community, and it is suggesting by its very presence that we should attend to our writing assignments with renewed care.

Unfortunately, inattention to test development is not solely to be found in classrooms. It is not unusual to find testing, evaluation, even research programs depending on writing tests developed in the most casual way—or even imported from a quite different environment with a different purpose. A few years ago, I agreed with pleasure to direct a holistic essay reading as part of an immensely expensive and important program evaluation; a prominent figure in evaluation was responsible for the entire project. To my astonishment, I discovered that both essay questions used in the evaluation had sprung fully grown from the head of this particular individual and showed not the slightest sign of systematic development: The unstated criteria were quirky and personal, quite unsuited either to the group of students tested or to the program being evaluated. There was no changing the situation; the questions had already been administered. We scored thousands of essays as well as we could, which is to say not very consistently, since the questions were as unclear and ambiguous as first-draft topics usually are. The prominent evaluator, of course, found it hard to understand the unsatisfactory results, since he was professionally committed to evaluating others and had little interest or practice in evaluating his own assumptions about testing.

Topic Types

We know surprisingly little about the differences in performance that are caused by different kinds of writing topics, but we do know that such differences exist. It is logical to believe that these differences are linked to the distinctions among modes of discourse on the one hand and to patterns of cognitive growth on the other. The latter two subjects have been much studied, but a convincing theory connecting them to writing test results has yet to emerge. We can say with some assurance, however, that some kinds of topics are more appropriate than others for some purposes and groups and that the choice of topic type will have an important influence over the score distribution obtained.

Richard Lloyd-Jones provides the most useful analysis of discourse types for testing in his description of the development of topics for the National Assessment of Educational Progress (Cooper and Odell, 1977). He briefly discusses some of the various schemes devised by Aristotle and his successors (with some particular attention to the complicated models developed by James Britton, 1970, and James Kinneavy, 1971) and presents the tripartite diagram shown in Figure 6.

This convenient model focuses on two aspects of discourse, its purpose and its orientation, and is intended to serve as an example rather than an inclusive design. Its very simplicity is its particular virtue, since it so clearly illustrates the different kinds of mental activity involved in different kinds of writing.

Figure 6. A Model of Discourse Types for Testing.

Explanatory Discourse

(Subject Oriented)

Expressive Discourse   Persuasive Discourse

(Discourser Oriented)   (Audience Oriented)

Source: Cooper and Odell, 1977, p. 39. Copyright © 1977 by the National Council of Teachers of English. Reprinted by permission of the publisher and the authors.

Since it has by now become a truism that there is a wide variety in individual styles of learning, and since the various stages of cognitive and moral development have been systematically described (Piaget, 1955, 1962; Bruner, 1960; Perry, 1968; Kohlberg, 1981), it should come as no surprise that an individual student's writing ability varies widely according to the mental operation demanded by a particular writing topic.

Some convincing evidence that this is indeed the case has been accumulated by the California State University English Equivalency Examination. From 1973 to 1981, that program tested over 31,000 students on nine different tests, requiring two different kinds of writing from each student at the same sitting. Essay 1 tended to be a form of what Lloyd-Jones calls "expressive writing," while Essay 2 was a comparison-contrast question, an analytic mode close to what he calls "explanatory discourse." During the first years of the test, Essay 1 had very little analytic demand; as years went by, more and more analysis was added to that question. In 1973, the correlation of Essay 1 scores with Essay 2 scores was a surprisingly low .37. By 1981, even with a substantial reading passage added to Essay 1, the correlation had reached only .57 (White, 1973–1981). These low correlations suggest strongly that the two different kinds of writing topics used for the two different essays each year produced quite different score distributions. Students who score in the high (or low) ranges on one kind of writing test will not necessarily receive high (or low) scores on a different one with a different kind of question.

While there is thus good reason to believe that different kinds of writing will elicit different levels of performance from individuals, it is not at all clear that certain modes of discourse are necessarily inherently easier than others. On the one hand, if we make a connection between Piagetian cognitive theory and writing mode, we might say that persuasive discourse, say, requires much more of a "formal operation" than expressive discourse (which is more "egocentric"). On the other hand, we would be entitled to use the same theory to demonstrate that any writing on any topic is such a complex and advanced skill that it requires formal operations in order to exist at all. And we can draw on the experience of any writing teacher to show that, while many students have an easier time writing about themselves than about abstractions, some students find it much easier to write about abstract topics than about their own experiences.

Until we know more than we now do about the connections among writing topic types, modes of discourse, and cognitive theory, we need to observe certain cautions in the development of writing topics. In the first place, we should attempt to measure anything we call "writing ability" by more than one writing sample and in more than one writing mode. If we use only one kind of topic, we will be disadvantaging those students who perform better in another mode and favoring those who do best in the one mode we test. If financial or time limitations make it impossible to test in more than one mode, we ought to be particularly alert to the validity problem contained in a single-mode test.

Secondly, we ought to resist assumptions about "easy" or "elementary" topic types. Typically, faculty tend to associate expressive writing with juvenility and explanatory modes with maturity. While there is some justification for doing so in the light of the "bad" expressive topics most of us experienced in school, the equation is improper. "What did you do on your summer vacation?" is a bad topic not because it is based on personal experience; it is bad because it is vague, unfocused, and pointless. The great value of a good expressive topic is that it demands that the writer relate the self to knowledge, find personal meaning in external objects, and communicate internal truth to an outside reader. Such an activity is not necessarily easier or less advanced (or less valuable) than another mode of discourse. When John Milton was assigned to write about his feelings on the death of a friend (not, we must confess, a particularly well-developed topic), he produced one of the greatest poems in the English language.

Once we dissociate, as we should, mode of discourse from level of difficulty, we become free to consider a wide range of topic types for any ability or age level. College preparatory students need to learn to demonstrate and take responsibility for their assertions, and hence they should receive more than expressive assignments. Complex expressive topics may be quite appropriate for upper-division college students; simple persuasive topics may be just the thing for a particular class in junior high school.

Finally, we need to remember that the writing of topics is, after all, *writing*. That is, all the problems and all the stages of writing are part of the process of devising topics, and no one should imagine it to be easy. The extraordinary compression of the form, the need for exactness of communication, the requirement that the topic elicit an immediate response that can be wide ranging and even creative, and the tense importance of the occasion all add to the unique difficulty of the writing of writing topics. It is no wonder that few of our topics meet this challenge.

7

Evaluating and Scoring
Writing Assignments

The three most prominent ways of evaluating student writing (holistic, analytic, and primary trait scoring) each have important implications for writing instruction. This chapter is designed to clarify the distinctions among these approaches to scoring and teaching writing, in part through examples of typical scoring guides. While each of these procedures has important uses for testing, research, and program evaluation, our principle concern here will be with classroom instruction, since theories of measurement both emerge from and develop into teaching practice.

We are reserving the term *holistic* for grading and teaching that treats writing as a whole. Primary trait scoring is based on such a premise, although it does isolate for scoring purposes the particular aspect of writing (such as coherence, say, or sense of audience) to be attended to in the holistic evaluation. The primary trait score is a single number representing the quality of the paper according to the scoring guide for that trait. Analytic scoring, however, is based on analytic premises and therefore ought never to be called holistic. The analytic approach to grading and teaching considers writing to be made up of various features, such as creativity or punctuation, each of which is to be scored separately; an analytic writing score is made up of a sum of the separate scores, often a weighted sum developed after multiplying each score by numbers representing the relative importance of the features.

Although primary trait/holistic and analytic scoring differ sharply in their assumptions about writing, they reflect a similar understanding of teaching: Since a teacher cannot do everything at once, writing instruction must deal with features of writing, traits if you will, much of the time. Since the teacher may be dealing with aspects of sentence structure one week and concepts of audience the next, there is a clear need for a scoring system that reflects this inevitable focus of pedagogy. If a class, or an entire program, stresses certain matters in relation to writing, a responsible measurement device also will emphasize those matters.

Since both the primary trait version of holistic scoring and analytic scoring take this need for pedagogical subdivision and emphasis into account, and since both of them attempt to provide more information about the papers being graded than the mere ranking supplied by holistic scoring, it is useful to consider them as contrasting methods of approaching the same problem.

Analytic Scoring

Most classroom teachers of writing tend to use a loose form of analytic scoring when they respond to student papers. They will read through the work, marking errors in spelling, sentence structure, coherence, and the like and writing notes in the margins (sometimes in code) to the student. A comment at the end of the paper will summarize the marginal notes, respond to the ideas in the paper, add a bit of encouragement (or, alas, sarcasm), and explain the grade as a sum of the different traits evaluated. Many conscientious writing teachers spend an enormous amount of time "red-marking" student papers according to this theory; one high school English teacher who, typically enough, saw such work as the tie that binds the profession concluded a friendly note to me by replacing the usual complimentary close with one specially created for colleagues: "Keep the red ink flowing."

Any teaching practice so widely accepted is bound to have its practical uses and to be rooted in a practical pedagogy.

Surely, no student can learn much from a mere holistic ranking of an essay (unless the class becomes used to the detailed discussion I propose in this chapter and in Chapter Thirteen) or even from a general comment about the writing as a whole. General exhortations to write better or to think more and more deeply have about the same value as sermons invoking virtue or pop psychology manuals calling for emotional honesty. We would all be better if we could reach such goals, but we need to be taught how to go about attaining them, particularly since parts of our nature protest against them. We recognize this problem as we teach writing and as we try to find and articulate achievable goals for our students. Thus, even if the thinking on the paper before us is fatuous, we can hope perhaps for improved sentence structure as an attainable goal; a student whose subjects and verbs seem eternal strangers can at least begin to work on the punctuation problem. Since a disorganized paper represents confused thinking, we can demand a coherent paragraph or a clear relation between parts of the sentence as a practical way to start untangling the sequence of reasoning.

Thus, the analytic grading that goes on wherever writing teachers have the time for it (and that afflicts with guilt those overloaded teachers who simply cannot grade papers as they feel they ought) is a reasonable response to the pedagogical need to do what one can for students with varying needs and varying capacities. If it is to be replaced, as I think it should, it can only be replaced by a procedure that meets that same need more effectively.

The problems with analytic scoring of papers have become increasingly clear in recent years. No large-scale testing program uses such scoring, for the practical reasons I considered in Chapter Two. Since there is little agreement on the definitions or importance of the various subskills to be measured, inter-rater reliability tends to be low; since the several repeated judgments of each piece of writing by each reader require much time, the cost tends to be high. Many idiosyncratic analytic scales exist, often shaped and used by committees of one, and from time to time other such scales surface at meetings of researchers, sometimes with categories for subskills that go into

three figures. But there has been no evidence of sufficient reliability or economy for such scales to make them useful for testing programs where scores must be demonstrably fair and obtained at reasonable cost. Even more serious is the theoretical
problem: There is no evidence that writing quality is the result
of the accumulation of a series of subskills. To the contrary, the
lack of agreement on subskills in the profession suggests that
writing remains more than the sum of its parts and that the analytic theory that seeks to define and add up the subskills is fundamentally flawed.

Furthermore, there are many practical reasons to question the effectiveness of the traditional analytic grading of student papers in the classroom. Many teachers substitute such
grading of papers for the teaching of writing, as if they were the
same activity; but few students actually make their way through
the analytic comments so painstakingly written on their papers,
and even fewer are able to make profitable use of those comments on succeeding writing assignments. Students will complain that teachers are so busy marking and adding up errors
that they do not take the time to respond to the ideas in the
writing. There is a confrontational air to the whole business,
sometimes conveyed with barely buried metaphors of violence.
Students will speak of teachers tearing their papers apart, while
teachers will talk about taking a set of papers home for the
weekend and "bleeding all over them."

The lack of reliability that is clear in analytic scales for
large-scale tests translates to vagueness in the classroom. The
devastating study of such grading I referred to in Chapter Five
(Sommers, 1982) shows that the same student paper will normally receive a wide variety of teacher responses, some of them
contradictory, few of them very useful. When one teacher rewards as creative what the next teacher punishes as unsuitable,
or when teacher comments appear to be quirky and hostile, students are justified in ignoring most of what their writing teachers tell them. Under such conditions, students are likely to feel
that judgments about their writing are largely a matter of
chance or personal taste and that revision is pointless.

Analytic scoring is uneconomical, unreliable, pedagogically

uncertain or destructive, and theoretically bankrupt. It nonetheless remains the dominant, almost universal, approach to the grading of student papers in the classroom. This curious situation reflects the common difficulty of connecting measurement to the teaching of writing and provides one of the principal reasons for the existence of this book.

The following analytic scale (Cooper and Odell, 1977, p. 24) is among the best of such devices: It has the virtues of simplicity and a certain amount of clarity. Nonetheless, it requires the evaluator to make eleven separate judgments about a piece of narrative writing and to make such evanescent distinctions as that between "wording" and "usage."

Table 1. Analytic Scale.

Reader _____ Paper _____					
		Low	Middle		High
I.	General Qualities				
	A. Author's Role	2	4	6	8	10
	B. Style or Voice	2	4	6	8	10
	C. Central Figure	2	4	6	8	10
	D. Background	2	4	6	8	10
	E. Sequence	2	4	6	8	10
	F. Theme	2	4	6	8	10
II.	Diction, Syntax, and Mechanics				
	A. Wording	1	2	3	4	5
	B. Syntax	1	2	3	4	5
	C. Usage	1	2	3	4	5
	D. Punctuation	1	2	3	4	5
	E. Spelling	1	2	3	4	5
				Total	____

Source: Cooper and Odell, 1977, p. 24. Copyright © 1977 by the National Council of Teachers of English. Reprinted by permission of the publisher and the authors.

Holistic Scoring

Although holistic approaches to evaluation have the built-in limitations that were described in Chapter Two, they have many uses in the classroom. They have several particular advantages: They require a response to the writing as a whole, they generally assume a positive attitude by rewarding the writing for what is done well, and they allow for as much criterion referencing (that is, definition of points on the scale to particular criteria) as one wishes to use.

Since holistic scoring guides need to be specific to both the question assigned and the level of ability of those writing, there is a great variety of such guides spanning the possible ability and difficulty levels of students and questions. For illustrative purposes, I will select one designed for entering college freshmen, one for students completing the freshman year, and one designed for upper-division college students; they represent a range from the fairly simple guide appropriate for a simple question to the more complex scoring guide needed for complicated purposes. Versions of these guides and their questions, particularly the first, have been used at the high school level as well, although always with careful revision to suit the individual context of the testing program. In addition, many faculty who have used these guides as test readers have taken them back to their classrooms and adapted them to their own classes and assignments.

The scoring guides that follow are all based on a six-point scale, a scale that is becoming more and more standard for such tests. Since reliable scoring of a test requires agreement by the raters on common standards, and since most teachers have an emotional commitment to their own personal definition of the usual letter grades ("A" to "F"), most scoring guides use numbers as a way of establishing a context for group agreement. The six-point scale is peculiarly useful and convenient, since it offers the simplicity of a two-point scale (the basic decision a grader makes is top half—a 5—or bottom half—a 2) with enough additional scores (all the other numbers can be considered pluses or minuses after the first decision) to allow a satisfying spread of grades for the readers and the statisticians. Other popular scales use four points, five points, nine points, and fifteen points. The four-point scale has turned out in practice to be less satisfying both to readers (who are often bothered by the compression of the scale to cover a wide range of quality) and to statisticians (who find that that same compression limits the value of results). Odd-numbered scales in general offer the disadvantage of a midpoint, an easy way out for readers confronted with perhaps half of their papers clustered around the center; an even-numbered scale does force a choice and hence force more deliberation about these mid-range papers than does a scale with a midpoint.

Some teachers have adapted the numerical scale for classroom use as well. They may develop, with their classes, such a scoring guide for a particular assignment and use it for the initial scoring of papers. By reserving more conventional grades for revised work, they can demonstrate the importance of revision and distinguish grades given at two separate points in the writing process.

The first holistic scoring guide (White, 1973) was designed for entering college students taking a large-scale placement test, one part of which asked for writing based on personal experience:

Assignment: Describe one or more objects that are important to you. Explain what values they represent and comment on those values.

Holistic Scoring Guide No. 1

The student should be rewarded for what he or she does well in response to the question. Here, the student is asked to *describe* one or more *objects* that are important to the writer. The student is further asked to *explain* what *values* the objects represent and to comment on those values. Note that the question does not demand that the object or objects be unusual ones.

Essays that misinterpret "objects" as "objectives" and that deal mainly with generalized abstractions (such as life or God) should be read sympathetically, but they should ordinarily not receive above a score of 2, since they fail to understand and properly respond to the question.

6: A superior response will not just name one or more object(s) but will *describe* the object or objects in some detail, and it will not just identify the values represented but *explain* and comment on them, their nature, and their source. A superior paper will be literate and orderly.

5-4: These scores will be useful for a well-handled paper that is deficient in one or two characteristics of the superior response (that is, in description of the object or objects and in explanation of the values represented) but that is otherwise competently written.

3-2: These scores will be useful for the following kinds of papers: those in which only one part of the two-part question is addressed; those in which the representativeness of specific objects is ignored; those that treat the subject in superficial or stereotyped fashion; and those in which the writing exhibits several important weaknesses in wording or structure or other respects.

1: This score is to be used for papers that are lacking in focus and substance, that depart from the assigned topic, and/or that exhibit consistent, serious writing faults.

9: Nonresponse papers and papers that do not fall into the preceding categories, that extensively argue with the question, or that are otherwise idiosyncratic should immediately be brought to the attention of the table leader and the question leader.

Neither the question nor the scoring guide is as simple as it appears to be at first glance. Both were the result of months of work and pre-testing by committees. The question is particularly suited for students leaving high school. It is designed to allow everyone taking the test to begin writing fairly quickly, since it draws on personal experience that all students may be presumed to have. It also examines descriptive skills, one of the less complex writing abilities, and asks for a description of objects rather than of people, which is a much more complicated task. A test of younger adolescents appropriately might stop at this point. But since this is a test for college applicants, the question requires the students to move beyond mere description into two levels of abstraction: They are asked to connect values to the object or objects described and then to comment on the values.

It is somewhat paradoxical that a scoring guide as general as this one can lead to substantial agreement among raters while the apparent precision of analytic guides does not. Nonetheless, that is exactly the case. After considering a series of sample papers representing the range of abilities demonstrated by the students writing to the assignment, a group of teachers will concur on such terms as "literate and orderly" or "serious writing faults" despite profound differences about concepts of grammar and usage. The student papers that illustrated the bottom half and top half of the scale for this scoring guide follow:

Score of 2: Heat, exhaust, fumes, burning rubber and smoke are all caused by a remarkable invention that has spured our society into being one of the most materialistic in this modern age. Our society today depends on the car for transportation. We overlook the bad side of this invention for all the wonderful things the car has done for us.

No longer are people confined to one small region for their entire lives. Trips to the coast or to a distant city for a day are not unheard of now. It has actually broadened our horizons for we can meet new people, go new places. People we haven't seen in along time are in easy reach.

Working days are shortened with the use of the car. Instead of walking many miles to work, it provides fast and easy transportation on highways.

Status is related to owning a car. Some people seem to feel that the bigger a car is, the better it is. Socioeconomic status is based on the number of high value materialistic things we own. Having four or five cars in a family tends to raise a family's status.

Cars come in all shapes and sizes. Big or small we can find one that fits the needs of everybody. Compact, economy and luxary cars are priced to fit people with even low income budgets as well as high.

There is a limit that people using cars must draw. Excessive use of a car can damage our enviornment. Taking a car into high mountain area can damage or even ruin flora and fauna. Pollution from cars cannot be stopped unless all cars are banned.

With all the good and bad sides to cars, which way can we turn? Cars can be used for destructive purposes as well as useful, meaningful reasons.

Score of 5: As I look back on my life, the object that I place the most value on is the house that I grew up in. For sixteen years I walked through its doors and lived in its rooms. That house became a part of me.

Now, almost nineteen years old, it stands in a middle-class suburb of Los Angeles. The surrounding streets are lined with well-kept homes and neatly-trimmed yards.

Children that I don't know play baseball on the avenue, and cars that I don't recognize fill the driveways. My dear house is in an alien world both to me and to it.

My family took pride in that home. We bought it new, put in all the landscaping, and made it a beautiful place to live. In all the years we lived there, I never once took its loveliness for granted. I would sit and look at it and know what a wonderful home we had.

That long avenue was my world. Little playmates moved in and out of the other houses, but I was the stable one. I didn't believe that we would ever leave our home.

That building saw my first step, heard my first word, and watched me fall off my first bicycle. It stood by when I was sick and was there for all the happy moments too. It became more like a person, part of the family.

Leaving it all alone for new people to run about in was next to impossible. Is it as lonely as I am?

Our new house is bigger and more modern than that one was. Still, this makes no difference. It will never be home.

When we look back to the scoring guide, the difference between these two papers becomes clear. The lower-half paper (score of 2) misreads the question's demand for a specific object, taking cars in general for a topic. The series of general statements that make up the essay is roughly organized, but the subject is treated "in superficial or stereotyped fashion" in writing markedly weak in logic, wording, sentence structure, and just plain good sense. The 5 paper not only chooses a specific object, the house, but makes us see its setting and the deep feelings of the author. Quite remarkably for first-draft writing under time pressure (forty-five minutes), the writer develops a consistent and reasonably subtle figure of speech, personifying the house as the principal means of description.

The scoring guide thus makes consistent rating of a clear question relatively easy. But it is at the same time an immediately useful teaching tool. Some teachers will want to use a scoring guide developed by question committees or by themselves; others, more daring and more creative, will lead the writing class to develop and understand a scoring guide as part of the writing assignment. In either case, the students' scoring of their own and others' writing then can become part of the writing class itself.

As more and more teachers at all levels and in all disciplines become accustomed to holistic scoring, more and more of them are asking their writing classes to develop and use scoring guides for the assignments they write. Since one of the best indications of an unclear assignment is difficulty in devising a clear scoring guide (a technical version of the student complaint, "I don't know what you want"), this procedure is also leading to improved assignments. And it is a great surprise to many teachers to see how consistently even young students can apply scoring guides after some training in the meaning of the score level distribution. It is often a great revelation to inexperienced writers that there are clear differences between good and weak writing; developing a well-designed scoring guide is often the first step to an awareness that writing actually can be improved by revision.

Students such as the one who wrote the 2 paper are familiar indeed to writing teachers. Such students do not attend carefully to questions before they begin to write; they dash off whatever comes into their heads without sifting, organizing, or considering the reader. They often talk much more fluently than they write, and they sometimes score in the upper ranges on multiple-choice tests, since they know more than they can well express. When given a poor grade on an essay such as this one, they are ready to challenge the teacher, asking to see the errors; they are accustomed to analytic scoring and look puzzled when their ideas are taken seriously or when their writing is seen as a whole piece of communication. Sometimes, they do not conceive of writing as communication at all but rather as a game of error avoidance, at which they try to beat the teacher. Revision, if required, involves correcting whatever the teacher objected to—without touching anything else and without thinking at all about whatever the paper has to say or what it might say.

When such students are asked to participate in the development and use of a scoring guide, they often are first stunned and then delighted. After all, they have been playing a game that denies them intellectual integrity, and, furthermore, they have been playing it under someone else's rules, which are at best half understood. The scoring guide sets out the rules for all to see, the class must understand the guide to use it at all, and the rules actually work in accord with instinct and common sense. The writer, along with virtually the whole class, can see why the paper is a 2, can compare it with papers earning higher scores, and can begin to learn ways to improve. Perhaps a 5 is out of reach, at least at first, but the 3 paper is not that much better and represents real advancement.

Scoring guides in the writing class remove the mystery and even the curse from grading, along with the worst of the labor. A holistic guide, urging, as most of them do, attention to what is done well and calling for attention to what is said, offers students the opportunity to learn how to evaluate their own work as well as the work of others. The teacher changes from inscrutable judge to guide as the students work to produce writing that will score in the top half of the scale; although the class cannot relieve the teacher of the responsibility for term grades, the use of scoring guides can shift the evaluation process into its rightful place as part of the writing process. While some students may never be able to or may not want to make the

effort to write top-ranked papers, almost all of them will be
able to assess the relative quality of their work. And when the
occasion calls for it, they will know what they need to do in
order to produce their best.

The practical use of scoring guides in classrooms often begins with the instructor returning a set of papers marked according to a guide distributed at the same time. A few duplicated papers illustrating the scoring guide clarify the process
and, incidentally, relieve the instructor of writing similar comments on many of the student papers. When the next writing
assignment is given, the instructor may want to make development of a rough scoring guide part of the pre-writing activity in
class; nothing clarifies an assignment quite as fully as a statement of the criteria for evaluating it. The next step in the application of this concept is the division of the class into small
groups to read and evaluate one another's writing according to
an agreed-on scoring guide. Since the goals are both the achievement of consistency (each student scores each paper privately
and the group then compares and discusses the scores) and the
application of clearly stated criteria (the students must defend
their scores according to the guide—or convince everyone involved to change the guide), the focus of the activity must remain on the quality of the writing.

Many writing teachers have found the development and
use of scoring guides along with writing assignments to have a
series of unexpected advantages: Not only does the scoring
guide accomplish the stated goals of clarifying the assignment
and the criteria for evaluation, but the classroom use of the
guide expands the audience for writing beyond the teacher, in-
creases student ability to read one another's and their own writing, leads to improved revision and improved motivation for
writing in general, and—possibly most delightful of all—reduces
the excessive time demands for grading on the conscientious
writing teacher.

The following scoring guide (adapted from a draft by
David Rankin; White and Polin, forthcoming) was used as part
of a research project evaluating college freshman composition
writing programs. It is far more elaborate than the first one, in

part because the question (designed for students completing freshman composition) is more complex and in part because it is derived from a set of definitions of the goals of freshman composition.

These goals were defined by the research team in terms of what abilities the topic was supposed to measure and what criteria for scoring should be included in the scoring guide. Four specific writing skills were to be tested:

Description. The topic should include a demand for descriptive writing, so that the student can demonstrate the ability to use concrete language in clear sentences. The topic should allow the student considerable range of choice, so that the student can choose a familiar and accessible object for description and so that weak writers will be able to perform.

Abstraction. The topic should ask the student to move from description into some form of abstraction, so that the student will be able to demonstrate the ability to move between the abstract and the concrete and to relate concrete description to concepts. The topic should allow room for inventiveness, even as it makes this demand, so that students who have been trained to work at various levels of abstraction will be able to demonstrate that skill.

Analysis. The topic should ask students to compare, evaluate, or otherwise analyze the material they have described and developed. A demanding question will make distinctions among the better writers, for whom freshman composition is frequently a course in systematic thinking.

Use of Standard Prose Forms. The student writing should be expressed with enough regard for the conventions of educated usage so that meanings are communicated clearly and unambiguously, without those distractions that are unacceptable even in first-draft writing.

The essay topic selected was carefully developed, using the procedures outlined in Chapter Six, to meet these specifications:

Assignment: Some changes or inventions intended as "improvements" turn out to have unforeseen or unfortunate consequences. Think about and select one such change in, for instance, a product, a machine, a procedure, a policy, or an institution. In an organized essay, briefly describe the situation before the change, explain the intended "improvement," and discuss the gains and losses resulting from the change.

The research team developed the scoring guide by connecting the general specifications and the writing assignment to four kinds of skills and processes taught in freshman composition courses: cognitive processes, heuristic skills, invention processes, and organizational development skills. The research team then expanded the criteria into an outline for scoring as follows:

1. Cognitive processes
   a. Perception of the paradox and/or irony in the topic
   b. Conception of a procedure for writing
2. Heuristic skills
   a. Perception of the problems to be solved in the topic
   b. Ability to follow directions through stages of the topic
3. Invention processes
   a. Selection of an appropriate subject within the topic
      • A particular "invention" (not a generalization)
      • A sufficiently complex and interesting subject
      • An invention with advantages and disadvantages
      • An invention reflecting a real change
   b. Selection of an appropriate controlling idea
      • Establishment of focus
      • Maintenance of focus
4. Development skills
   a. Selection, organization, and presentation of some relevant details that support the controlling idea of the paper
   b. Demonstration of control over levels of generality
      • Ability to move between more abstract and more particular levels of argument
      • Ability to use rhetorical markers to guide the reader through levels of generality
      • Ability to maintain cohesion through use of markers
   c. Control over organization and paragraphing
   d. Demonstration of ability to use

- edited American English
- vocabulary appropriate to subject and purpose
- syntactic structures and patterns appropriate to the complexity of the task, that is, subordination, transitions, coordination, devices for cohesion that accurately convey abstract relationships, and so forth

The following elaborate scoring guide was then prepared for the holistic scoring of the essays. A quite different guide for a primary trait scoring of the same question appears later in this chapter.

Holistic Scoring Guide No. 2

6: A paper in this category will complete all the tasks set by the assignment. It will be distinguished by lucid and orderly thinking—and may even introduce an original interpretation of the writing topic. It will be virtually free from errors in mechanics, usage, and sentence structure. And there will be evidence of superior control of language.

5: A paper in this category may slight, but not ignore, one of the tasks of the assignment or deal with it only by implication, but the writer will demonstrate a clear understanding of the writing topic. It may not be as thoughtful or as carefully reasoned as a 6 paper, but it will not be characterized by mere statement and restatement of ideas at a high level of generality. Although the paper may have minor weaknesses in paragraphing, it will contain evidence of the writer's ability to organize information into unified and coherent units. It will be largely free from serious errors in mechanics, usage, and sentence structure. And it will be generally well written, characterized by clarity if not by felicity of expression.

4: Although a paper in this category may execute the assignment less completely or less systematically than a 6 or 5 paper does, the paper will come to terms with the basic tasks of the assignment. The reasoning may be less precise and less discriminating than one would expect to find in a 6 or 5 paper, but it will not be flawed by logical fallacies. It may insufficiently develop a point or two, but it will give evidence of the writer's ability to support key ideas. It will be organized and paragraphed well enough to allow the reader to move with relative ease through the discourse, though there may be some disjointedness and lack of focus. It may contain errors in mechanics, usage, and sentence structure, but not so frequently as to call into question the writer's command of the conventions of the standard dialect or to consistently distract the reader from the content. The paper will display generally accurate use of language.

3: A paper will fall into this category if it shows serious difficulty managing the tasks of the assignment; OR if it shows definite weaknesses in analytic thinking; OR if the paper is so markedly underdeveloped that key ideas stand virtually without illustration; OR if errors in sentence structure, usage, and mechanics seriously interefere with readability. There may be distinctive weaknesses in paragraphing and organization, but the total effect will not be chaotic. The writer's control of language may be uncertain.

2: A paper in this category may fail to come to terms with the assignment; that is, tasks may be ignored, misconstrued, badly mishandled, or redefined to accommodate what the writer wants to say or is able to say. There is also likely to be a combination of the following defects: serious errors in reasoning, little or no development of ideas, and no clear progression from one part to the next. There may be serious and frequent errors in sentence structure, usage, and mechanics, giving the impression of distinctly inferior writing.

1: This category is reserved for the paper in which a combination of errors, conceptual confusion, and disorganization creates the impression of ineptitude. There are, however, definite indications of the writer's attempt to deal with the topic.

9: This paper is obviously "off-topic" by intention, whatever its writing quality.

Both the question and the scoring guide are more elaborate than usual here, since the researchers were not interested merely in a pass/fail or placement decision. The goal was to generate a wide range of holistic scores that might indicate narrow but significant differences among a variety of writing programs. The question was also designed to generate two different kinds of primary trait scores, one of which will be discussed shortly.

This question is similar to the first in its demand for initial description. But whereas the college applicant was asked to choose and describe an object, the college freshman must select a change or invention with two characteristics: It was intended as an improvement, and it has had unintended consequences. This choice of topic is crucial, for the four parts of the question all revolve around that choice: (1) Describe the situation before the change; (2) explain the change itself; (3) discuss resultant gains; and (4) discuss resultant losses.

Some students gravitated to the obvious choices, such as automobiles, television, and nuclear power, while others reached for arcane, witty, or hopeless topics such as certain medicines, unusual sexual practices, and even the introduction of Eve to the garden of Eden. An "unintended effect" of the question was the production, in response to the call for description of the situation before the change, of a quantity of dubious invented history. Only the unusually well-trained student was able to deal with all parts of the question. Those who were accustomed to plunging in without much planning or pre-writing tended to get themselves in severe organizational difficulties and sometimes found themselves explaining matters about which they were wholly ignorant.

The question, however, did achieve its goal. Those students with weak writing ability showed just where they were weak, while the better-trained and more effective writers were able to produce better and more effective responses. Whereas many of the more general topics, with more general scoring guides, will produce a peaked bell curve with a low standard deviation (that is, scores will accumulate mostly in the middle range), this question was able to generate distinctions among the weak writers and also among the strong ones.

The scoring guide, in typical holistic fashion, begins the description of each score level by considering the degree to which the writer was able to manage the tasks of the assignment.

It proceeds next to levels of development and logical thinking, paragraph and sentence structure, and, finally, control over language. The highly experienced team of college faculty who used this scoring guide required four hours of practice scoring and training before reaching substantial agreement on the wide variety of papers the question elicited; by the end of a three-day reading, the readers were grading rapidly and sensitively, still interested in the complex problems presented by the question and the guide.

While this kind of scoring guide is valuable as a reference, its major use must be in research. Most in-class essay assignments need not be so complicated, and most scoring guides should not be so complex. Classroom teachers would be wise to resist the temptation to create such a guide, for few students would be able to use it holistically. I have chosen to present it here as an example of the way in which holistic scoring can reflect a highly sophisticated research design and a complex view of writing instruction at the college freshman level.

The last holistic scoring guide I will give was designed to score a proficiency test for college students at the upper-division level (taken from unpublished materials from the upper-division writing program, the California State University, San Bernardino, California). Since the students taking the test are both mature and already committed to various academic majors, the question needs to be both advanced and general. It cannot be based entirely on personal experience for at least two reasons: Students and faculty would find such a question too elementary, too similar to freshman composition assignments and placement tests; more seriously, such a question would fail to measure the analytic writing ability most faculty expect of college graduates. However, the question also needs to be devised so that no particular major field of study will advantage a particular group of students; the exam needs to be, and must be perceived as, fair to all.

Thus, questions for this purpose tend to be text based so that analytic skills can be tested without using material more familiar to some majors than to others, although some allowance for personal experience often enters. The question needs to offer scope for advanced students, and it need not make much allowance for the very weak reader or writer, who is insufficiently proficient to be awarded a college degree in any event.

The scoring guide to this relatively complex question, however, does not need to be particularly complex, since the decision to be made is basically pass/fail. Thus, the following question and scoring guide offer a peculiarly useful combination for use in the classroom: the question, though general enough for anyone to answer, is complex enough to examine advanced writing skill, while the scoring guide is an economical one, quite easy to use.

Reading. Read carefully the following passage, adapted from an essay by Jacob Bronowski (1966, p. 112):

> The process of learning is essential to our lives. All higher animals seek it out deliberately. They are inquisitive and they experiment. An experiment is a sort of harmless trial run of some action which we shall have to make in the real world, whether it is made in the laboratory by scientists or by fox cubs outside their earth. The scientist experiments and the cub plays; both are learning to correct their errors of judgement in a setting in which errors are not fatal. Perhaps this is what gives them both their air of happiness and freedom in these activities.

Preparation. Consider the following questions about this passage:

Just what is Bronowski saying about the role of experiment in learning? How does he define "experiment"? How does he explain the process of learning? How does his writing ability (consider his use of words, repetitions, examples, and so on) help make his point convincing? To what degree is his point sound? Do you find his definitions of "experiment" and "learning" useful? Can you think of examples that confirm or deny his conclusions?

Assignment. In a well-written essay, discuss and evaluate Bronowski's view of the role of experiment in learning. Include a detailed and well-supported account of your own observations about how learning takes place.

Holistic Scoring Guide No. 3

The student should be rewarded for what he or she does well; we need to remember that we are scoring first-draft writing to a demanding assignment, and everyone is likely to make some minor errors under such conditions.

The assignment requires the student to accomplish two tasks: (1) discuss and evaluate Bronowski's argument and (2) include an account of his or her own observations about learning. Ordinarily, an essay that does not respond to both parts of the question should not be scored in the upper half. Both parts may occur simultaneously, or even implicitly rather than explicitly. Papers that are unusually well written may be scored a point higher than they otherwise would be.

Upper-Half Scores. The 5 paper responds to both parts of the question, using both generalizations and specific details to make its own case. It will analyze the Bronowski passage, perceiving several aspects of his argument, such as his equation of experiment and play, his odd description of animal and human nature, and his assertion that experiment is a natural activity. It will include specific detail in the personal part of the response and connect both parts. It will demonstrate the ability to write coherent and fluent paragraphs, direct and clear sentences, and an organized paper. It is generally free from distracting sentence, diction, grammar, or spelling errors, although it will not necessarily be error free.

The 6 paper adds to these characteristics a unity of tone and point of view, a sense of depth in the analysis, some creativity, and some sophistication of style.

The 4 paper may lack a unified argument, although it will still respond to both parts of the question, and show flaws in coherence and development. Not all parts of the question will be treated very well, and there may be a few noticeable errors.

Lower-Half Scores. The 2 paper will show an incomplete response lacking in coherence, direction, or focus. It will tend to use generalizations without supporting detail or details without organization or conclusions. These papers sometimes wander off into a simple summary of the passage or a very weak analysis; they may use restatement rather than development or narration rather than analysis. Important problems with diction, sentence structure, punctuation, and the like distract the reader.

The 3 paper remains in the lower half because it slights or ignores one part of the question, uses little detail, or has serious organizational or mechanical difficulties. But it is better than the 2 paper.

The 1 paper shows incompetence in writing, with many serious errors, lack of comprehension of the task, or inability to arrange thoughts into minimally acceptable prose.

Faculty teaching the advanced writing course that used this examination found the scoring guide particularly valuable in class. The course existed in various forms (one in the humanities, one in natural sciences, and so on), but, typically enough for a program meeting a graduation requirement, it was expected to enforce a reasonably consistent standard of writing for the college as a whole. The examination, devised by a committee of those teaching and graded holistically by the entire staff, had become the principal means of obtaining and demonstrating consensus on these standards. The scoring guide thus became a definition of the college's criteria for judging the writing proficiency required of its graduates, not merely a means of scoring a common examination reliably.

Most instructors distributed sample papers at the various score levels along with the scoring guide; they asked their students to evaluate these papers and to understand the scoring guide before the examination papers were returned. This procedure forced the students with low grades to confront their writing without the usual excuses; no one could blame the teacher's unfairness (since each test had been read twice by other faculty), and no one could claim that quirky or hidden standards had been employed. The teacher had, in fact, become a kind of coach, helping the student master the skills called for in the scoring guide, instead of an antagonist to be outsmarted in order to gain a good grade.

Furthermore, the use of the scoring guide in class helped

undermine the common belief that good writing in various academic specialties is somehow fundamentally different. The undeniable fact that the faculty from these disciplines were all able to agree on, and use reliably, that single scoring guide enforced the holistic concept of writing: Superficial differences in style or format from one field to another do not materially affect judgments about effective writing, since the whole is greater than the sum of its parts.

When faculty with little or no training in the teaching of writing find themselves teaching writing, either in a proficiency course of this sort or as part of their own departmental courses, grading often looms as a particularly forbidding problem. Many such faculty remember the hostile red marks their student work received from the analytic graders of their youth. Sensibly enough, they resist that model, but since it is the only model most of them know, they then feel that they simply cannot grade student writing in a respectable way. Sometimes that feeling alone prevents good writers and excellent teachers in the various disciplines from teaching writing. And, since writing is one of the principal means by which students learn anything, the entire educational enterprise suffers.

Participation in holistic group scoring tends to break down this destructive attitude toward the grading and teaching of writing. It also, of course, leads to discussion of standards and many other matters. When the instructor takes the scoring guides from the group grading session back to the classroom, the benefits of the procedure multiply. Now the students as well gain from the process: They begin to internalize the standards for evaluation, which they can use in revision; they become more able readers of their own drafts; and they can see that better writing is both definable and attainable.

Primary Trait Scoring

Since primary trait scoring is conceptually the same as holistic scoring, we need not review its assumptions in detail. Indeed, all that would be necessary to change the three scoring guides I have just presented into primary trait documents is a sharpening and narrowing of the criteria listed. However, the team that developed primary trait scoring was heavily involved with rhetorical theory, as opposed to the strictly practical bent of those who developed holistic scoring at the Educational Testing Service. The best summary of the conceptual history of primary trait scoring is given by a member of the group convened by the National Assessment of Educational Progress (NAEP), Richard Lloyd-Jones (see Cooper and Odell, 1977, pp. 32-66), who exemplifies the wit, sensitivity, and pedagogical experience that were part of the entire enterprise.

The problem with holistic scoring, particularly when the scoring guides are quite general or not specific to the question at hand, Lloyd-Jones points out, is the general nature of the rating: "At times one has the sense that a household yardstick is being used to measure the diameter of a cylinder in an automobile engine." As primary trait scoring narrows the focus and shortens the yardstick, "to some extent one must know less to know more" (Cooper and Odell, 1977, pp. 46-47). Thus, the team developing this procedure returned to the history of rhetorical theory in order to come up with ways of focusing measurement according to a consistent understanding of the goals of writing. A review of discourse models from those of Aristotle to those of James Kinneavy (1971) led the team to decide on a three-part scheme consisting of expressive, explanatory, and persuasive modes. (See Chapter Six.) The theoretical and conceptual work in turn led to a set of exercises and scoring guides intended to elicit particular and restricted kinds of information about the writing produced.

For example, in order to measure what the team called "imaginative expression of feeling through inventive elaboration of a point of view," the students were shown a photograph of five children playing on an overturned rowboat. The writing assignment directed those taking the test to imagine that they were one of the children in the picture or someone standing nearby and then to tell a good friend what was going on "in a way that expresses strong feelings." The papers were scored only on the writer's ability to use dialogue, manage point of view, and control tense structure, all as ways to discover the writer's ability "to project him/herself into a situation, find a role and an appropriate audience, and then reveal an attitude toward the material in relation to the role." The detailed attention to certain aspects of the writing can only be achieved by ignoring all the other aspects of the writing; such matters as spelling or diction or organization (aside from coherence) had no part to play in the scoring. (Several of the NAEP questions and scoring guides are printed in Cooper and Odell, 1977, pp. 47-66.)

The particular advantage of this method of scoring for classroom use is obvious: It allows an entire assignment to focus on one issue at a time. Particularly in a situation in which the surface features of writing are not important, as is often the case in early grades, it is valuable to have a method of scoring that does not allow too wide a scope. Writing is so complex an activity that such primary traits as the use of the imagination or (for more mature students) the development of an argument are well worth special attention in class and special focus in scoring.

While the NAEP materials (now available from the Educational Testing Service) give a wide range of primary trait topics and scoring guides, most writing teachers will want to use the concept rather than the particular materials in their classes. The great advantage of primary trait scoring is that it adds the option of a narrow focus to holistic scoring and thus allows teachers to fit such methods of assigning and responding to student work into their curricula. In simple terms, the primary trait theory supports every teacher's knowledge that we cannot do everything at once, nor need we try.

The primary trait scale I am presenting here (White and Polin, forthcoming) does not come from NAEP, although its precision and focus derive from the theories developed by the NAEP team. The scale was used as part of the research project in college composition programs described earlier in this chapter. After essays written to the question on "changes or inventions with unforeseen consequences" were scored holistically, the papers were scored again according to two primary trait scales designed to gather more precise information from the student writing. The scale printed here therefore allows a comparison between the holistic and primary trait approach to the same question, as well as an illustration of the kind of focus that can be achieved.

This particular primary trait scale was designed as a high-level measure to make distinctions among the papers likely to have already gained upper-half scores on the holistic scale. Since the goal of the research was to find the most effective writing programs for strong as well as weak writers, the primary trait scale in "Development and Focus" measured the writing feature most commonly stressed in college composition classes for students who are already competent writers. Classroom teachers will find this scale valuable when they are teaching paragraph development, essay structure, or the use of evidence to support generalizations. The concepts of structure and levels of development contained in the guide are based on those developed by Francis Christensen (1967), as revised and adopted by a former student of Christensen, David Rankin.

Development and Focus
Upper-Half Scores

6: 1. There will be movement to at least a third level of development.
2. There will be at least (a) one shift back and forth between levels of development or (b) movement to four or more levels of development.
3. A distinct richness will be achieved within levels of development, either within sentences, by various means of modification (embedding, free modifiers, initialized adverbials), or in successive sentences that represent coordinate amplifications of an idea already expressed on a higher level of generality. For example:

```
        1                       1
          2                       2
            3                       3
          2                           4
            3
```

4. Use of focusing devices will indicate awareness of the need to keep the audience oriented. Functional markers are present and used correctly.

(The major distinction between 6 and 5 is quality of development (richness).)

5: 1. There will be movement to at least a third level of development.
    2. There may be shifting between levels or movement to four or more levels of development.
    3. There will be some richness within levels.
    4. Use of focusing devices will indicate awareness of the need to keep the audience oriented.

(The major distinction between 5 and 4 is focus (quality of markers).)

4: 1. There will be movement to at least a third level of development.
    2. There may or may not be shifting between levels.
    3. There will be little or no richness within levels.
    4. These papers will be less focused than 5 papers.

(The major distinction between 4 and 3 is development (3 levels, all under control).)

Lower-Half Scores

3: 1. There will be movement to a second level of development. If there is apparent movement to a third level or beyond, the reader will be distracted by irrelevant details or ideas. Generalizations, abstractions, or important ideas may remain undefined or not illustrated even if the prose seems to move to a third level.
    2. There will be little or no richness within levels.
    3. Some focusing problems will cause the reader to work a bit to stay on track.

(The major distinction between 3 and 2 is focus (3 papers still have a grasp on focus).)

2: 1. There will be movement to a second level of development or to a misconceived third level.
    2. There will be little or no richness within levels.

3. There will be a distinct lack of focus, with the result that the reader must supply the connections in the prose if, indeed, the writing is in any sense consecutive discourse.

(The major distinction between 2 and 1 is development.)

1: 1. There will be no movement beyond one level of generality. The prose will consist of undeveloped generalizations or meaningless specifics that support no clear-cut controlling idea.
2. There will be no richness.
3. There will be a distinct lack of focus.

Notes

Lower-half papers are characterized by their tendency to stay on one level or to jump levels without awareness of the need to signal the reader or to make connections. Low-level specifics are never gathered into a larger meaning, or their meaning is (or is imagined to be) self-evident. Although the reader may have to infer generalizations, this will not affect essay scores, as long as such inference is a clearly intended product of the writing and not simply evidence of the ingenuity of the reader. However, it is not acceptable for the reader to have to infer the support (for example, details) for generalizations.

The Christensen model of paragraph organization, from which this primary trait scoring guide is derived, provides teachers with an effective way of helping students develop their ideas. Once students understand different levels of abstraction and the ways in which lower levels of abstraction allow them to illustrate, particularize, and develop their more general ideas, this pattern of paragraph analysis (as illustrated under the score of 6 description above) becomes a powerful way for them to see what they have written or might write. Those who are familiar with this method of teaching are likely to be surprised to see it embodied in a scoring guide, not at all what the author had in mind as he sought to discover the "generative rhetoric" that formed successful paragraphs.

However, the great value of primary trait scoring is precisely its direct connection with classroom teaching. Valuable aspects of teaching should develop into measurement devices that both evaluate and support the work going on in class. Primary trait scoring guides offer the opportunity to focus on what is being taught—without breaking writing into pieces or diminishing its importance for human expression.

Conclusion

When we consider the relative usefulness of primary trait and holistic scoring, their strengths and weaknesses become clear. Holistic scoring, with its attempt to encompass the full range of components that go into writing, generally will be preferred where conclusions about that evanescent skill called "writing ability" are made: most testing programs, many research programs, and often in the classroom. When more narrow judgments are called for, as in many program evaluations, much research, and the most common teaching situations, a carefully designed primary trait scoring will lead to more useful (if less global) information. Sensible and informed people will spend time and energy developing or discovering the appropriate measurement device for their needs, and they will insist that scoring systems and scoring guides confirm and support their teaching.

8

Organizing and Managing
Holistic Essay Readings

Those who are charged with organizing a holistic essay reading can find little to help them in the literature. The development of the procedure over the last decade or so has been so rapid, and those involved have made themselves so generally available, that word of mouth and traveling consultants have satisfied much of the need for information about setting up such a project. The primary source of this information has been the team that originated the process at the Educational Testing Service in Princeton, New Jersey. That team helped shape the holistic scorings begun on the West coast in 1973 by the California State University English Equivalency Examination; as director of that project, I made presentations to various groups (such as the Bay Area Writing Project), which further disseminated the concepts and procedures. The CSU English Placement Test readings, begun in 1977, were modeled on the English Equivalency Examination program, by that time well known and accepted by English faculty in the CSU; and, to complete a geographical circle, they became the model for the New Jersey Basic Skills testing program. ETS consultants have remained prominent in this development, with such sophisticated specialists as Gertrude Conlan, Evans Alloway (from the Princeton office), and Alan Seder (from the Berkeley office) supporting the organization of many readings.

The purpose of this chapter is to make generally available the experience of those who have been developing and refining the management of holistic essay readings. While there are some differences in procedure on some matters, a general consensus has developed as to the best practices to be followed. I will assume here that a placement or proficiency test has been given to a large group of students—the entering freshman class, say, or prospective graduating seniors fulfilling a proficiency requirement, or all students completing freshman English—and that a faculty member has been given the responsibility of directing the scoring of the test. This increasingly common situation may lead the inexperienced director into a surprisingly complicated task with many ulcerous traps. However, careful planning, with an awareness of the experience of others, can clear the way to a successful reading.

Planning the Reading

Anyone who has been part of a badly planned scoring session will remember the irremediable sense of chaos it engendered. Before the scoring could begin, someone had to make the coffee (or find the coffee pot) and locate the pencils. Instead of being told where to record scores and how the first score would be covered before the second reading, the readers had to debate the procedure and come up with a system. The movement of papers from reader to reader was haphazard and uncertain. The chief reader scurried about finding materials and dealing with organizational matters instead of concentrating on developing a consensus on grading standards. The reading started late and the last hour was as confused as the first, since no one seemed confident that the scoring would be finished before dinner. The experience seemed unprofessional and unsatisfying, and few would be ready to repeat it.

A well-run reading, in contrast, begins with a sense of calm and order. When readers appear, they find folders and name tags at their places and everything ready to start on time. They can concentrate on the taxing work at hand without being distracted by irrelevant detail, and they are kept informed about the pace of the reading and the expected finish time. The chief reader is calm and good humored, confidently expecting agreement and ready to give full attention to the scoring of papers. There is ample time for discussion of the papers at hand, and some time is allowed for consideration of the implications of the test and of the scoring procedure for teaching. Such matters as meals and honoraria are attended to in a way that makes the readers feel special. At the end of such a reading, faculty leave with a sense of satisfaction, an enhanced sense of professionalism, and a willingness to repeat the experience.

The planning that makes the difference between a good and bad reading can be broken down into three categories: facilities, personnel, and materials. A well-planned scoring session shows care in all three areas.

Facilities

It is sometimes a surprise to discover how few facilities are well suited for an essay reading. Typically, a room for a scoring session is arranged with tables of readers as illustrated in Figure 7. This room arrangement can accommodate eighteen

Figure 7. Room Arrangement for an Essay Reading.

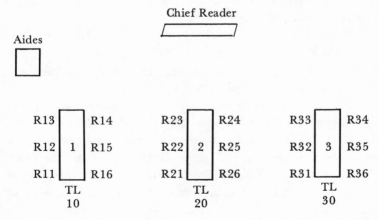

readers at three tables, with three table leaders. The chief reader, or room leader if there is more than one room, directs the reading from the front of the room. The aides need working space in order to distribute and collect batches of papers, cover and uncover scores, discover discrepancies, and check the count of tests (to guard against misplacing one). The table leaders, whose function is to maintain a consistent grading standard at their tables, need room to walk around their tables in order to check randomly selected papers scored by readers. Since all these activities require some space and some whispered conversations, the room needs to be of ample size, with excellent lighting throughout and, if possible, carpeted to reduce noise. Readers need enough room for comfort, so the reading tables should be of good size. Just outside the reading room should be an area for refreshments, with convenient rest rooms. A photocopy machine needs to be at hand; if none is nearby, one can be rented for a reading at low cost and installed at a convenient location.

Few schools have rooms suited for an essay reading. Classrooms and libraries usually cannot be rearranged suitably, and cafeterias and gymnasiums tend to be noisy and badly lit. Many universities will discover an appropriate location in a trustee meeting room or other conference room. Sometimes an auditorium can be made suitable, although lighting is often inadequate. The best solution may be found in a hotel meeting room or a local conference center. If compromises must be made, the highest priority should be lighting; second comes quiet; third is space.

Before the readers arrive, the room should be prepared to receive them. Place cards not only facilitate quick seating but allow the director to arrange readers to advantage. Inexperienced readers can be placed between helpful old hands or next to the table leader; noisy or gregarious personalities can be put next to unresponsive workaholics. Every reader and table leader should be assigned a number to record next to grades both for record-keeping purposes and to ensure that second or third readings of a paper will always go to a new reader, preferably at a different table. A folder at each place could contain a copy of the essay question (often forgotten), the scoring guide, sample papers, rosters of readers, pencils, and the like. The presence of coffee and doughnuts encourages early arrival and sets a pleasant tone.

Considerations of food and drink are by no means trivial

for a longer reading. A hearty lunch on site saves reading time otherwise lost to restaurants, and a cocktail party planned at the end of the day keeps readers going through the long afternoon hours. Extra attention to these creature comforts says more loudly than do words that the readers are special people doing a special task, and it reinforces the importance of the enterprise. The conversation at these social occasions and at breaks during the day (at least five minutes every hour or so) invariably centers around the task at hand, supporting the professional cohesion of the group and reinforcing the standards (and implications) of the reading.

Only one question can be scored in a room at any one time. If the test consists of two or more questions, two or more groups of readers in separate rooms will need to be set up. The same result will be reached if the same group completes the grading of question one and, after a break, undertakes the grading of question two. Only in this way can unwanted variables be kept out of the scoring process and reliable scoring be maintained.

Of course, the perfect facilities may not be found or, in the case of a small or a classroom essay reading, may not be needed. The many teachers who involve their classes in essay readings will group their students in casual ways, and many of the strict procedures I am detailing in this chapter will give way before sensible compromises and pedagogical alteration. I hope the classroom version of holistic scoring will not attempt to duplicate the machinery of large-scale testing. At the same time, anyone involved in holistic scoring ought to know the most strict and careful methods for it, even if they are not necessary at the moment, for the reasons behind the procedures do apply to any essay reading, however informal.

Personnel

Since a reading is only as effective as the people involved, particular care needs to be given to the selection of participants, particularly the chief reader, the table leaders, and the chief aide. Once chosen, these people should be given enough time to accomplish their tasks (not asked to add the scoring to already full teaching days or to volunteer weekends) and paid professionally for their extra time. Excuses for exploitation are always available and never convincing; ETS, for example, pays readers the merest token wage on the asserted grounds that it is a professional privilege to read essays eight hours a day for a commercial (if nonprofit) testing firm. It is idle to imagine that readers—or others—treated unprofessionally will develop the professional consensus and professional attitude that are absolutely essential to a reliable essay reading.

The chief reader, who is often but not always the program director, needs to possess a strong combination of flexibility and authority. This central person effectively runs the reading, choosing the sample papers, moderating and ending debate over standards, arbitrating differences of opinion, and accepting final responsibility for a reliable scoring session. In the conduct of the initial training session for readers, the chief reader needs to allow enough discussion of the scoring standards so that readers internalize and come to "own" the scoring guide, but discussion has to be cut off when it becomes unproductive. During the reading, the chief reader constantly scores papers culled from the tables and compares scores with the table leaders; the essential task is to make sure that all table leaders have the same standards and that, therefore, the readers at the various tables do not drift up or down in their scoring.

From time to time during the reading, generally three or four times a day, additional brief training sessions will deal with particular problem papers that have emerged. For example, a very good paper in very bad handwriting will be distributed for scoring, or a good short paper will be contrasted with a weak long paper. Sometimes during a reading, superficial or empty papers with few mechanical errors will receive higher scores than they deserve, or unusual original approaches to the topic will receive lower scores than they should. The chief reader will need to be alert to these potential problems and others like them and deal with them in a calm, authoritative way, eliciting rather than commanding assent.

Since there is no substitute for experience in a chief reader, those beginning new programs may want to import an experienced outsider for a first reading; the next chief reader can be chosen from the best of the table leaders. But sometimes it is politically wiser to select the most appropriate person available on campus as chief reader and let experience accumulate on the job. It is a rare academic who has the sensitivity, tact, self-confidence, and quick wit to accomplish this job well; a good first choice should be considered a most lucky hit.

The table leaders need to have many of the same qualities as the chief reader. They need to be quick and steady readers, for it is their function to check-read papers scored by readers at their tables throughout the entire scoring session. They will identify readers who are scoring higher or lower than the room as a whole, and it is their delicate job to ask these readers to adjust their standards; these requests must somehow be made without damaging the self-confidence of sensitive professionals who are not accustomed to having their judgments evaluated or challenged. A good table leader will be intuitive enough to find a way to do this and will quickly locate the problem readers who will require the most time.

It is easy to spot the good table leaders at a reading. They are seen as valuable allies by their readers, who take problem papers to them for consultation. They establish a cordial tone at the table, even as they keep noise down, and they remain very busy check-reading six or eight papers from each reader in turn. On the other hand, the inept table leaders see themselves—and are seen by their readers—as overseers; they tend to make everyone a bit edgy. These table leaders spot-check only occasional papers and never seem to have much to do; their readers are unconvinced when asked to review or change scores that are out of line. An experienced chief reader knows that the quality and tone of a reading depend on the skill of the table leaders and will take particular pains to appoint the best that can be found.

The chief reader and the table leaders form a team that must work together comfortably; if they cannot reach agreement on the issues that emerge, the readers will never come to agree on consistent standards. But a team that works smoothly will be able to cope with problem questions or problem readers with aplomb and deliver reliable scores in a pleasant, professional environment.

A competent chief aide is as important to an essay reading as the chief reader and needs to be as carefully chosen. This aide will be responsible for the preparation of papers for scoring, for the movement of papers throughout the reading, for the identification of papers with discrepant readings (requiring a third reading), and for the pacing of the scoring session. The aide prepares copies of all sample papers, at the direction of the chief reader, and sees that readers have these samples for scoring when they should. The aide usually oversees the preparation of travel reimbursements, payroll, time sheets, and the like, and sees to it that all supplies (including those for refreshment breaks) are at hand when needed. In short, the chief aide is responsible for all aspects of the reading outside of the actual scoring, and he or she makes it possible for the readers to focus their attention on the scoring.

Chief aides thus belong to that bureaucratic infrastructure that allows most enterprises in America to function: the special group that includes administrative assistants, department secretaries, assistants to the president, and so on. These people know how to fill in the forms, order the supplies, reserve the rooms, send out and monitor the replies to appointment letters, and (when needed) make the coffee. No reading—indeed no organization of any sort—can get along without such an aide, and one should be identified early, paid well, and honored fully. After two readings, the aide will know everything that needs to be done, maintain a small group of assistant aides as needed, require no instruction, and be indispensable. The only problem then becomes an occasional reminder to the aide that the chief reader must appear to be in charge and that the machinery of the reading must always support the reliability of the reading and not become an end in itself.

The choice of readers is fraught with difficulty, particularly for a new program; established programs keep records of reader speed and accuracy and so can be more sure of getting a critical mass of good readers for any one scoring session. The ability to read essays accurately and quickly demands a peculiar skill not necessarily associated with other academic skills. Some excellent teachers never get the hang of it, while the least likely individuals often turn out to be amazingly talented as readers. Excessively rigid teachers or those who are insecure often have difficulty adopting group standards, and faculty who take pride in their differences with their colleagues may resent the entire process. But even such apparently unsuited readers sometimes turn out to be delightful at readings, while some highly recommended people read erratically and inattentively.

Those appointing readers thus should be careful about making premature judgments before giving people a chance. Careful record keeping will identify those who read inaccurately or too slowly to carry their weight (although speed is much less important than accuracy and should not be overvalued). The experience of participating in a well-run reading is so valuable to faculty that rotation should allow virtually all who are interested to take part. Even a weak first reading may be followed by a strong second showing, as a teacher feels increasingly comfortable with the process. Over time, in a continuing program, the natural leaders will emerge to be chief readers and table leaders, and the best readers will form a steady cadre to help shape a new community each time a reading convenes. If the leaders of the reading have been well chosen, and if they can count on having a number of experienced readers at each table, the reading can accommodate as many as one third new readers without losing control.

Materials

An essay reading is a specialized form of conference, and all the usual supplies for a conference need to be on hand: pens, pads of paper, aspirin, and the like. The chief aide should make up a list of such materials and add to it as needed. The special materials associated with a reading have to do with the arrangement of test booklets for scoring, the preparation of sample papers and scoring guides used to develop consistent standards, the system of concealing prior grades for second and subsequent raters, and the plan for recording scores and other data from the reading for future use.

Arrangement of Test Booklets for Scoring. It is so convenient to handle tests of uniform physical size and shape that virtually every testing program of any size requires students to write in a standard test booklet. While such "blue books" are available from every college bookstore, many programs will design their own in order to develop a cover suited to their particular needs. Such a cover will have not only spaces for the students to fill in identifying information but also locations for the assignment of grades. The lower half of such a cover may appear as in Figure 8.

Figure 8. Sample Test Booklet Cover Design.

First Reading		Second Reading	
Score	Reader No.	Score	Reader No.
1 4		1 4	
2 5		2 5	
3 6		3 6	
9		9	

This design allows readers to circle the scores they decide on instead of writing them in in more or less decipherable handwriting. The score of 9, meaning an off-topic or otherwise unscorable paper, may in some programs be given only by table leaders in order to be consistent in an area of inconsistency. If the test booklet contains more than one question, additional boxes for scoring will be needed; if a third reader is used to resolve discrepancies between the first two, an additional set of boxes will be included for the reconciliation reader. In short, a well-designed booklet cover will allow for the needs of the particular test and simplify the recording of scores.

It is usually a good idea to randomize and batch test booklets in preparation for a reading. Batches of twenty or so can move from reader to reader as a unit much more conveniently than can individual tests; it is easier to keep track of

200 batches than 4,000 tests. Each batch should contain tests randomly chosen from the entire test group in order to avoid concentrating certain groups in special batches. Even a small campus reading of an exam from, say, eight sections of freshman composition should randomize and batch the 160 test booklets into 10 batches of 16, with 2 papers from each section in each batch. Readers scoring randomized batches thus will not be distracted from the scoring guide by the peculiar characteristics of particular batches, and the reading will more fairly represent the group standards of the readers to all those taking the test.

In a large reading, batches will be numbered and every test booklet in the batch will be stamped with the batch number. If that is done, any booklet removed from the batch (to serve as a sample, perhaps, or to be used during check-reading) can be replaced; if batch numbers are included with final score reports, it will be easy to locate any test, as long as the batches are stored sequentially. In the last hour or so of a reading, it becomes necessary to break up batches in order to even out the work that remains; if every test has a batch number, the booklets can be readily restored to order and counted at the end.

Preparation of Scoring Guides and Sample Papers. A tentative scoring guide should be prepared by the test development committee. Then, shortly before the reading, the chief reader and table leaders should meet to select sample papers to illustrate the several score levels and to refine the scoring guide in light of the actual test results. (Only the most strict purists require these samples to be inserted in the batches and scored again during the reading.) The final version of the scoring guide they approve then will be duplicated and made available to all readers, usually in their folders at the table. It is always possible that some changes will be made in the scoring guide during the initial training session, but once actual scoring of the test has begun no more changes can be made. All papers need to be scored according to the same criteria.

The length of the reading and the complexity of the question will determine the number of sample papers that are needed. An initial set of samples should be chosen to serve two purposes: to illustrate the range of quality, from the best to the

worst, in the actual test group, and to illustrate as unambiguously as possible the distinctions in quality described by the
scoring guide. Thus, a set of six samples would be chosen as the
first set of "anchor papers" on a six-point scale, each paper representing the most typical example of one of the scores. After
scoring and discussing the scores for these papers in light of
the scoring guide, another set of typical anchor papers would
follow.

Relatively few additional samples will need to be used if
agreement is high and there are few problems. But usually several additional groups of samples are used in the initial training
session. A set of four or five papers may be used to clarify the
distinctions between papers at the top of the bottom half of
scores and those at the bottom of the top half. Another set may
illustrate the difference between narratives that respond to the
question and those that do not. Perhaps it is important for readers to see papers that answer some portions of the question indirectly as opposed to papers that neglect some portions of the
question.

At some point, the chief reader will decide that the reading is ready to begin with "live" batches, and the scoring of the
test will begin. But additional samples will be used for training
sessions after breaks or meals, and the table leaders should be
particularly alert to problems that call for discussion during the
early hours of a reading. A one-day reading will often use
twenty or more sample papers before it is finished; the typical
three-day reading may well use forty.

Sample papers are usually identified by letter, as sample
"G" or sample "BB." Aides should be prepared with sufficient
copies of at least fifteen samples at the start of a reading, and
they need to be ready to produce copies of additional samples
rapidly throughout the reading.

The System for Concealing Scores. It is essential that
every test paper receive at least two independent readings. If
this basic rule is not followed—and economic pressures always
urge this unprofessional shortcut—two serious problems occur:
In the first place, the relative unreliability of any essay test will
be exaggerated to the point that all test scores will be open to

question; in the second place, the essential data needed to demonstrate the reliability of the scoring will not exist. But it is not enough merely to generate two scores for each essay: Those scores must be reached independently. Therefore, the score given by the first reader must somehow be concealed from the second reader. Furthermore, the system for concealing scores must allow for ready comparison of the two scores after the second score is registered so that a reconciliation score may be added if necessary.

Small, informal essay readings can accomplish this goal in simple and informal ways. The first score can be written on the cover of the test booklet, which is then folded back; the second score is recorded on the now-exposed inside front cover. Or readers can privately record their first readings, which can be entered by a clerk after the second reading. However informal the arrangement may be, some system of concealment is necessary, since the temptation to look at the first reader's score is almost irresistible.

Larger readings have come to use more formal methods. Most commonly, aides will pick up a scored batch of papers from a reader and cover all scores with a specially constructed tape, which is unglued in the center. These tapes, nicknamed "band-aids" because of the perforations that allow the center portion covering the grade to be ripped away, come in rolls of 500 and are quickly and easily applied to the cover of the test booklet.

Readings conducted at ETS in Berkeley, California, are now using invisible ink as a less cumbersome way to conceal first scores. Special pens allow the reader to see a marked score for a few seconds after it is written; the score than fades away and can be read only when exposed to black light. The table leaders, chief reader, and aides have black light lamps at their places so that they can do their work. Once all the equipment is obtained and set up, this system works more quickly and easily than do the band-aids, but some readers maintain that the impression on the paper left by the special pens remains readable even though the ink has faded.

Whatever system may be used will require special materials, and some foresight is required to obtain them well in advance of the reading.

Recording of Scores. When my colleagues and I get together to score the common examination we administer each term in the twenty or so sections of our upper-division writing class, each of us brings a copy of the class roster. As the reading approaches the end, a graduate student aide busily unmasks first scores (we use band-aids), bringing discrepancies (a difference of more than one point on the six-point scale) to the chief reader for reconciliation and reorganizing the scored tests from their randomized batches into class sets. Each instructor then receives the tests of his or her own students, records the scores on the extra roster for our records, and records them again on the class roll book. At that point, the job is finished.

However, when the number of tests reaches into the thousands or even the tens of thousands, more formal methods of recording scores are needed. In recent years, scored essay booklets for many tests have been sent to teams of keypunch operators, who record the scores along with student identification on punch cards, which then can be read by a computer. The computer, when properly programmed, produces rosters in various kinds of order (alphabetical by student name, high to low score, and so on), individual score reports for each student, and various statistical data at the same time. Thus, score reporting and record keeping are part of the same operation, and files for additional score reporting can be easily kept and readily reproduced. This procedure is, at this writing, the usual way scores of large-scale testing programs are handled.

Advances in technology suggest that much simpler procedures soon will become standard. Punch cards are even now giving way to direct entry of scores into computer files through keyboard-controlled data management systems. As these new systems develop, they will require less and less complicated equipment, and the rather simple software will be available everywhere, as personal computers now are. Testing programs will not have to choose between simplicity and sophistication; every school and college campus will be able to manage test scores and records of essay readings with ease. In order to en-

sure this manageability, any faculty director of a testing program needs to involve the local computer specialist in planning
for the use of test scores. With careful communication and
planning, the problem of what to do with scored tests and how
to handle the mass of data produced by an essay reading can be
solved. Without this proper and orderly planning, one can expect to be inundated by tons of paper and unanswerable questions.

Conduct of the Reading

The central concern for an essay reading must be to establish what the literary critic Stanley Fish calls an "interpretive community": a community of readers responding in the
same way to similar texts. The procedures involved in such a
reading are all designed to set up such a community—within the
constraints of a budget and a limited amount of time to accomplish a taxing and tedious job. This suggests not only decent pay
and comfortable working conditions but a sense of collegiality
among all those at the reading.

The most common mistake in the management of holis-
tic essay readings is losing sight of the need for this collegiality.
It is easy to see why this delicate sense of joint participation
and professional respect is so difficult to maintain. Very often,
readings do not proceed by consensus and joint decision making, which is a requirement if readers are to feel that they are
grading properly. Some test administrators see the discussion of
standards for grading as a waste of time better spent in generating scores. Coffee breaks, cocktail parties, and the like are seen
as luxuries and frills instead of the community-forming activities they need to be. Gracious treatment of readers or even professional pay for readers are considered to be expendable costs
instead of essential ingredients for a professional working community. But readers are not merely employees; they must form
a working team committed to group judgments and to the entire process of group scoring.

Even sensitive academics who run essay readings may
make the same mistake if they are not careful, since the process

of determining standards puts them in a position to coerce others in a good cause. Before readers come together to score a test, the chief reader and the table leaders will have met to read through many student papers in order to get a sense of the range of papers to be scored. These experienced readers will have spent a day or more reading several hundred papers, choosing papers to be duplicated for the readers to use as "range-finders," and developing the scoring guide describing the different points on the scale to be used at the reading. By the time the readers arrive, those responsible for the reliability of the reading will have already reached substantial agreement on standards. Every temptation exists, therefore, to tell the readers what to do and what standards to apply so that the reading can get under way efficiently.

But to do so is to ignore the need for a community of assent, which is what a holistic reading must become if it is to function responsibly. Those who understand the process will use their advanced knowledge of the student papers cautiously. Readers will have no problem granting the representativeness of sample papers if they trust the leaders of the reading. But readers must have the opportunity to grade those papers, to argue out differences, to come to an understanding of the ranking system, and even to make changes in the scoring guide if they agree to do so. The training of readers, or "calibration" as it is sometimes called, is not indoctrination into standards determined by those who know best (as it is too often imagined to be) but rather the formation of an assenting community that feels a sense of ownership of the standards and the process.

Maintaining the standards of the reading and of this sense of community go hand in hand even throughout scoring sessions that last many days. Retraining on new sample papers must occur every few hours to prevent reader drift up or down, and readers must see this process as a group endeavor to work together, not as a check by management on the accuracy of the readers. When leaders of a long reading organize social activities such as play readings, poetry readings, special films, and the like, they are not serving as entertainment directors so much as they are helping to hold the group together. When chief readers can use confident humor to acknowledge legitimate differences of opinion or admit that they might change their minds or even be wrong, they are not giving in to reader demands (as I heard one hard-nosed administrator put it); rather, they are admitting that they are human and part of the group that must accept that leadership willingly.

I have been stressing the need to develop a sense of community for a holistic reading and the various problems created by those who fail to see the need for that community. However, I do not mean to imply that the tone of a reading should be excessively casual. The best readings have a decidedly businesslike atmosphere, and the collegiality is part of the business to be accomplished. No one should imagine the reading to be a vacation or a social occasion: This is a hard and tedious job that must be done well in a limited amount of time. Establishing an "interpretive community" is simply the most efficient way to get the job done properly. It is an unexpected and even unintended result that the need for collegiality demands that the reading be a pleasant social and professional experience as well.

A well-run holistic scoring is the result of careful planning, with particular attention to the matters discussed in this chapter, combined with full sensitivity to the communal nature of the collegial enterprise. Visitors to such a reading tend to be struck by the intensity of the work going on, usually with great rapidity, in an environment of relaxed cordiality. They will see a room full of readers working through batches of essay booklets at a rate of from twenty-five to forty-five an hour (depending on the length and complexity of the question and the scoring guide). The table leaders will be standing by or moving around their tables, check-reading papers, or crouching beside a reader in a whispered conversation about the score of a particularly troublesome essay. Aides will be picking up scored batches from readers and replacing them with batches to be scored; other aides will be masking scores at their work tables or unmasking completed batches to discover discrepancies. The chief aide may be checking the pace of the reading and waiting to talk with the chief reader about how long the afternoon break should be. The chief reader may be talking quietly with the ta-

ble leader of table 2 about reader 24, who has been reading consistently high and has had half a dozen discrepancies with reader
13. Meanwhile, one of the aides is duplicating a paper scored at
the 2 level that ought to have received 4s; another aide is waiting to duplicate a hasty playbill for the play reading to occur
after dinner (as it happens, a "world premier" of a new play to
be produced by a major theater next month, directed by reader
36, who smuggled the script into the reading because he thought
it would be just what the readers needed after a tedious day of
scoring).

The eighteen readers pictured on the room chart given
earlier in this chapter (see Figure 7) will average twenty-five papers per hour for a seven-hour workday (8:30 A.M. to 4:30
P.M.), including several training sessions with sample papers, if
they are grading the typical college essay question—a forty-
five-minute expressive or analytic paper. That adds up to 175
scores a day for each reader, or 3,150 scores for the room.
Since each test requires two readings and about 10 percent of
the scores will be more than one point apart and require a third
reading, such a room will grade reliably about 1,500 tests a day.
(The first day of such a reading will require about two hours for
initial training and thus allow only a five-hour scoring day.) If
the test consists of a twenty-minute writing sample, which
allows for little development of ideas, the scoring pace will be
almost twice that of the more complex test.

The budget for an essay reading often appears high at
first glance. But it is important to understand, and to argue
with funding authorities, that the well-run holistic reading does
not only produce test scores at a reasonable price. It has two
major additional advantages—products, if you will—that are
being purchased at the same time. The reading allows a writing
test to be given and hence makes a major contribution to the
educational enterprise at its most crucial point; the reading deserves funding support from the instructional budget for this
reason. Furthermore, a holistic essay reading is the most effective in-service training for the teaching of writing yet discovered. It accomplishes more for the education and morale of the
faculty involved than would a series of lectures, seminars, and
retreats—indeed, it combines the virtues of various schemes for

faculty development most creatively. The budget for faculty development or in-service training could hardly be better spent than in contributing to the costs of an essay reading.

Holistic readings, in common with any aspect of testing, do not exist in a vacuum. Their influence on curriculum and teaching is what makes them important, and their positive effects on our work with our students are what make them valuable. Most readers of this book will not find themselves in the position to direct an essay reading, and hence they may not be able to take direct advantage of the technical experience that has been summarized in this chapter. But many faculty will take part in essay scorings, and the more informed they are about what is happening and what ought to be happening, the better those readings are likely to be. And these teachers can take away from the reading and to their work in class or with students in any capacity a sense of the validity of writing as a legitimate test of writing ability (and thinking ability) and an awareness of the ways in which reliability in such testing can be achieved. Such an awareness enriches our approach to whatever subject we may teach, at whatever level, and allows us to use writing as a means of learning, a means that can, if needed, serve as a refined and valuable measurement tool.

Program Planning

Chapter Eleven of this book outlines in considerable detail the steps and pitfalls in planning a writing testing program. Those who are in charge of a holistic reading need to be aware of these program planning issues, even if most of them do not seem to apply to the particular situation. I do not mean that faculty need to become test officers or statisticians in order to direct a holistic reading; but they do need to understand the kinds of issues that occur and to be sure that someone is taking care of them, or no amount of care with the reading itself will ensure success for the test. Just as a reading needs a room with good lighting and access to a supply of coffee before a reliable essay scoring can start, a testing program requires substantial planning before the test begins.

The planning issues become increasingly complex as more

people become involved. Teachers usually have a clear sense of the criteria and goals for a final examination of their students in freshman composition, but as soon as they combine with the other faculty teaching other sections of the same course, they discover a set of competing goals. For instance, one class may attend to analytic writing, while across the hall a different class works on the research report and down the corridor some maverick focuses on the lyric poem. In such a situation, one should forget about a common examination until the faculty have agreed on common goals and not imagine that any holistic scoring arrangement can solve such a program problem. Or—to take another example—one teacher may be convinced that writing proficiency at the high school level means the ability to write coherent paragraphs about concepts, while the assistant superintendent for instruction talks to the community about the need for better spelling and what he takes to be grammar. Again, it would be foolish to undertake holistic scoring without some clear agreement about the function, criteria, and meaning of a test for writing proficiency.

Of course, one of the great advantages of deciding on a testing program is that such a program invites—even requires—discussion about goals. The unprofessional situations I have just described (I wish I could call them hypothetical, but they are painfully common) must be changed if there is to be a single responsible test. But no one should be put in the position of administering a test until agreement on the goals of that test has been reached.

Similarly, other test administration issues should be in order before the reading. The test questions should have been developed with care (see Chapter Six), and the test should have been given under similar conditions and time limits to all of the students being examined, with appropriate attention given to test security. Decisions about the uses of the scores, the storing of the data and the tests, and the evaluation of the program should have been made to prevent such problems from interfering with the reading. Tentative scoring guides for the questions ought to have been prepared by the test development committees, and the scoring scale should have been determined.

It is important to clear away beforehand as much of the program detail as possible, because the direction of the reading itself is a job involving both considerable detail and a conscious grasp of the overriding goal of this group operation—the development of a consistent professional consensus about the writing standards to be applied to the particular test. All aspects of the reading need to work together to achieve this goal. The professional satisfaction of directing a successful reading is analogous to that of directing a symphony orchestra: The mastery of an enormous number of details leads to the team performance to which every player makes an essential contribution. The best conductor knows how to elicit the best from each participant and knows that a fine performance depends on all the small parts fitting together smoothly.

9

Understanding and Using
Recent Writing Research

Many of those who use writing in their classrooms neither know
nor care much about writing research—often for very good reasons. In the first place, much of this research has focused on
fairly young children, with uncertain application to adolescents
and adults and hence unclear value at the college level; those
who teach young children, and who thereby might profit directly from the research, tend to major in college in such subjects as education or liberal studies and thus receive very little
training in any aspect of writing. In the second place, college
teachers of writing generally conduct literary research, an activity so different in kind from writing research that the two
seem at best distant cousins. Graduate students in literature are
not trained to read or respect writing research, which often
looks suspiciously like the kind of thing done by social scien-
tists—a kind of practical, experimental activity utterly foreign
to their experience. Thirdly, writing research is often badly
written, unclear, clogged with data, and self-evident. The most
highly regarded writing research of the 1970s dealt with the
writing process; a series of detailed and expensive experiments
discovered what all writers and most sensible writing teachers
have always known: Writing demands a recursive process of considerable complexity. While the kinds of complexity the research has discovered open some interesting teaching possibilities, competent writing teachers can be forgiven for sighing that
they need no charts and statistics to prove the obvious. The

fourth and most common objection to writing research centers on its most common flaw: Too many of the studies' results turn out to be elaborated show-and-tell, not generalizable beyond the particular classroom or teacher with a special teaching idea.

There are less respectable reasons for ignoring writing research, however. Some of the research, such as that arguing that the teaching of grammar fails to improve writing or that which builds on an understanding of error to help rather than condemn unskilled writers, suggests strongly that it is time to abandon certain kinds of conventional teaching. Those committed to the teaching methods and materials under attack are often unwilling to consider abandoning familiar procedures. Even when a writing teacher decides to pursue some research question, the quest is often discouraging because studies are not concentrated in a familiar field; in order to follow most research, it is necessary to move into uncomfortable new areas and to discover difficult new journals. And finally, much research depends on measurement of results—one aspect of writing about which teachers know very little and toward which they tend to feel boredom and even hostility.

Nonetheless, writing research, like research in any emerging field, is extremely important. The portion of it that turns out to be significant—and no one can quite be sure which research that will be—becomes the new knowledge of the discipline, determining its textbooks as well as its directions. Process research may have demonstrated what every writer already knew, but not until this research gained prominence did writing textbooks and handbooks begin to reflect this knowledge. Those teaching writing to less skilled students now use materials that draw on research done by biologists on the brain, by second-language specialists on the development of language functions, by psychologists on writing anxiety, and by linguists on dialectology. Furthermore, we must look to research to evaluate the effectiveness of the latest panacea, such as word processing equipment, or the latest reborn concept, such as the supposed importance of the hemisphericity of the brain.

The purpose of this chapter is to provide those who assign and evaluate writing in their classes with a summary of some current writing research, with particular emphasis on the measurement applications involved. Teachers, particularly at the college level, have an obligation to be informed about the state of knowledge of the subjects they teach. Many teachers feel keenly this obligation in relation to writing research, despite the problems I have just cited, and this chapter is designed to make their professional concern less of a burden. The following overview is not intended to be inclusive but rather to exemplify the measurement issues teachers need to consider as they look at the findings of writing research. Indeed, if this chapter helps demystify some of those measurement issues, more teachers might become willing not only to read critically writing research but to conduct classroom research themselves. Teacher-conducted research is a particularly promising activity in the teaching of writing, a field in which practice often precedes and generates theoretical knowledge.

A review of theoretical and experimental writing research suggests three distinct perspectives from which writing is studied and discussed: The first focuses on the text and is product based; the second focuses on the interaction between writer and reader and concerns itself with the way that communication takes place; and the third attends principally to what is going on inside the writer's head, looking closely at cognitive operations or processes. It is obvious that each of these perspectives describes an important aspect of writing and that no one perspective should be seen as necessarily the best or worst. But since each perspective has different and important implications for measurement, teaching, and research, we need to look at each perspective separately.

Writing as Text

Traditionally, educators and measurement specialists have felt it to be axiomatic that writing skill is revealed in written products, or texts. Those conducting the research or measurement would learn about the writing and the writer through scrutiny of the features of the text, often focusing on syntax, diction, punctuation, and other scribal or grammatical matters as indicators of fluency and proficiency. Holistic scoring of writing samples is a sophisticated example of the same theory at work.

Three Approaches to Text Analysis. One method of text analysis that has been prominent in both research and teaching is Kellogg Hunt's concept of the "T-unit" (Cooper and Odell, 1977). The "T" in "T-unit" stands, Hunt tells us, for "terminable": "Grammatically a T-unit can be terminated with a period or other terminal mark" (p. 93). He defines the T-unit as "a single main clause (or independent clause, if you prefer) plus whatever other subordinate clauses or nonclauses are attached to, or embedded within, that one main clause" (pp. 92-93). The T-unit thus allows the researcher to analyze the complexity of sentence structure of a text. Simple prose and prose written by young children tend to consist of many short T-units; as children get older and prose becomes more complex, the T-units become longer, reflecting the increased ability to subordinate and otherwise embed ideas within other ideas.

Hunt's T-unit is a much more useful measurement tool than the sentence, which depends heavily on punctuation. He cites evidence to show that the T-unit, in various permutations, works as well with Dutch and Japanese children as with Americans, and he connects lengthening T-units in all cultures with what he calls "syntactic maturity."

The influence of Hunt's work has been pervasive. Many studies of the teaching of writing, particularly in the lower grades, use the comparative length and frequency of T-units as the touchstone for success. The practice of sentence combining, the most effective tool for teaching embedding (and hence lengthening the T-unit), developed as a pedagogical by-product of the measure; books by John C. Mellon (1969) and Frank O'Hare (1973), whose sentence-combining feature in Scholastic's *Voice* magazine is widely distributed in American grade schools, helped promulgate the teaching procedure.

In sentence-combining activities, students are given a series of short T-units (for example: (1) Aluminum is a metal. (2) It is abundant.) and asked to create one sentence from them (for example: Aluminum is an abundant metal.). Although the T-unit was developed and validated for young children, it has become generalized as both a research tool and a teaching device; Hunt reports finding in university-level writers certain "late-blooming" syntactic structures that allow complicated sentences to emerge with very long T-units.

As the T-unit moved from its role as a research measurement tool for children to that of a pedagogical device, a certain negative reaction set in. Numbers of teachers began to complain that sentence combining easily became a bore since it asked students to "write" other people's sentences rather than their own; and while the exercises seemed to teach certain kinds of grammar effectively, their contribution to writing ability was by no means clear. When writing time was taken up by sentence combining, the actual effect (as with other grammar exercises) was to reduce the amount of real writing students accomplished. Frank O'Hare has told me in conversation that he cautions teachers about this problem, as too many of them feel that sentence combining can accomplish much more than it does.

An even more profound attack on sentence combining and the T-unit was launched by Joseph Williams, who, in conference presentations and articles, pointed out that complex sentences do not necessarily lead to better writing for adults. Some of the worst bureaucratic writing is "syntactically mature," since it contains long T-units, while some of the best modern English writing consists of short and direct statements. One of his articles, brilliantly defending this position, is written throughout in short T-units (Williams, 1979).

It is instructive to note that Hunt's measurement tool, unquestionably useful and appropriate in a limited research context, became increasingly open to question as it moved out of that context into, first, a pedagogy (sentence combining) and, second, a general qualitative measure for writing. The college writing teachers who object to the murky sentences many of their best students produce find themselves fighting against some effects of the pedagogy, and some of the more appalling examples of obfuscatory prose printed in *The Quarterly Review of Doublespeak* (published by the National Council of Teachers of English) rate very high indeed on the T-unit test of "syntactic maturity." The history of the T-unit exemplifies not only the inevitable relationship between research measurement and classroom practice but also the problems that occur when assessment devices change contexts. The T-unit is thus an excellent example of both the value and dangers of using measurement experimentally in research in writing.

A similar movement of a measurement device from research through pedagogy to disrepute has occurred with error analysis, probably the most traditional of research tools. Error analysis measures writing quality by frequency counts: The fewer the errors (and there is some variety of definition here) per sentence or word count, the better the writing is defined to be. Much of the research dismissed as inadequate by Richard Braddock and his team of evaluators depended on simple-minded forms of error counting (Braddock, Lloyd-Jones, and Schoer, 1963); once we move beyond the lower grades, it becomes more and more difficult to relate error to writing quality. The great attraction of error counts, as with the T-unit, is the appearance of quantitative objectivity; once the parameters are set up, almost anyone can add the numbers and strike an average. Most multiple-choice tests of writing ability still depend on the supposed relation between identification of error (however defined) in testwriter prose and the production of good prose. Those who are proficient writers, according to this text-based theory, will avoid making errors in their own writing and will show this ability by identifying errors in others' writing.

The teaching that follows such a theory of measurement leads to error avoidance as a basic principle of writing, one of the more destructive pedagogies in the schools. The process research we will look at shortly and psychological research into writing apprehension (Holland, 1979; Rose, 1983; Smith, 1984) tend to blame an error-oriented pedagogy for many students' inability to write as well as they might. By the same token, however, every writing teacher has been confronted by students outraged because their empty but error-free writing has received less than the best grades; it seems to be an unfair shift in the rules of the game to ask these writers to take risks with complex or original ideas, or, sometimes, even to have any ideas at all.

Mina Shaughnessy's encounters in the learning center of the City University of New York with the error-filled writing of many students led her to reconsider the phenomenology of error. In her *Errors and Expectations* (1977), she asked writing teachers to seek to understand the reasons behind errors of various sorts and to use the insights gained by this understanding to help students rather than merely to condemn them. For example, she found that student errors revealed three different kinds of problems that kept students from successfully revising their work: Some students did not know what needed revision; others knew what needed revision but did not know how to take care of the problem; still others knew what was needed and what to do but were unsuccessful in their attempts. Shaughnessy felt that a teacher who moved beyond the counting and marking of errors to this kind of reading of the meaning of error would be able to use error as a guide to instruction.

A third prominent approach to text analysis is that of Francis Christensen, whose articles detailing a generative approach to sentences and paragraphs are collected in *Notes Toward a New Rhetoric* (1967). Christensen noticed that the usual handbook rules for reading and writing did not seem to apply to most professional writing, and he sought to describe more accurately the kinds of structures writers actually use. Although Christensen was concerned with reading and responding to student writing, his method of charting levels of abstraction lends itself to measurement; the primary trait scoring guide given in Chapter Seven uses his concept of the ways ideas develop to measure the trait called "development and focus" as part of a research design. A parallel theory of the way ideas emerge in written texts was developed by Kenneth Pike and given by him the unfortunate name of "tagmemics." His theories became part of the influential text he prepared with Richard Young and A. L. Becker, *Rhetoric: Discovery and Change* (Young, Becker, and Pike, 1970), which argues that writing should be seen as a means of problem solving and that various kinds of rational problem-solving techniques (called "heuristics") can lead to well-developed writing. This rhetoric not only developed the text-based tagmemic theory but added to it a process-based pedagogy. These rhetorical theories have entered both the classroom and the research room, and they allow for sophisticated approaches to the definition of text quality.

I have by no means exhausted the many versions of text analysis that have been proposed in ancient and modern times, all of which have led to both measurement and pedagogical procedures. Whenever either research or evaluation assumes that the text in hand will reveal essential information about the writer, such a theory is at work. Whenever the teaching of writing focuses on the end product as a thing in itself without much concern for either its audience or the process by which it was created, a text analysis theory lies behind both pedagogy and measurement.

Reliability Problems in Text-Based Research. As Chapter Two suggested, holistic scoring could only become a useful text-based research measurement tool after it developed high levels of reliability. Since it is easy to exaggerate both the reliability and unreliability of this measure—and hence the value (or lack of value) of the text-based research it frequently evaluates—we need to consider closely the concept of reliability in relation to holistic scoring.

The reliability of a measure is an indication of its consistency, of its simple fairness. In common with most simple concepts in measurement, reliability is subject to a large variety of complex forms and subdivisions, many of them dependent on statistical manipulations. Happily, there is considerable agreement among statisticians about appropriate ways to assess and report the reliability of such standard measures as surveys, multiple-choice tests, and the like. Faculty can expect to see clear statements about the reliability of these measures in any research using them and should require high reliabilities before trusting any claims made by the research. While high reliability in a measure or in a study ensures only consistency—not validity—no results can be meaningful if the measure used is not consistent.

However, more and more text-based research is now dependent on direct writing measures, and there is as yet no standard way to measure the reliability of these measures. Meanwhile, those using these direct measures are caught between the
familiar suspicions of essay test reliability on the part of those
accustomed to conventional measures and the naive confidence
in the accuracy of essay tests on the part of many English faculty. It is common today for research results to be reported
using essay test measures, perhaps even giving reliability coefficients, but without clear statements of how these numbers are
derived.

When reliability is reported in terms of the degree of difference in scoring by several raters of the same student paper, it
is well to be suspicious of almost absolute agreement. One way
to ensure agreement, for example, is to use a scoring scale with
very few points on it; a two-point pass/fail scale, or even a four-
point scale, will induce much more agreement than a six-point
or a fifteen-point scale. But the statistical agreement that is so
easy to obtain on compressed scales makes it very difficult to
discern the fairly small differences among student writers that
most research seeks to discover. Scrupulous researchers may
well trade the very high reliability they know they can achieve
on such a compressed scale for the more refined distinctions
that emerge from a scale that offers raters more decision points.
For this reason, it is important to look closely at the rating scale
used in the research (and, of course, at the procedure for rating)
before accepting the reliability of a study as convincing evidence for its findings.

It is not necessary to use complicated statistical methods
to check on the reliability of one's own or (if the data are given)
of others' research. Paul Diederich (1974), for example, gives a
simple formula for calculating reliability coefficients for classroom research. In Figure 9, I give a study of inter-rater reliability for one test program I directed to show how easily this can
be done for a larger-scale study. The chart is also useful because
it makes clear the nature of scoring reliability on a moderate-
sized (six-point) scale: Under carefully controlled conditions,
most readers will agree quite closely, but there is a real possibility of substantial disagreement about any one particular paper.

Figure 9. Reliability Study: CSU English Equivalency Examination, 1976 Sample Papers.

Distribution of 1977 Scores

(Vertical axis: Distribution of 1976 Scores)

1976＼1977	4	5	6	7	8	9	10	11	12	13	14	15	16	17	18	19	20	21	22	23	24	N	X̄
4						1																1	9.0
5	1		4																			5	5.6
6		2	1	1	2	2																8	7.1
7				1	1	4	1	1	1													9	9.3
8				2	2	6	5	1	2	1												19	9.6
9				2	3	10	9	11	4	3	1	1										44	10.3
10				1	5	9	6	15	10	1	1	2	1									51	10.7
11					1	5	10	22	26	9	8	2	1									84	11.7
12						3	12	16	22	18	14	4	2	1	1							93	12.3
13					1	1	2	8	15	20	26	13	4	2								92	13.3
14							2	3	11	20	21	13	9	4	3							86	14.0
15							2	2	6	12	13	17	4	6	2							64	14.2
16								2	3	7	11	13	12	7	4	1						60	15.0
17										1	3	8	13	4	4							33	15.9
18									1	1	5	3	4		2		1	1				18	15.6
19											2	1	1	3	3	2	1					13	17.1
20												1		1	3	4	1					10	18.2
21													2		1	1		2	1			7	19.0
22																	1					1	20.0
23																					1	1	24.0
24																							
N	1	2	5	7	15	41	49	81	101	93	105	78	53	28	23	8	4	3	1		1	699	
X̄	5.0	6.0	5.2	8.1	9.1	9.2	10.7	11.2	12.0	13.2	13.9	14.6	15.6	15.8	17.0	19.6	19.3	20.0	21.0		23.0		

1976 Data
Overall Mean = 12.991
Overall standard deviation = 3.087

1977 Data
Overall mean = 13.017
Overall standard deviation = 2.774

Source: White, 1977, p. 56.

This study involved the rescoring of 699 test papers from the 1976 California State University English Equivalency Examination by a similar, though not identical, group of essay readers one year later. Each test contained two separate essays, and each essay was scored independently twice on the six-point scale; thus, the best score a paper could receive was four 6s, or a total of 24, while the worst was four 1s, or a total of 4. The vertical axis of the chart shows the 1976 score distribution for those papers: One paper received a score of 4, five were scored 5 (three readers gave it a 1, while the fourth generously gave it a 2), eight were scored 6, and so on until we reach the one paper with a score of 23. The horizontal axis gives the 1977 scoring of those same papers. The numbers that appear between the diagonal lines represent exact agreement between the two scorings. Thus, of the ninety-three tests that were scored 12 in 1976, twenty-two received the same score in 1977; an additional thirty-four of them received either 11 or 13. At the extremes of disagreement, three were rescored as 9s and one received the very high score of 18.

Both the original scoring in 1976 and the reliability check scoring were done under ideal conditions, with well-trained and experienced readers, table leaders, and chief readers using identical test papers, scoring guides, and procedures. Thus the reliability shown in this study is not likely to be much improved on with six-point or higher scales. For this reason, it is well to summarize what the study shows. Approximately one fifth of the tests (20.7 percent) received identical scores after rescoring on the twenty-four-point scale; 58 percent of the scores varied by one point or less, 82.7 percent by two points or less, and 92 percent by three points or less. For the group of papers as a whole, this represents a quite remarkable stability of scores and gives a firmer meaning to the reliability coefficients (1976: .85; 1977: .78) derived by a statistician from the scorings. Nonetheless, these reliable results for group scoring become rather less dependable for individuals, since one can never know just which students are in fact included in the 8 percent whose scores changed radically in the experiment. (A full discussion by project statistician Robert Bradley of the statistical issues of the experiment and of essay test reliability in general may be found in White, 1977, pp. 51–56.)

Reliability is a major concern for text-based writing research, but all research, indeed all measurement of any sort, needs to consider and demonstrate reliability if results are to be convincing. All of those who read and seek to profit from research have the right to demand more than impressive correlation coefficients from researchers; the context, scale, procedure, and criteria for scoring often will be the most valuable information for assessing the consistency by which results have been obtained.

Writing as Communicative Act

The second perspective on writing views writing as a "vehicle" for communication; the main focus is not the written product but the act of communication in a social setting. Writing is seen as a social and communicative act, an interactive and inherently meaningful, motivated activity. From this view, writing serves one or more functions that make sense in a particular setting. Studies and measures focus on the social context (made up of writers and readers) in which writing occurs and on the successful communication of intended meaning to the intended reader. In this sense, writing is now a transitive "verb," an interactive activity with a direct object, rather than a noun, as it is with text analysis.

Field Research. Research conducted from this perspective, as might be expected, is usually carried out "in the field." The field is the natural setting in which the activity of people to be studied can be found. Thus, the researcher will study writing by observing writers and their texts in the environment and manner in which they normally occur, as opposed to the analysis of the written text or to laboratory studies of single writers who "think aloud" (in a way they almost never do naturally). Those who do field research tend to compare their procedure favorably with the intensive and controlled work done in laboratories by process researchers. While the laboratory experiment can offer the process researcher greater control over variables and precision in measurement, field researchers claim greater validity. Laboratory studies of writing always invite the possibility that the experimental conditions generate or influence the results: "Composing out loud" may change the way the writer thinks and thus the way he or she writes. However, studies carried out in the field invite a parallel problem—unintended researcher "bias"—since it is the on-site observers who select what is worthy of attention in the setting and whose notes and video/audio tapes "make data." Those reporting both kinds of studies must be wary of overgeneralizing their findings to sites that are not similar to the one at which the data were collected.

One key study of school writing in context is that carried out by James Britton and his colleagues (1975) for the London Schools Council, who studied the nature of writing tasks in school. They did not look only at English classrooms, and they did not rely on the teachers' or students' self-reports of writing activities. Instead they collected all writing assignments. In trying to organize these assignments into meaningful categories, they discovered that a good deal of school writing was not a truly communicative exchange between reader and writer; rather, students mainly wrote to prove what they had learned in a subject area (a genre Britton calls "pseudo-informative") or to demonstrate their writing skill (a "dummy run"). Similar categories described the implicit "audience" for school writing ("pupil to examiner") and the writing itself as "a demonstration of material mastered or as evidence of ability to take up a certain kind of style; a culminating point rather than a stage in a process of interaction and with the expectation of assessment rather than response" (Britton and others, 1975, p. 122).

The Britton studies have much to offer teachers who find themselves bored with the writing their students produce. One such teacher told me of her surprise at the quality of some surreptitious notes she confiscated from a mildly rebellious teenager; instead of the dull and flat writing of the usual schoolwork, the student had turned out lively, stylish, witty prose of exceptional quality for the eyes of a close friend. The teacher, accustomed to thinking only of writing products, was genuinely puzzled: How could the student turn out texts, the measure of writing proficiency, that differed so drastically? When she began to consider, in the light of Britton's study, the communicative nature of the writing she was comparing, the problem changed its shape. Now, instead of blaming the student for inconsistency and bad schoolwork, the teacher started to seek ways of improving the kind of communication she asked for in her assignments. Certainly, university teachers, so often bored with the quality of term papers, master's theses, and other generally toneless prose, can apply this teacher's experience and the Britton studies to their more advanced level.

Another, more recent classroom-based study of writing

(Kroll, 1978) was conducted over an entire school year in one classroom. Although the focus of the study was on writing, the definition of writing included such informal work as notes between students. In this study, which was conducted at a lower elementary grade level, the classroom teacher devised a special setting for writing: the classroom became a "town" (named "Betterburg") and writing became an important tool to get things done. Students wrote letters to each other either as friends or in their town roles. Students also wrote to outsiders (for example, to a toy manufacturer to persuade him to provide free toys for the town store). The researcher gathered samples of writing done in this context and was able to demonstrate that the students produced a quality of writing well beyond normal expectations: Any kind of audience awareness is exceptional for such young children, particularly in persuasive writing.

Another classroom research study focused on the interactive journal writing, or "dialogue journals," produced in a single class during an entire school year (Staton and others, 1982). Although the teacher who required the student journals did not expect them to be part of actual writing instruction (they were much too unstructured and there were no workbooks), they did, in fact, turn out to teach writing very successfully. The research clearly demonstrates that this unplanned success was directly related to the teacher writing an entry in each student's journal in response to the entry the student had written. The teacher's response commented on or asked questions about what the student had written and generally refrained from correcting or marking errors, thus removing the work from the genre of school writing. This reader response, with its evidence of the degree of understanding the prose had won, also provided the student with a genuine and familiar audience and turned the journal writing from a merely private act into real communicative writing. Staton calls the teacher's formative role in this process a matter of providing "scaffolding" for the student to use in developing writing skill.

These three examples of researchers studying writing in its context provide insights for writing teachers that could not have emerged from more traditional experimental procedures.

These researchers did not limit themselves by defining good writing only in terms of essay scoring criteria, nor did they take writing out of its normal setting in the way large-scale writing assessments do. They looked at the context and purpose for writing, and their findings reveal some discrepancy between common school writing assignments and "meaningful" tasks in which students can learn and display their learning.

The application of this kind of research to college-level writing is far from clear. The generally low prestige of writing courses directed to practical communication ("business writing," "technical writing," "professional writing," and the like) is due to many causes and often includes allegations of low standards and low intellectual challenge. It would be interesting to discover the degree to which this low prestige emerges from distrust of the communicative model for writing at the heart of such courses, a model that determines curriculum and evaluation. And it would be more interesting still to explore ways of adding some of the energy of that model into the more usual writing curriculum.

Validity Problems in Communication Research. The principal claims made by research into writing as a communicative process depend on its supposed validity: What is observed is not a sample or a symptom or an indirect measure but the real thing itself in its natural habitat. While it is far from clear that school writing needs to be artificial—those who assume that schools and colleges are not a real world make different assumptions about the meaning of reality than I do—these claims for validity deserve to be respected and hence tested.

Those who are not specialists sometimes confuse reliability with validity. But reliability in the scoring method does not ensure that the resultant scores will be indicators or descriptors of students' competence; only measures of validity can demonstrate that aspect of assessment. Research that stresses its validity, or, indeed, any measurement at all, must demonstrate that validity, and those of us who read research need to be alert to the particular problems of validity measures.

Specialists have developed many kinds of validity and many ways of measuring validity, but the issue is considerably less complicated than it appears to be: Construct validity and content validity are the most important kinds of validity, while measuring concurrent, predictive, and face validity is the most usual procedure for determining validity.

Concurrent validity refers to the degree of agreement between scores on two different tests of the same skill; newly developed tests often establish their validity by correlating students' scores on the new test with their scores on well-known and widely accepted tests of the same skill. For example, ETS researcher Paul Diederich (1974) correlated new tests of writing skill with a measure made up of the average score from five separate writing samples gathered from each student over a nine-month period. Less meticulous developers of multiple-choice tests of writing may justify their indirect approach by demonstrating a moderate or high correlation with students' scores on an experimental sample of a single holistically scored writing sample, on some other multiple-choice test, or (least dependably) on grades in certain courses. Obviously, there are potentially serious problems with validity claims based on correlations between test scores. There is always the possibility, especially strong in tests that seek to measure verbal fluency, of the correlation reflecting the two tests' ability to measure some third, undefined trait, such as "general intelligence" (if such a trait exists; see Gould, 1981) or "socioeconomic status" or "urban sophistication."

Predictive validity is an alternative, more defensible method of establishing test validity by referring to an external standard. In this case, rather than using other test scores, the point of reference is the degree of accuracy the test scores exhibit when used to make predictions about student performance in another setting. The Scholastic Aptitude Test has continued to be widely used and relied on in college admissions decisions, despite various challenges, because the scores continue to correlate quite highly with success in college as indicated by grade point average, course load, and dropout rates. The SAT scores turn out to be valid indicators of likely success in college, and as long as that is the purpose to which they are put, students' scores do seem to be valid.

But two particular problems need always to be considered in relation to predictive validity. The first is similar to the problem with concurrent validity: The two measures might both correlate with some other measure that is unrelated to education. Thus, it is possible that both college success and the SAT relate highly to some trait such as "middle-class cultural conditioning"; if so, the SAT still would be a valid predictor of college success, but one might argue that it should be renamed. More serious is the problem of measuring predictive validity when an educational effort is under way to change the prediction of the test; a remedial writing course is specifically designed to lower the predictive validity of the placement test that forecasts failure for its students. Low predictive validity for a placement test might just as well indicate the success of the course as the invalidity of the test.

Face validity is a simple common sense measure. Those determining validity ask if the test, on the face of it, seems likely to yield valid scores according to what it purports to measure. Obviously, this sort of validity depends entirely on the judgment of the evaluators and hence is not likely to be accepted by those looking for much statistical support (or by those who may have professional or personal differences with the evaluators). Nonetheless, every teacher trusts his or her own judgment, and all of us tend to apply "face validity" criteria when we first pick up and peruse a test or scoring system we are considering using. Face validity is frequently used in writing research, particularly for studies that define writing as a communicative act, and the use of face validity represents one of the major reasons that these research projects are difficult to replicate; writing that seems obviously better on the face of it to one observer may look quite different to another.

Content and construct validity are the most convincing, though also the most difficult to establish. Content validity refers to the degree of match between the material covered by some measure and the definitions and interpretations assumed by the reported score. This is a particularly critical issue in instructional program research, where the customary short test cannot possibly include all that has been covered in instruction.

Content validity requires a demonstration of the representative-ness of what can be and is included in the test or a demonstra-tion of other ways of measuring the omitted important content.

The problem of establishing content validity is a particu-larly thorny one for essay tests of writing proficiency. Even when careful test committees establish test criteria and specifi-cations and offer a well-developed set of questions in several modes of discourse, we remain uncertain that we have defined the representative "content" of the material we are examining. And when a writing test offers students only one topic repre-senting one content area, one mode of discourse, one reader audience, and one short period of time for response, our uncer-tainties are compounded. We need to be particularly cautious when we generalize about the meaning of research based on test scores so obtained. When we move to evaluation of writing con-ceived as a communicative act, the danger of simplifying the meaning of content becomes acute and is likely to jeopardize the validity of research.

Typically, the issue of content validity is established by testimony. Most popularly, test developers obtain endorsements from "experts" in the field of study the test covers. Experts examine the test, its items, methods, scoring, and interpretation of scores. Although many people define experts as specialists from out of town, the notion of expert is a relative one. If we are developing a common final for our composition course or an interdepartmental common writing exam, our colleagues, those who are teaching the course or who will be making use of the test scores, are the experts whose judgments of validity should be sought.

In the measurement of writing ability, content validity is a difficult and central problem, and there are no easy ways to make that problem go away. Research designs that purport to demonstrate that some method of instruction or approach to writing has improved student work are particularly obliged to deal with the content validity of their measure. When the writ-ing that has supposedly improved is defined as a communicative act in a social context, careful readers are likely to look very carefully at the content defined by the validity measure. It is possible, for example, for impressive communicative acts to take place that disregard or flout such possible criteria as logical argument or appropriate use of evidence.

Finally, construct validity is the most important and most difficult kind of validity to establish for any measurement device. This term, *construct,* is most often used in psychology to describe an unobservable trait that is hypothesized to underlie and account for observable behavior. For example, achievement motivation is a construct presumed to underlie and account for the tendency to persevere at a task or to select a task that is neither too simple nor too difficult to complete. Constructs, then, are measured not directly but indirectly, and yet they may be what test scores in fact are measuring. Rarely is it possible for us to test all possible exhibitions of skill, knowledge, aptitude, or ability in any given area. Yet, we often talk as if we do when we measure constructs as complex as writing ability.

Tests and other assessment methods reflect our ability to do experimental research, that is, to translate abstract theory into concrete behavioral demonstrations. And construct validity is a measure of our success at that. Test scores are "construct valid" to the extent that research confirms or empirically supports the link between the construct (writing ability) and the test (perhaps the holistic assessment of an expository essay written in response to a given topic). The extent to which theory—of development of writing skill, for example—explains differences in test performance also affects the validity of the use of test scores for labeling an individual's writing skill.

Questions about construct validity arise most frequently when students are judged "below mastery" or "not competent" on the basis of their test scores. Such labels are valid if they reflect actual inadequacies or incompetence in students' performance and are not instead partially or predominantly the result of other unrelated qualities in the student test takers or the test items. For example, some will challenge the validity of scores derived from a single essay on certain kinds of topics because they feel that differences in scores may be related to differences in the amount or quality of relevant knowledge the student writer had available in formulating a response or because the student's selection of a topic greatly affected his or her likelihood of success as defined by the rating scale.

Unlike the other forms of validity, construct validity is not easily established by expert ratings or correlation coefficients. Instead, it calls for direct connections between measurement techniques and theory and the use of research findings that support those links. Thus, to measure student competence or achievement in composition requires a workable definition of "good" writing and a theory of how competence in writing develops.

While the various definitions and problems associated with validity may seem technical, we cannot dismiss the concept of validity as merely a concern for test specialists and researchers, nor can we simply allow statisticians to turn validity into a matter of correlation coefficients. And while validity is a crucial concept for research into writing as a communicative act, it is also a central issue for all testing and all teaching as well. We need to be sure that writing tests and writing research are valid, because we want our teaching to be valid. We cannot separate teaching from research any more than we can separate it from measurement, and the validity of our teaching is a central professional issue. We must be concerned about whether we are teaching what we think and say we are teaching and whether our measurement in fact measures what we like to imagine it does. These are validity issues as well as research and teaching concerns, and, in the final analysis, matters of personal and professional integrity. Such integrity, a holistic concept in etymology as well as morality, calls for regular examination of the "construct validity" of the theoretical grounds and the pedagogical practice of our teaching.

Writing as Mental Process

The third perspective on writing also employs the word *writing* as a verb—but now as an intransitive verb looking back to the writer rather than to the writer's audience. In this case, the underlying concepts of research and measurement derive from cognitive psychology. Writing is studied as the writer's use of strategies for carrying out the tasks and meeting the goals of the assignment. Writing now becomes a skilled performance, and process research has focused on identifying covert mental operations and their behavioral indicators. In observations of writers at work, usually in a laboratory setting, researchers use these indicators to distinguish between skilled and unskilled, expert and novice writers.

Development of Process Research. The first widely reported process research studied six "good" and two "not particularly able" high school student writers (Emig, 1971). Emig asked her writers to "compose aloud," that is, to verbalize their thoughts as they arose before and during writing. These monologues were taped, transcribed, and analyzed along with Emig's observations of the writing behavior and the actual text produced by the students. Her study was aimed at discovering the distinctions between the way in which more or less skilled writers responded to writing tasks in different rhetorical modes (in this case labeled "reflexive" and "extensive"). Her data did indicate some interesting differences, mainly in length of pre-writing time and amount of starting and stopping and reformulations during writing.

By choosing to look at the act of writing, Emig was able to compare directly the nature, duration, and sequence of the writing activities her writers carried out from the product-based, linear perspective on writing to be found in many writing handbooks. The handbooks at that time tended to assume that writers moved more or less neatly through a series of steps: Writers first plan, then write, and finally revise and edit their writing. Emig found that her writers paused during drafting to do some of each of these activities, spending little time in formal planning before writing. Indeed, Emig is probably the first researcher to declare and give empirical support to what professional writers and good writing teachers have always known: "The composing process does not occur as a left-to-right, solid, uninterrupted activity with an even pace. Rather, there are recursive, as well as anticipatory, features; and there are interstices, pauses involving hesitation phenomena of various lengths

and sorts that give . . . composing aloud a certain . . . tempo"
(1971, p. 57).

Many of the research implications Emig elaborates in her
final chapter turned up in subsequent studies—for example, the
use of time-lapse photography and a special stylus to record
more accurately the stops and starts occurring during writing and
their relationship to elements of the text (see Hayes and Flower, 1978, 1979; Flower and Hayes, 1980, 1981). The work done
by Flower and Hayes, though similar in methods to that of
Emig, adds an additional psychological component to the writing process: writing as a skilled, cognitive activity. They applied
existing cognitive theories in designing research and analyzing
the resultant descriptive data. In fact, the technique of asking
experimental subjects to "think out loud" has been used extensively in cognitive experimental research on problem solving, a
field of study for which John Hayes is best known. In the Flower and Hayes model of the writing process, we find frequent references to strategies, goals and obstacles, and writing as problem
solving, concepts that moved rapidly from research design into
the contemporary writing curriculum.

Hayes and Flower also asked their college and expert
writers to compose "aloud"; tapes of the writers' remarks were
later transcribed and analyzed. In their descriptions of skilled
writers and good writing, these researchers do not talk about
overall text qualities or rely on writing samples to make judgments about writers. Instead, skill is defined and measured by
the presence and quality of evidence that the writer understands
the writing process. Proficient writers come to be described as
those who make particular kinds of plans, pause to reread, and
carry out recursive planning and revising as they work.

The research of those studying the writing process has
made it clear that the linear model of that process enshrined in
the old writing handbooks has little relation to the recursive
method of composition used by most skilled writers. These
writers are constantly moving back and forth from one part of
the process to another and rarely stop one activity even though
they may have moved on to the next. Thus, the skilled writer
will engage in drafting or revising very early in the writing pro-

cess and may delay outlining until editing has begun; some pre-writing is likely to go on during the entire period for writing, and active invention does not stop just because proofreading has begun.

It is the unskilled writer who boxes himself in with formulas for invention, and it is the halting worker who feels that he or she alone has missed learning the rigid series of steps that all good writers must use. Many of the least able writers are paralyzed by the conviction that every good writer produces perfect first drafts, since good writers have learned the secret rules for writing; so these unskilled students will linger painfully over one or two sentences, or one or two words, in a hopeless attempt to render them flawless before proceeding.

In an unpublished paper, Morris Holland (1979), of the UCLA psychology department, speaks of his attempts to interrupt the destructive writing process of these anxious or blocked writers, many of whom have demonstrated remarkable abilities at other academic subjects (and at avoiding the writing assignments that strike terror to their hearts). His interesting concept of the "therapeutic classroom," which retrains such students by, for example, teaching them new and positive interior monologues to say to themselves as they write, is one example of the innovative teaching of writing that can result from this view of writing as process. A recent "Theory and Research into Practice" booklet published by the National Council of Teachers of English (Smith, 1984) exemplifies this same concern. Called *Reducing Writing Apprehension,* it provides a series of structural writing exercises and useful suggestions for responding to them in a way that reduces student writing anxiety.

Sampling Problems in Process Research. Sampling, the selection decisions and process that determine who will participate in a study, is one of the most overlooked and yet most critical aspects of research, affecting the greater utility of research findings beyond the context in which they were produced. One of the main criticisms of many laboratory studies of writing is that the sample of writers is either too small for generalization or not representative of the population the researchers claim to be studying. Consider, for example, the Flower study of expert/novice differences just described. In that study, the novices were selected from the freshman population at Carnegie-Mellon University. Many would argue that even low-ability freshmen at so selective a university are hardly novices and that freshmen at the local junior college (or perhaps a non-college population) would have made up a superior sample for the purposes of the study. Those using the research need to be cautious about the conclusions they draw about the abilities of novice writers because of this sampling problem. And those reading other research with very small numbers of specialized participants (as, for example, much split-brain research) ought to be skeptical of overgeneralization.

When certain kinds of teacher experimentation are dismissed as show-and-tell, the objection is really to the sampling involved. Readers have the right to ask if the same kinds of results will take place with other teachers, other students, other settings. However, the claims of the study on test bias in Chapter Four rest in large part on its sampling size and representativeness. Indeed, careful attention to sampling issues would be more likely to reduce the number of minor, contradictory, and self-evident research publications than would any foreseeable reduction in government support for the research community.

Measurement Issues in Research

It is common for researchers, as with evaluators, to postpone issues of measurement until all other aspects of the research have been considered. This is a sensible procedure—after all, there is no point in thinking of measurement until there is something to measure—but measurement ought not to be left for a last-minute decision. It is also common for readers of research to skip over the descriptions and charts that set out the sampling plan, the reliability checks, and the validity measures that let us know if the findings are generalizable, consistent, and meaningful. Yet no one is in a position to cite or use research without attention to such matters.

Measurement issues are crucial for research, and a weak measurement design will be detrimental to an entire study. The literature of research is filled with inventive plans whose results cannot be taken seriously because of poor measurement. Classroom teachers need to be cautious about accepting the claims of research, at least until its perspective on writing has become clear and its measurement justifies its generalizations.

10

Evaluating Writing
Programs and Projects

Evaluation of writing programs (which includes writing projects, research and grant designs, and in-service training seminars, as well as regular instructional programs), like so many other issues in this field, seems on the surface to be much easier than it actually is. Using familiar medical metaphors, those unaware of the special complexity of writing simply want to "pre-test" students before they receive the "treatment" (that is, the writing instruction) and then "post-test" them when the treatment is complete. (The concept of "remediation" comes out of the same metaphorical pharmacopeia.) Except for those with some experience with educational research or with the recursive nature of the learning of complex skills, this routine pre-test/post-test model seems the natural way to evaluate the success of a program.

Unfortunately, this model almost invariably fails for writing programs, even for the best ones in which the value of the program is so generally recognized that it seems impossible to miss. The evaluation of a writing program does not simply consist of a combination of individual evaluations of the performance of students in the program, nor do the problems of program evaluation simply consist of the sum of the individual problems of individual measurement. The issue is not only that the wrong kinds of measures are normally used or that those doing the measurement are normally unaware of the complexity of the subject and the ways it is being taught; the problems in program assessment are deeper than any one test or kind of test and are intimately related to the complex nature of teaching and learning how to write. It is quite wrong to imagine that the only important goal of a writing instruction program is to improve the first-draft writing products of individual students or that a successful writing program will necessarily (or only) make easily measurable gains in those products.

The usual failure of the usual writing program evaluation to obtain statistically meaningful results should not be taken to mean that writing programs are failures. The inability to get results ought to be seen, in general, as a conceptual failure deriving in part from a failure to understand the state of the art in the measurement of writing ability. For example, if you go on a diet and lose ten or fifteen pounds, take in your belt two notches, and fit nicely into an outfit you previously could not button, you have pretty good evidence that your diet has been a success. But suppose that you then decide to employ a more quantitative pre-test/post-test model as an added rigorous statistical check, and you use the truck scale beside an interstate highway as your measure. Since the truck scale weighs in one-hundred-pound increments, it does not register your weight loss. Alas, you would say—if you were to follow the usual unsophisticated program evaluation model—I must have been deceiving myself; I have not lost any weight, since the truck scale does not show that I have, and the truck scale is, after all, an objective measure.

Strange as it may seem, this truck scale measurement model is still the dominant form of program evaluation, and it has led to much absurdity. For example, about twenty years ago a study of the composition program at Dartmouth College gave much evidence to demonstrate that graduating seniors wrote worse than they did as entering freshmen. The definition and measure of writing skill was an elaborate error count in student prose. The evaluation showed that Dartmouth seniors make more errors in writing than do freshmen (an unsurprising finding, since many writers who handle complex subjects tend, at least on early drafts, to make more errors than they would writing on simple subjects), but the measure, elaborate though it was, made little attempt to evaluate complexity of idea, depth of thought, integration of knowledge and opinion, or any of the other higher-order skills that are presumably part of a Dartmouth education. Nor did the study consider other possible program effects beyond the reduction of errors in student prose. An inappropriate measurement device was used to "demonstrate" a finding contrary to much available evidence (and to common experience). Nonetheless, those findings are still widely cited and have entered academic folklore (Kitzhaber, 1963).

Program evaluation is a serious matter, and serious financial and personnel decisions often depend on its results. Most grants require at least a gesture toward evaluation, research findings require validation before dissemination, and instructional programs of all sorts depend for their funding on a demonstration of their value. Since the more sophisticated measurement models frequently seem to be as ineffective as the simpleminded ones, we need to look closely at the usual evaluation models in order to avoid committing the same mistakes. A program evaluation that fails to show results is a damaging document, and it is far better to avoid such an evaluation than to engage in one that will seem to demonstrate that no measurable good is being done by an effective composition course, grant program, or research study.

We will look first at four general models of program evaluation that can be applied to writing programs. In the first place, we need to review—and dismiss—the norm-referenced pre-test/post-test evaluation model, which is certain to show no results. Secondly, we will look at the criterion-referenced pre-test/post-test model, which is much more supportive of the curriculum but is still not normally sensitive enough to show results. A third model often seems to obtain results but does so by avoiding the serious questions of program evaluation, using outside experts or survey devices. Finally, I will outline the kind of program evaluation that uses a variety of measures, that is not irrevocably tied to the pre-test/post-test model, and that is very likely to yield results if they are there to be found. After this discussion of general models, I will suggest some current resources now available for program evaluation.

Program Evaluation Models

Certain Failure: Norm-Referenced Testing. The great appeal of a standard norm-referenced test is its supposed objectivity. Some publisher or testing service produces a multiple-choice instrument with an impressive name, such as the Test of Standard English Usage, and, even better, publishes norms and statistical tables along with the test. Furthermore, some local education professor is heard to say that the test is unexceptionable, or something like it, so it must be good. So the college testing office or the assistant superintendent for instruction administers the test to students before and after the composition course, only to find that scores do not change. When the results are published, the composition staff finds itself in a difficult defensive position.

Now, the basic problem with using someone else's norm-referenced test is that it probably is not the right test for your situation. It may define writing as spelling and punctuation, while your program defines writing as originality and coherence; it may be normed on a population with characteristics quite different from your own students, without regard for the special economic or ethnic groupings you are teaching. It is also more likely than not to have been constructed according to the usual procedures for norm-referenced tests—that is, so that it yields a bell-shaped curve. Such test construction needs a preponderance of questions of middle-range difficulty, since the bell curve is its goal, and hence tends inevitably toward the kind of question suitable for aptitude rather than achievement testing. It is the nature and goal of many norm-referenced tests (the SAT is the best-known example) *not* to show the effects of short-term instruction.

Thus the use of a norm-referenced, multiple-choice test following the pre-test/post-test model (the kind of program evaluation that seems to come first to the mind of the uninformed) gives an almost certain negative prognosis. The test is designed *not* to show what is sought, it will most likely examine that which has not been taught, and it is probably normed on an inappropriate population. Furthermore, it defines the effects of a writing program in the narrowest possible terms. And all this is accepted in the name of "objectivity"! We should certainly demand of any instrument used in program evaluation that it be appropriate to the material and the population in the program and that it be designed to measure the specific kinds of improvement the program is designed to bring about.

Probable Failure: A Single Essay Test. More sophisticated program evaluation in writing will respond to the problems I have just summarized. Careful evaluators will bring together the administrators and faculty responsible for the classes, work out test specifications that correspond to the writing skills being taught, develop and pre-test writing topics, and grade the writing test according to the state of the art of holistic or primary trait scoring. More and more program evaluators are following this more responsible model, which they then use as part of the pre-test/post-test design in order to show (as they fully expect) that student writing performance as they define it has improved as a result of that particular writing program.

Such evaluators deserve applause. The faculty benefit from the discussion of and added sophistication in the assignment and measurement of writing; the students benefit from a consistent emphasis in class and in assessment on actual writing; the program itself benefits from the considerable evaluation of goals and procedures that must take place. Only one important benefit is missing: Normally the post-test shows that no statistically significant improvement has taken place in student test scores.

The disappointment brought about by this kind of result, after all the work of the assessment, can be devastating. Sometimes it becomes hard to realize that the fault is still with the evaluation design, since all the problems with norm-referenced multiple-choice testing have been avoided: The essay test is a criterion-referenced device designed specifically for the local population and for the goals of the particular program. Why has it failed to measure the improvement in student writing that every teacher in the program knows has occurred? Or is it (the hidden fear buried in every American intellectual) all a delusion that education has an effect, that students can be taught to write, that we have really earned our salaries, such as they are?

No, the problem remains with the evaluation model—with

the pre-test/post-test model, to be precise—with its assumption that the only program effect worth measuring is the short-term learning that may show up in first-draft products on a writing test. While such a model may well be effective for measuring lower-order skills, such as counting or spelling, or for evaluating limited kinds of learning, such as the declensions of Latin nouns or theorems in geometry, writing is in itself too complex and multifaceted to be measured in such a way. The amount of improvement that can occur in so complex a skill in a few months is likely to be submerged by such statistical facts as regression to the mean or less-than-ideal reliability.

A carefully designed essay test ought to be a part of any composition program evaluation design: The more careful it is, the more likely it is to show the effects of instruction. But everyone involved in the evaluation should be aware of the strong odds against obtaining statistically meaningful results from this one instrument. Therefore, a simple pre-test/post-test model using actual writing scored holistically should never be the entire evaluation design. As *part* of the design, such a test has many beneficial effects and just might document the improvement that has taken place; as the *whole* design, the test is asked to carry more weight and more responsibility than it can well bear.

Those using a writing sample as part of the evaluation design should attend to the following procedures in order to give themselves the best chance at obtaining results:

1. Those teaching the classes must be involved in developing the test specifications, and at least some of them should take part in selecting the writing topics. If the test is to be truly criterion referenced, energy, time, and money will have to be spent on test development. A primary trait scoring guide will help those scoring the test focus on the aspects of writing that are being taught in the program.

2. The test should give the students the opportunity to write using the forms of writing that are being taught. Unless the program being evaluated teaches only one mode of discourse (as some business or research writing courses do), the test should give all students the opportunity to do their best by

requiring at least two different kinds of prose: for example, a personal experience essay *and* an analytic essay. The test should recognize that some students learn some kinds of writing much more quickly than others.

3. Two separate forms of the test should be prepared so that half of the student group can take each form as pre-test and the other form as post-test. Raters then will be unable to distinguish pre-tests from post-tests by topic.

4. After all the tests have been coded, all identifying marks should be removed from them, and all the tests (pre- and post-tests) should be scored at the *same* controlled essay reading. After the scoring has been completed, the tests should be grouped once again by test date, school, class, and so on, so that statistical processing can take place. Never score pre-tests separately from post-tests.

5. The test needs to have enough administrative, clerical, statistical, and computer support so that its various components can be carried out professionally. It is a foolish economy to ask an English professor to do statistical work or to ask secretaries to grade compositions. In testing, as in life, we get what we ask for and usually what we pay for. If you have elected or been chosen to direct this limited evaluation design, you need to recognize the strong odds against achieving results and to resist the kinds of economies that lower reliability and validity.

Pretend Results: Outside Experts and Opinion Surveys. Just as the pre-test/post-test model seems to come readily to the minds of those with little experience, so do the two other means of avoiding the complex questions of program evaluation: hiring an outside consultant and administering an opinion survey. While neither of these devices is improper in itself as part of an overall evaluation plan, they are usually adopted as substitutes for an evaluation plan. By their very nature, they also can be depended on to produce positive results whether the program is an effective one or not. Unfortunately, such results normally are not to be depended on.

Outside "experts" may have some expertness (or may not) in some aspects of composition and may even have some experience in evaluation. Some, such as those trained by the evaluation team of the Council of Writing Program Administrators, may even have some systematic questions to ask. While such qualifications may or may not enhance the value of the expert, two characteristics are invariable: The expert must be from out of town, preferably even from out of state, and the expert must be "friendly" to the program being evaluated.

The outside expert, for a nominal fee, is usually expected to spend a day or two on campus and to write a brief report about the program in question. An astute and experienced visitor can discover a great deal about a program even under such disadvantageous circumstances and can prepare a modest document for the use of the program administrators. Such documents are usually highly laudatory of the professionalism of the program, citing its best features and most qualified personnel. Negative matters, if reported at all, are likely to be hinted at, buried in the praise, and covered with qualifiers unless these items may be used by program administrators to gain more funds or other advantages in future negotiations with campus officials.

The reports produced by these experts (I have prepared several, so I speak from experience) are better called subjective impressions of a program from an individual than program evaluations. Since the expert is from out of town, he or she can hardly be expected to understand the program very fully in the time allowed, so recommendations can easily be ignored if they are not convenient.

It is possible, of course, to contract for a serious evaluation by an experienced evaluator or evaluation team. But few institutions are willing to find the major amount of money such an evaluation team demands (running into the tens or even hundreds of thousands of dollars) or the many months such an effort would take. Those seeking serious but economical evaluation, understandably enough, prefer to use evaluators who already know the program and its context and who can find legitimate evaluation devices at modest cost. That usually means selecting an on-campus evaluator who cannot be "expert" since he or she is local but nonetheless may have considerable expertness.

Surveys of faculty and students about writing programs

are sometimes part of responsible program evaluations, but normally surveys substitute for such evaluation much as outside experts do. Those without much experience at such surveys imagine them to be much easier to prepare and analyze than they in fact are and often will ask local faculty to prepare one on short notice. Such quick and cheap surveys are almost sure to have numerous flaws, most prominently a clear indication of the answers the evaluators are hoping to obtain. It is relatively easy to accumulate favorable opinions of a writing program from those teaching in it and from the students who have invested time and labor in it; even faculty and administrators who have little contact with the program are often ready to say positive things about their friends and colleagues if a questionnaire urges them to do so.

Those who develop questionnaires and surveys professionally have learned how to protect such instruments from the usual abuses: ambiguity, suggested or even forced choices, oversimplification, and so on. They develop the instruments over a considerable period of time, pre-testing, evaluating, and revising them, and subject the results of the drafts to intense analysis for reliability and validity. Even after such labor, however, the data produced by surveys must be seen only as opinions; statements of belief are not the same as program descriptions or program effects, though in some cases they may be said to reflect or anticipate behavior.

Thus, outside experts and superficial surveys of opinion ought not to be considered solutions to the problems of program evaluation. Indeed, since they are easy substitutes for a program evaluation, and since they are even used occasionally as if they were program evaluation, they are more deceptive than the pre-test/post-test models. The worst one can say about these latter models is that they generally do not live up to the expectations of those who employ them, while experts and surveys tend to be sympathetically misleading.

Probable Results: Evaluation of Varied Results by Varied Measures. Writing programs have many goals, all of which have something to do with the improvement of student writing. An evaluation design that attempts to define and acquire information about a wide range of these goals will be more responsible and much more likely to identify measurable results. While every program will be somewhat different from every other one, the following list gives examples of some of the effects that might well be evaluated:

1. *Student Outcomes.* This book argues for the value of measuring student writing skills by means of several holistically graded writing samples. Unfortunately, the demands of program evaluation on such a test are particularly severe, since what is needed is a "gain score," that is, a measure of the fairly narrow improvement to be expected on first drafts as a result of a relatively short writing program. As I said earlier, although such gain scores are very difficult to obtain, they normally ought to be sought. However, an early indication of improvement to come is an attitude change. Measures of student attitudes may show that students have more positive feelings about writing after passing through the program, even if their writing skills have not yet improved very much. A number of other desirable student outcomes—such as improved grades in some or all other classes, a lower dropout rate, a willingness to take other English courses, and so on—may be identified in the process of discussion with faculty and students in the program. Long-range outcomes, such as changed attitudes and behaviors years after the program has been completed, have not been much attended to but offer real possibilities under the right circumstances.

2. *Faculty Effects.* It is surprising that the effects of a program on teachers are generally ignored. There is considerable evidence that programs that value and challenge the faculty and that leave them feeling effective and appreciated are more successful than those that do not. A set of faculty outcomes can be identified and measured, all of which will impinge directly on the students in the program: attitudes toward the subject and the students, morale, conference attendance, publications, and so on.

3. *Spread of Effect.* Writing programs, particularly the most effective ones, may have a wide circle of effects beyond the immediate impact on students and faculty in the program. Sometimes faculty outside the program will show their support of the program by adding writing assignments or essay tests to

their own curricula. Perhaps a special college program at the freshman level will call forth other programs at the upper-division level, or an extraordinary program at a junior high school will elicit changes in the elementary schools that send students to it and in the high school that receives its students. Sometimes writing programs lead to changes in the way students, or even their parents, deal with writing or reading outside the classroom.

A further advantage to an evaluation design not limited merely to a pre-test/post-test model is the formative effect the evaluation itself can have. The very act of gathering information from a variety of sources leads to new lines of communication and new thinking about the program. There is no need to wait years for data analysis; some findings result directly from the evaluation activity. The principal of the school discovers that the new materials he or she proudly ordered still have not arrived; the freshman composition director is dismayed to find out that half the staff are teaching literature instead of writing; the English teachers are amazed to hear that they are held in high esteem by their colleagues in the sciences, many of whom require writing in their classes.

The resources to be described in the next section of this chapter provide a wide range of possible effects of writing programs and of sample measures for these effects. We will return to the implementation of a multilevel evaluation design after looking in more detail at the available resources. The essential point here is that an evaluation design should resist the simple and deceptive answers that have become traditional and consider multiple measures for the many and varied effects that writing programs can, and usually do, manifest. Such a procedure will show an appropriate respect for the goals and implications of the writing program and, even more important for the short run, achieve believable documentation of the program's value.

Sources and References

The decade of the 1980s has provided those involved in program evaluation with theoretical structures and practical materials never before available. Four new guides to program evaluation have recently become available and now, for the first time, it is a matter of a few hours of reading to become up to date in this unexpectedly complex subject. However, since each of them emerged from quite different kinds of projects and contexts, it is well to be aware of the important differences among them.

The most generally useful handbook is by Barbara Cross Davis, Michael Scriven, and Susan Thomas (1981): *The Evaluation of Composition Instruction*. This 229-page volume is available only by direct mail from Edgepress, Box 69, Pt. Reyes, California 94956. It developed from a large Carnegie Foundation grant directed by Michael Scriven to evaluate the effectiveness of the (then) Bay Area Writing Project. A compact yet comprehensive book, it attempts to organize and define all the issues that the evaluation team encountered as well as to list the many sources consulted.

The Scriven evaluation was probably the most extensive (and expensive) evaluation of a writing program ever undertaken, resulting, as the *Carnegie Quarterly* put it, in "no less than 32 separate reports on [Bay Area Writing Project] activities, none of which was able to present direct cause-and-effect statistics" ("Teaching and Learning the Art of Composition," 1979). It is some comfort to those with only a fraction of the resources of the Scriven team to notice (in the reports filed with the foundation) the frustration the team members felt at the complexity of the evaluation task and their reluctant conclusion that only a wide-ranging series of statistically inconclusive measures could demonstrate the effectiveness of a program widely recognized for its major impact on teachers and students.

The handbook, as the authors call it, remains the most comprehensive single source of information on the topic, bringing together the approaches of the professional evaluator and an unusually capable research team. Its bibliographies are unusually complete, and the emphasis on proper statistical and other procedures is most appropriate; the book is designed for evaluators at all levels of sophistication and includes useful definitions of concepts and terms throughout. It presents case studies of evaluations, with discussion of more and less appropriate methodologies, and some twenty-five pages of model question-naires of various sorts.

Unfortunately, the handbook is an irritating little volume to use, designed for reference rather than reading and written in a committee style of imperial impersonality. Numbers of the statements reflect struggles within the assessment team rather than judicial wisdom: "The general qualities that composition teachers tend to weight in holistic scoring may be only remotely related to the commonsense requirements of functional prose writing, because teachers may be preoccupied with stylistic con-siderations" (pp. 89–90). It is unhappily clear that the authors of the handbook shared this "functional" view of style, and lit-erate faculty will need to overlook consistent stylistic crudities and considerable social scientific jargon in the interest of under-standing the important concepts summarized in the book. Emerging as it does out of an assessment of a program designed for the most part (at that time) to improve the teaching of high school writing teachers, it focuses almost entirely on student and teacher outcomes. But despite its limitations of style and angle of vision, it is an indispensable reference for writing pro-gram evaluation.

Even more interesting but rather less comprehensive is Stephen P. Witte and Lester Faigley's (1983) *Evaluating College Writing Programs.* This seventy-eight-page booklet (with thirty-eight additional pages of notes and bibliography) should be studied carefully by anyone responsible for the evaluation of a writing program at any level. Those planning program eval-uations will want to check their tentative designs against the flawed evaluations that the authors analyze; the series of four major pre-test/post-test quantitative projects should serve to warn even the hardiest practical types of the hazards of writing program evaluation. The theoretical structure for program eval-uation that the book endorses emerges from the grant the authors received from the Fund for the Improvement of Post-secondary Education (FIPSE). The series of documents pub-lished (through ERIC) as a result of that FIPSE project, based at the University of Texas at Austin Department of English, is particularly useful for evaluators (Witte and others, 1981b).

The great advantage of this booklet is that it is written

with unusual grace and clarity. The authors are well aware of the great complexity of the issue and are nonetheless able to present the state of the art in two hours of interesting reading time. They comment on the handbook produced by the Scriven team, which they see as too limited in its perspective, and they share my distaste for the simple pre-test/post-test model of evaluation. While they have less respect for the use of writing samples in evaluation than I wish they had, they present a five-level view of the components of a writing program that is extremely valuable: the cultural and social context, the institutional context, program structure and administration, content or curriculum, and instruction.

The Conference on College Composition and Communication (CCCC) Committee on Teaching and Its Evaluation in Composition (1982) report, "Evaluating Instruction in Writing," was first given at the 1979 convention of the National Council of Teachers of English. Its major concern is that the evaluation of teaching be done responsibly and fairly as part of a program evaluation. There is, of course, a substantial literature on the evaluation of teacher effectiveness, and this committee was particularly careful to review that literature in relation to the teaching of writing. The value of the report stems from its large conception of teacher evaluation and teacher effect, which too often are narrowed in practice. A series of evaluation forms is provided for use by those involved in the evaluation of writing teachers.

As this book goes to press, a five-year study of the effectiveness of college composition programs, of which I served as director, will be drawing to a close (White and Polin, forthcoming). Funded by the National Institute of Education, the research is attempting to find evidence connecting various aspects of writing programs to successful (and unsuccessful) student and faculty outcomes. The study uses the writing programs on the nineteen campuses of the California State University, with their variety of campus types and student characteristics, as samples of the kinds of writing programs on most American campuses. The first-phase report (White and Polin, 1983) offers a highly developed "taxonomy" of writing program structure, a series of questionnaires and interview protocols for gathering information, and some analysis of the information collected to date. The final report should present those program features that are associated with success (or lack of success) for particular kinds of students on a wide variety of campuses. The materials from the study, entitled *Research in Effective Teaching of Writing,* ought to be of particular value to campuses that lack the resources to develop their own questionnaires or writing topics and that want to compare aspects of their programs with baseline data from a large and diverse university system.

Steps in Program Evaluation

Most of the literature on program evaluation consists of warnings, bad examples, and explanations of ineffective procedures. Valuable as these ill omens may be, they are not much help to the faculty member directing the evaluation of a writing program; something, after all, must get done, and successful evaluation designs, while difficult, are not impossible. The following steps, suggested with due caution, outline the procedures that can lead to a successful evaluation.

Initial Planning. It is realistic and sensible to consider the scope, funding, audience, and function of the evaluation design as early as possible. If resources allow only a gesture toward evaluation and the audience for the report is sympathetic, evaluation can be avoided or pretended. However, such a situation can allow for an evaluation that is essentially formative—that is aimed at the improvement of the program with its primary audience being those who can effect such improvement. The Davis, Scriven, and Thomas handbook states categorically that "formative evaluation is a crucial part of doing anything worthwhile, if the project takes any period of time at all" (1981, p. 7). Since less rigorous procedures may be used (as long as they are sufficiently convincing to the participants), even sparse resources will allow for enough formative evaluation activity to urge reconsideration of goals and procedures.

However, an evaluation designed primarily for the improvement of the program may turn out to be exactly the

wrong plan for a funding agency looking for demonstrated results. In this case, the limited resources must be devoted to a
summative evaluation, documenting the effectiveness of the
program. Numbers of funding agencies expect 10 percent of a
grant to be used for evaluation, for example, and will expect
some statistical verification of the findings.

Since the distinction between formative and summative
evaluations is basically one of audience and purpose, an understanding of this distinction is only the start of the planning process. Most evaluations tend to be both formative and summative
in result if not design, since any evaluation leads to reconsideration of the effectiveness of what is going on as well as to a judgment about its effects. Some basically formative evaluations
may even be held to a much more rigorous standard of proof
by the participants than are some summative evaluations delivered to genial funding agencies. The problem, in short, is for
those responsible for a program to give the evaluator they engage the most precise indications possible of the task. While
it is not proper to tell evaluators what they are to find, it is
absolutely necessary to make clear the audience, function, funding, and timing of the evaluation report.

A final consideration in the initial planning stage should
be the designation of those responsible for the evaluation.
There is some professional difference of opinion here. I have
suggested that outside "experts" ought not to be considered,
and Witte and Faigley support that position in the strongest
terms (1983, pp. 5–7). However, Michael Scriven, a professional
outside expert, disputes that view, arguing, in effect, that only a
"goal-free" outsider is in a position to distinguish what is in fact
occurring (1973). Those close to a program are inevitably corrupted by their knowledge of or even commitment to intended
effects, according to this view, and thus have trouble seeing
with the needed clarity. The handbook produced by the Scriven
team takes a more moderate position, calling for evaluation
teams with maximum credibility, containing both insiders and
outsiders.

Under most circumstances, the best solution is to select
as evaluator someone with expertness in the field who knows

the program involved but is not directly connected with it. An evaluator who knows little about the teaching of writing cannot be expected to understand the issues involved in writing program evaluation; an "expert" who needs to spend a great deal of time learning the context of the program is less valuable than one who can begin right away. Thus, usually, someone can be found locally to direct the evaluation effort. But, of course, this person should have little direct connection with the program being evaluated and ought not to be the director of the program. An evaluation team representing various perspectives is an obvious advantage, if one can be recruited. However, a team needs a leader, and some one individual needs to be responsible for the entire evaluation effort.

The evaluator needs both the appearance and the fact of independence from the program if the evaluation is to be credible and useful. If, as is sometimes necessary, the only one available to serve as evaluator is the program director, unusual steps (such as use of an outside statistician) need to be taken to establish the authenticity of the final report.

Background for Evaluation. Whoever is chosen to direct the evaluation now has the obligation to avoid the routine errors of the past. That means that the four sources listed earlier in this chapter must be required reading, particularly the Davis, Scriven, and Thomas handbook and the Witte and Faigley booklet. No one should attempt to design an evaluation without studying in detail chapter 2 of the booklet, particularly its review of the University of Texas plan, which was unsuccessfully designed by the authors in an attempt to avoid the most common evaluation flaws. If we are to claim respect as professionals, we must build on the accumulating knowledge of measurement and evaluation that is now so readily available. There is simply no excuse for the repetition of invalid or discredited procedures.

Goal Definition. Once the basic decisions about the purpose and audience of the evaluation plan have been made and an evaluator has been selected who has read the basic texts, the next step is to develop a clear sense of the goals of the program itself in as precise terms as possible. If improved student writing is a goal, it is well to ask what "improved" means to the participants; if better teaching of writing is called for, there had better be discussion of ways to identify (if not to measure) that teaching. Unintended goals or spread of effect need to be noted. The goals of the program, in short, need to be put in the context of the goals and audience of the evaluation report as early as possible.

The discussion of goals is central to the evaluation process and requires a substantial amount of time and thought. The evaluator should keep in mind the "Framework for Evaluating College Writing Programs" developed by Witte and Faigley (1983, chapter 3), a wide-ranging view of five components moving from the instructional activity itself outward to the social and cultural context. The list of over thirty "questions for evaluators" with which the booklet concludes (pp. 74–78) should keep any evaluator from taking too narrow a view of the subject.

The evaluator needs to compile a list of goals, including unintended goals and spread of effect, before setting out a plan for measuring program effect. Since most writing programs will have more—and more complicated—goals than evaluation funding can encompass, these goals will have to be arranged in some sort of hierarchy of importance. The most important goals will need particular attention in the evaluation report, though all goals should be listed with whatever evidence may be available as to their achievement.

The Evaluation Design. In constructing the evaluation design, every evaluator is constrained by time and money. Before making the decisions about generating new sources of data, the evaluator should see what "found" data may already be available. (The Davis, Scriven, and Thomas handbook, 1981, pp. 76–95, makes several useful suggestions for finding such materials.) Very often, certain kinds of baseline data are on hand from, say, placement tests or admission tests of one sort or another. Instead of developing an end-of-course essay test, the evaluator may be able to use a course final examination. Certainly, there is no longer any need to develop questionnaires for most occasions, with the plethora of available ones on hand.

As the evaluator decides among the most important goals

for detailed examination, he or she needs to consider available resources, data, time, and cooperation (teachers will give up only a little class time for evaluation). The most important principle to keep in mind is to use a variety of measures that reflect the various goals of the program and not to put all the funds in one measure or narrow the goals of a complex program.

Thus, if you are collecting student writing samples in an attempt to find gain scores as a result of the program (don't forget to include a control group not in the program), you ought to collect a student attitude questionnaire at the same time. While teachers are watching the students doing this task, they can also fill in a report on their attitudes or activities. Or, again, if you are depending on a faculty questionnaire for data on a faculty development program, you might select every tenth faculty member for a structured in-depth interview as a way to validate the questionnaire and gather additional information.

There is plenty of room for creativity in the development of a research design. Indeed, one of the small comforts to be derived from analysis of the failures of very elaborate and expensive evaluation plans is the awareness that most of what has been attempted in the past ought not to be repeated. Witte and Faigley (1983, p. 38) are very clear on this point: "Evaluation studies, including our own, which were based on the quantitative model have yielded few major insights concerning the teaching of writing or the operation of writing programs. Indeed, the findings of most evaluations of writing programs and courses hardly justify the massive efforts required to conduct the research. The implications for would-be evaluators of either writing programs or writing courses is clear enough: no matter how carefully conceived and constructed the design or how sophisticated the methods of analysis, evaluations must be based on more than pretest and posttest writing samples. Evaluations of writing programs and courses, if they are to result in valid and reliable judgments, must employ a variety of methods and procedures."

Follow-Through. Since most program evaluations cover an extended period of time, sometimes years, it is essential that the evaluator keep written records of discussions, decisions, and plans. It is a common experience for replacement evaluators to come on the scene with little to guide them, for data to be misplaced or destroyed by accident, for evaluation reports covering years of work to be patched together hastily at the last minute. Since the most energy, creativity, and support for evaluation usually occur at the beginning, that is the time to prepare background chapters of the final report, time lines for later evaluation activity, and detailed descriptions of how the design is to proceed. One generally ignored obligation of the evaluator or the evaluating team is to prepare enough documentation for the design so that it can proceed in their absence.

The Value of Evaluation

While a negative program evaluation or a badly done evaluation report can be most damaging, a well-handled evaluation has many advantages. The consideration of goals and ways of approaching those goals that evaluation demands is a formative activity; it asks those teaching writing to consider what they are doing and why—questions that need to be asked far more often than they usually are. The gathering of information for an evaluation is itself a valuable activity; it not only makes those producing the information see it with new eyes, but it makes statements about the importance of the information being collected. (Imagine an item on a faculty questionnaire asking about the number of professional conferences on the teaching of writing attended or the number of conference papers read.)

Finally, of course, a careful evaluation leads to a reexamination of the way things are being done, the way human and financial resources are being spent. It may suggest that some of us have found more successful ways of doing our jobs. It may even suggest that we are so enormously effective at what we do that we should spend rather more time than we do at self-congratulation. Or it may suggest that we are not very effective at all. In any case, the evaluation of writing programs need not be threatening or destructive; if it is done in a sensitive and intelligent way, using a wide range of measures and involving those teaching in the program in the substantive issues of the evaluation, it can be a valuable experience for everyone.

Program evaluation ought never to be seen as a mere measurement issue, unrelated to conceptual, contextual, and curricular issues that define the writing program; behind program evaluation lies our responsibility to our students and to the central role of writing, in all its complexity, in education. Whenever writing teachers involve themselves, as they should, with writing program evaluation, they must be fully alert both to the dangers of oversimplification and to the large possibilities for constructive change offered by any evaluation program.

11

Avoiding Pitfalls in the Testing of Writing

This chapter provides an overview of many of the issues dealt with in this book. The procedures and findings of writing assessment at various levels, from the large-scale test involving many thousands of students to a single classroom assignment, offer valuable applications to teachers of all subjects at all levels. The pitfalls present in these testing programs also suggest important cautions to anyone involved in teaching or evaluating writing. This chapter focuses on these pitfalls and on how to avoid them, taking them sequentially as a testing program might proceed from its basic planning through dealing with the political repercussions of its score reporting. Thus, the first section deals with problems in the planning steps of testing, the second with test development and test administration, the third with test scoring, and the last with pitfalls in both the evaluation and the use of test results.

Planning

The usual problem with the planning of tests or testing programs is simple: Either there is not enough of it, or it is done after problems develop instead of beforehand. The first large-scale test program I administered worked fine until the end of the essay scoring session. As thousands of scored essay booklets emerged from the two separate reading rooms, I realized that no one had planned a system or location for combining and recording scores, and no one had reserved space for the ton or so of paper that we had to store and keep accessible for at least a year. We, of course, improvised: Our resourceful statistician came up with a workable solution to the first problem on the spot, and I took the test home to store in my basement until better storage could be found. In succeeding years, we made sure to plan more carefully.

In the classroom as well, we often fail to give adequate attention to planning. Unclear and apparently purposeless assignments burden students in too many classrooms, and unreliable final exams are common in writing classes. We teachers often receive bad writing from our students because that is what we call for, in spite of ourselves. For example, our most frustrating task as writing teachers is the teaching of revision; yet one important reason so very few students take revision seriously is that we often fail to plan time for the revision process and rarely plan to reward revisions as highly as first drafts.

An understanding of the kind of planning necessary for careful testing will improve classroom practice in all these areas. The issues for planning that follow are illustrative rather than inclusive; particular programs or classes will come up with different lists. But the topics that follow all illustrate the need for planning and the need to expand the team of planners, if the program is large, to include both faculty and staff specialists.

Goals. A common pitfall in writing testing results from inattention to the purpose and function of the test. Chapter Four of this book speaks to the differing goals of placement, proficiency, and equivalency tests and to the ways these goals lead to different kinds of tests. Classroom teachers generally have no trouble with this planning issue when they give exams, since their goal is clear: to find out if students have learned the materials of the class. But few teachers are as clear about the goals of the writing they ask students to complete outside of class. And those involved with tests of larger groups often find that there are unspoken and sharply different goals below the surface of many disagreements with their colleagues. Many faculty are likely to think that a writing test is, well, a writing test, and that a clear definition of the purpose and meaning of the measure is not really necessary. Those who take measurement and its effects on teaching more seriously will insist that a goals statement with test specifications be established before, not after, the test is designed.

Sometimes testing seeks to measure group performance rather than individual ability, as when a writing program, a research grant, an in-service project, or the like needs to demonstrate to a funding agency that its program has positive benefits. Chapter Ten reviewed the various pitfalls involved in program evaluation, where ineffective methods of measurement seem to be the rule. The most common form of program evaluation uses a simple pre-test/post-test model, employing some form of writing testing of individuals in the program. This model is generally inadequate, since most such programs have many more effects than a short multiple-choice or even an essay test can show. Effective program evaluation calls for a multiple series of measures for the multiple effects, including the intangible ones. This more complicated and extensive evaluation process need not, however, lead to very long testing of individuals, since group scores are what count. For example, matrix testing, which divides a long test into short segments to be taken by different students, can provide reliable group scores even though no single individual takes the whole test; a three-hour test can be broken into six half-hour segments, and, if the groups are well chosen, no individual need write more than one segment. Whatever form of measurement may be used, if an evaluation is attempting to measure the comparative effectiveness of two programs or of a program in comparison with a control group, the measurement should focus on the aims of the program being evaluated and should avoid testing matters that are irrelevant to the programs. Thus, a freshman writing program that focuses on the development of analytic skills, say, ought not to be evaluated by a multiple-choice usage test or by an expressive writing essay.

In all cases, the most important aspect of planning is to consider with care the goals of the testing program. When that complicated job is done, much of the rest of the work flows naturally from it. When that job is not done or is done badly, we can expect most of what follows to be confused, undefined, and ineffective.

Specifications. Test specifications usually appear as a direct and unambiguous written statement of the goals of a testing program. Those accustomed to putting together multiple-choice tests construct charts listing those goals in order to be sure that all are tested. Thus, a reading test may have a list with specifications of skills down one side, such as "understands metaphors" or "comprehends implied meanings"; across the top will be a set of content specifications, such as "short poems" or "Shakespeare." Every item needs to fit both a skills and a content specification, and the more important specifications will be represented by proportionally more items.

Such a grid, of course, is not really appropriate for essay tests, although the demand for precision of specification is always a worthy goal. Experienced writing faculty must accept the responsibility for developing specifications for essay tests, and that responsibility should be taken seriously. These faculty need to know that different kinds of writing assignments test different kinds of abilities, and they need to develop clear enough specifications from the goals statement so that a test development committee will be able to evaluate its questions in light of precise requirements. For example, a specification such as "use concrete language in descriptive prose" would lead to different questions than would "analyze the structure of a modern poem" or "summarize and then evaluate a given complex argument." A failure to articulate clearly and to record in writing test specifications (often because at the moment they seem self-evident) is an important omission that can lead to confusion or worse, particularly after some time has passed.

Personnel. It ought not to be necessary to point out that it is both sensible and economical to recruit appropriate personnel for the various activities called for by a testing program. But often English teachers who wind up in charge of testing programs are not aware of how much support is at hand, sometimes just for the asking, and poor personnel planning can lead to most unfortunate results. For example, I witnessed one school district essay reading in which English teachers were used to handle the statistics while secretaries were asked to score the papers. An able statistician slipped a disk hauling boxes of essay booklets at the same reading.

Consultation. A major destructive result of many badly planned testing programs is the separation of teaching from testing. A particular benefit of careful planning comes from the mutual support teaching and testing give each other when teachers are fully consulted. (The College Board's Advanced Placement Program is a fine example of this mutual support; the high school courses generated by the tests are more important than are the tests themselves.) When those teaching writing are carefully and regularly consulted, and when their ideas are both heard and used by those developing the test, there are many beneficial results: The test will both seem and be appropriate, the tone of classroom discussion of the test will be positive (since the teachers will gain a sense of ownership of the test), and the students will find the test a meaningful part of their education. Those outside the field of education will wonder why this logical and obvious situation is exceedingly unusual in the testing of writing; in fact, serious consultation among those working at different levels is rare in most American enterprises. If procedures for consultation are not built into the planning process, consultation probably will not occur and potential support will turn into covert or even overt opposition.

Budget. No one ever forgets to deal with money during the planning of a testing program. The problem is that there is never enough money to do all that one would like to do and that constant budgetary decision making threatens to dominate planning. In addition, excessive attention to cost cutting can have disastrous effects on a testing program. Two national testing programs have cut budgets by eliminating second readings on test essays, for example, thus not only reducing the scoring reliability of the test but also eliminating the way to ascertain and measure that reliability. For a grueling day of scoring papers, another national testing service pays essay readers the salary earned by a journeyman plumber for an hour of pipe cleaning; those in charge of the essay scoring then wonder why some of the readers may act in less than professional ways.

After over a decade of planning testing programs, I have come to some highly personal conclusions about budgets. Since the difference in cost between a well-funded and a badly funded test program is relatively minor, budgeting in this area is almost always a statement of priority, not finance. If underfunding becomes a serious problem, it is a symptom, not a cause, of the weakness of the program. When the cost of a writing test, particularly the written part of a writing test, is challenged, most often it is writing itself that is under attack. If possible, the testing program should be abandoned rather than rendered ineffective or trivial by those who do not value writing. Those planning a program need to decide on the minimum funding allowable (including professional wages for essay readers) and to arrange for appropriate action should the money available sink below that figure.

It is important to remind those in charge of budgets that test costs include development as well as scoring. Although multiple-choice tests cost far less to score than do essay tests, it is far more costly to develop multiple-choice tests and to keep them current, secure, and valid. Thus, the relatively high cost of scoring writing samples can be balanced by the relatively low developmental costs. The weakest testing programs can give very cheap tests by avoiding the development costs of a multiple-choice test through the purchase of out-of-date and inappropriate exams, which are available everywhere. But responsible professionals will have little to do with such tests.

Reporting and Use of Test Results. From its inception, the plan of a test program needs to attend to the reporting and use of test results. It is pointless to gather more information than can be well used; it is mischievous to report results in ways that can (and hence will) be misinterpreted and misused. No one should underestimate the concealed power of a test score, nor should anyone underestimate the readiness of various publics and the press to misread, misunderstand, oversimplify, and distort test results.

Unfortunately, it is common to postpone planning for

score reporting until much too late; but it is even more common to ignore the need for evaluation of the test itself until many valuable data have been lost. Evaluators for the test program should enter the planning process right from the start. For example, it may be valuable to gather information about writing ability before the testing program begins so that a comparison is possible later on; once a program is under way, such information can no longer be obtained. There may be ways of designing forms, such as essay booklets or answer sheets, so that data are available when needed by the evaluator instead of requiring an expensive later data collection effort. Finally, planning should attend to record keeping (distribution of rosters, machine-readable results, security, privacy laws, availability of transcripts, and so on) and storage long before the test is given. The sheer bulk of an essay test, and the convoluted laws on the release of test results, must be seen to be believed, and these matters ought not to come as surprises at the last moment, though they often do.

Scored essays often impress those who have labored over them as precious resources for research, even after the scores have been recorded and reported. Unfortunately, researchers with funding for and interest in someone else's test are rare, while great mounds of scored essays sit in faculty offices and garages from coast to coast. Unless a local study is under way, plan to ship tests that are more than a year old to a paper recycling center.

Time Lines. Organizing planning is important if all key issues are to be considered systematically. Participants at initial planning meetings should develop overall strategies and construct time lines for activities. This is the place to guard against a major pitfall in testing programs: the failure to allow sufficient time, money, consultation, and energy for adequate attention to planning.

Planning committees will discover many options in laying out time lines. One time line might begin with the development and printing of information about the test, the distribution of these materials, test registration, and the printing and distribution of test results. A quite different time line, probably under the supervision of a different individual, might follow the selection and development of the test itself, beginning with the designation of a committee to draw up test specifications, then moving to pre-testing and printing schedules (with extra proofreading!), and then covering distribution of the test to test centers, the return of the materials to the central office, and the payment of the proctors. Yet another time line might consider the scoring of the text as the central temporal element.

If student writing is involved, a choice site for the essay reading needs to be reserved many months ahead of time, and a team should develop procedures for selecting current readers (including chief readers, room leaders, table leaders), for identifying a cadre of future readers, and for determining all costs for the reading. An essay reading is similar in many ways to a substantial conference and requires at least as much attention. Any post-test activities, such as publication of sample papers and scoring guides, should be included in these time lines, since nobody will think to collect materials for such a purpose as a matter of course during the heat of test administration and scoring.

The preparation of time lines is important for any testing program for several reasons: It allows the cool consideration of tasks in advance (instead of during the confusion of other activities), it calls for the establishment of clear lines of responsibility so that those involved will know who is supposed to do what and when, and it helps break down a complex job of administration into a series of discrete tasks with deadlines.

Planning sessions may sound cold and uncreative, but in practice they are quite the reverse: Exciting, creative, contentious meetings, they blend people, theories, and practical activities into the pattern that becomes a testing program. They turn the chaos of an idea into the order of a plan, they share responsibilities among those best suited for the various tasks, and they anticipate problems before they occur. Even in the best-planned testing program, of course, one will encounter unexpected turns and unpleasant surprises; planning can never obviate all problems, nor can it be expected to do so. Still, it can allow time and money to meet those problems should they appear. A program that fails to plan carefully is an inevitable disaster just waiting to begin.

Test Development and Administration

Test Development. More and more institutions are becoming ready to choose an essay testing program, but it is a common pitfall to establish such a program without the test development that is absolutely necessary if the program is to meet its goals. As Chapter Six describes in detail, test development requires time, money, and the appropriate people before it can work properly. The most common mistake in test development is to assume that it is easy and that most of us who teach (since we give tests regularly in our classrooms) can do it well. Unfortunately, test development is difficult to do well, and, even more unfortunately, most of us do it rather badly. (One of the great benefits to an institution that moves into careful testing is the indirect training of its faculty in better evaluation techniques.)

Some institutions ask faculty to develop a multiple-choice test of writing skill. But even professionally developed multiple-choice tests in this area tend to be uneven at best; tests created without professional support tend to be unmitigated disasters. No individual should accept the responsibility of putting together such a test without a committee of colleagues. This committee should work together regularly for at least a year and should have at its disposal a professional test consultant, substantial computer support, clerical support for production and administration of try-out test items and norming tests, and a very large budget. None of these provisions is exaggerated. Unfortunately, they guard only against the most obvious pitfalls of multiple-choice testing (ambiguity, invalidity, unreliability); they do not guarantee that a very good test will result.

The development costs of multiple-choice testing are not well known and are usually ignored when arguments for the economy of such testing are presented. As I pointed out earlier, multiple-choice tests, though cheaper to score than essay tests, are far more costly to put together; if we add in the necessary costs of multiple forms and revisions (required by many of the new truth-in-testing laws), essay tests turn out to be far more cost effective. And when we consider the advantages to the curriculum and to the professional development of the faculty of essay testing, direct measurement of writing skill becomes a clear "best buy."

Under ordinary circumstances, then, test development will mean essay test development, and that is the kind of test development procedure that was detailed in Chapter Six. The steps, from appointment of a test development committee to embody the goals statement in questions through pre-testing of the questions, allow systematic review of the test as it takes shape over a period of months.

The fact that test questions must themselves be tested is not well understood and leads to many pitfalls in testing. But, given sufficient time and support, test developers will come up with test questions that will work. With such a test in hand, scoring the questions reliably becomes a manageable matter. Unfortunately, most testing programs spend insufficient time developing the questions and then expect those scoring them to produce fair scores on an unfair test. Anyone who has been placed in such an unfortunate position will insist that those responsible for the question development also be present at the scoring. If readers suffer scoring a stupid or impossible question, they have the right to be able to attack the perpetrators at the reading site, without delay.

Finally, essay test development can never be considered finished as long as a testing program continues. Just as a conscientious classroom teacher is always revising his or her exams, improving, clarifying, updating, or expanding them, so test development committees can never rest. The challenge to these committees is not only to produce new topics on the model of successful past topics but also to keep abreast of writing research, which is now slowly moving into the area of measurement and cognition. We know much more about essay testing now than we did a decade ago, as this volume demonstrates; five or ten years from now we will know much more than we do today. For example, as Chapter Six pointed out, we do not know why some students perform much better in one form of writing than in another or why there is a surprisingly low correlation between scores on personal experience and on analytic topics. (Personal experience topics may be more accessible to most students, but they are not "easier" for all students.) We can compensate for this by including at least two modes of discourse on any important writing test, so that students will have the opportunity to do their best. But research in this area will probably lead to better answers and thus better tests than we can now produce. Even within single modes, the difficulty of topics can vary greatly: Many writers find it considerably more difficult to "describe your favorite person" than to "describe your favorite place." Essay tests need constant renewal from new topics and from new ideas for kinds of topics, and test development committees need to be alert to both obligations.

Test Administration. Many institutions have diligent test officers, sometimes with statistical or psychometric training, who can be trusted to see to the many details involved in the administration of tests. The test officer should identify and deal with such matters as the appropriate time and place for the test, the proper handling of test materials, the control of the testing environment, the hiring and paying of proctors, and the handling of dishonest test takers.

But there are other issues in this general area of test administration as well: How long should the test be? How many essay questions should there be, and of what kind? Is there to be a multiple-choice portion of the test and, if so, how much weight should it have in the total test score? What kind of information about the test should be distributed to students ahead of time, and when? If there is a test fee, what is it to be, how is it to be managed, and under what circumstances are refunds to be made?

These questions are meant to be exemplary, not by any means inclusive. They are questions that require the attentions of a professional test administrator, and no faculty member should undertake responsibility for a large testing program without such staff support.

Test Scoring

Essay Test Scoring

There is no need to repeat here the theory or practice of the system of holistic essay scoring that is widely accepted today as producing reasonably reliable scores at an acceptable cost. Chapters Two, Three, and Eight of this book detail the present state of knowledge for this method of testing. Our concern here is with the pitfalls into which those directing essay scorin̦ may fall. Problems in essay scoring can be divided into three ɛ ˙eas: procedures, personnel, and statistics.

Procedures. The most common pitfall in the management of holistic essay readings is the loss of collegiality among the readers. Chapters Five and Eight speak in detail to both the theoretical and practical issues involved in the maintenance of the essential community of a reading.

A second procedural problem often centers around the use and origin of the scoring guide. This description of the qualities to be found in papers at different score points is normally written by those in charge of the reading after they have read a large sample of the work to be scored and after they have reached agreement on the ranking of many typical papers. The scoring guide is particularly valuable for several reasons: It sets out the standards for judgment so that they can be debated, it establishes the theoretical grounds for the ranking, and it encourages the use of the full range of scores by giving reasonable descriptions of the strongest and weakest papers. Since the scoring guide is derived in part from the actual range of papers written to the particular question, it reinforces the particular job to be done—that is, to rank order the set of papers at hand according to specific criteria devised for the writing topic at hand.

Some essay readings proceed without a scoring guide, in the mistaken conviction that debates over abstract descriptions will distract readers from practical decisions. Since readers will rarely refer to the scoring guide after the reading is well under way (the goal is to help readers internalize the standards), some practical administrators argue that the considerable time and effort required by a scoring guide are wasted time and money. All readers, the argument goes, can intuit common standards from sample papers just as well as the table leaders can. However, this argument ignores the need for an assenting community, one that can act in agreement because its members have reached agreement. The scoring guide not only accomplishes the useful tasks I have summarized, but it also symbolizes this community agreement by its explicit statement of standards. The discussion of those standards welds the community together and gives individual readers ownership of and a stake in the outcome of the reading. My most uncomfortable readings have been those conducted without a scoring guide; I felt more like an employee trying to follow established rules than like a professional using delicate judgment for a goal I understood and approved.

An even more common pitfall in relation to scoring guides also stems from a desire to avoid the cost and trouble of devising a new one for each reading. Some test directors will simply import a scoring guide from some other testing program on the supposition that if it worked well elsewhere it must have some inherent virtue. Almost certainly, such borrowed goods will not fit the test question or the essay responses at hand. Even more problematic is the use of an all-purpose scoring guide developed to meet the requirements of all questions designed for a particular testing program. A number of programs use such a guide not merely or even principally to avoid creating a new one but in the belief that the questions and student populations change so little from test to test that a new guide simply is not needed. In effect, this procedure discounts the influence of norm referencing on the scoring and makes the test wholly criterion referenced. It also assumes that it is in fact possible to create equivalent questions by using the same question format— an assumption I believe is unfounded; if this term's question is harder (or easier) than last term's and the scoring criteria remain the same, the meaning of the two sets of scores will be different. Those who use the same scoring guide for a series of questions cannot simply assume that they are maintaining the same standard. They also need to be careful that the all-purpose scoring guide, which cannot focus on the issues raised by particular questions, does not wind up emphasizing the more superficial aspects of writing at the expense of the more substantive ones. While it is true that such a procedure gains a standard document, it loses the discussion and revision process that allows a question-specific scoring guide to contribute to the precision of scoring, assist the formation of an interpretive community, and influence the criteria by reference to actual test performance.

Personnel. If the selection process for essay reading personnel is given careful attention, many of the pitfalls of bad choices can be avoided. Of course, one can use academic position or other existing structures, such as elections or selection committees, to select appropriate people. But one needs to be sure that the qualifications of those selected in fact match the demands of the job; often the existing procedures do not take into account the special nature of essay readings.

I remember well one university faculty I observed scoring placement tests. The dean was chief reader, the department chairs were table leaders, and the faculty became, of course, the readers, grouped at tables by department. The hierarchy continued with the aides: the dean's secretary was chief aide, and lesser secretaries were table aides. The confusion in the room was truly remarkable, since some of those chosen were spectacularly unsuited for their tasks. For example, the dean was extremely soft-spoken and mild and could not make himself heard in the reading room; some long-standing departmental quarrels continued unabated at some tables over neglected student papers; and the table of readers from a vocational education department looked askance at their unlettered chair, who, in turn, looked helplessly back. The dean's secretary disappeared in the middle of the reading, never to return, and the movement of test papers ground to a halt. Fortunately, a small group of extraordinary graduate students was on hand to learn from their professors; they quickly sized up the situation, took over, and made things work.

It is usually a good idea to convene a small and informed committee to choose the personnel for a reading. This committee should develop a set of criteria for the various jobs and then seek the best available candidates, wherever they may be found.

Choosing the chief reader is always the most difficult

task, rather like finding the perfect department chair. The individual chosen needs to be a firm and forceful leader, well-experienced and clear about the goals and criteria for the program. He or she needs to take charge of the meetings preparing for the reading, to work effectively with and through the table leaders, and to be the final authority on scores. Although the chief reader in fact runs the reading, setting the tone and making key decisions, he or she needs at the same time a sense of proportion and humor, an ability to work comfortably with sensitive colleagues, and the capacity to juggle competing important demands for attention. Such individuals are rare indeed, and the temptation to settle for less than the very best available should be resisted. No one can earn a position as chief reader by longevity, publications, or academic title.

The criteria for selecting table leaders, readers, and the chief aide were discussed in Chapter Eight. As with the chief reader job, these are difficult and responsible working positions, not to be seen as honorific. An abrasive or indecisive table leader will be the cause of an unreliable essay reading; an inefficient chief aide will waste much time and money; a seriously disruptive reader will have to be dismissed.

While some personnel difficulties are to be expected during a large reading, no matter how careful the selection committee was, serious attention to choosing the right people for the various jobs is the best way to avoid major problems. Every faculty and every support staff has good candidates for these jobs, and every test program can recruit them to work in an essay reading, under the right conditions and with enough planning.

Statistics. Many pitfalls are associated with the use of statistics in essay readings, but two particular problems are so common that they deserve special mention here: the temptation to score papers only once and the confusion between ranking papers and deciding on the meaning of the ranking.

Standard practice in essay scoring requires two independent readings of each paper. The first score is often concealed by a label of some sort, usually with a detachable center piece that can be torn away at the end of the scoring to reveal scores. Whatever the system, the second reader must be unaware of the first score. When the two scores for a paper disagree (at many readings this means that the scores are more than one point apart), a third reading then takes place to resolve the discrepancy. Continuing programs use these comparisons, as they accumulate, to gather data on the reliability of the reading itself, as well as on the accuracy of individual readers. Without double readings, it is impossible to gather these figures or to verify the fairness of the test scoring. Although there is a constant temptation to reduce costs by reducing the second readings to samples or by eliminating second readings altogether, such an economy renders the reading unaccountable and unprofessional.

The second problem has to do with the setting of passing scores on the test, a complex issue with an interesting relation to the debate over the all-purpose scoring guide. Those who prefer an entirely criterion-referenced test use such a guide for all essay scorings for a particular program, in the belief that the various scores on the guide will represent the same level of writing ability whatever the question or the student group. Under these circumstances, the passing score can be set in advance and can even be made a part of the scoring guide itself. However, those who prefer to introduce some norm-referenced aspects into the test or who are uneasy at the differences among questions and student groups will argue that the determination of the meaning of the holistic ranking must be made after the ranking, not before. Statements of scoring criteria that include references to passing and failing, this group argues, invite readers to go outside the scoring criteria into their own individual experience and so reduce scoring reliability; it is a difficult enough job to rank papers reliably according to the criteria of a given reading, and that job should not be confounded with matters beyond the ranking. Certainly, if you are including a norming sample in the test scoring (to see, for example, how freshmen with certain grades score on a placement test), referring to previous pass-fail rates, comparing percentile scores, or using other norm-referenced concepts, you should delay the decision on passing scores until the ranking is completed. And if you suspect, as I do, that this year's total score of seven may represent the same level of ability as last year's score of eight and next year's score of six, you will want to decide on passing scores after reviewing score distributions and norming data and whatever else may be available to increase the fairness of the passing score decision.

Multiple-Choice Test Scoring

The great convenience of multiple-choice testing is, of course, ease of scoring. With sensible planning, well-designed answer sheets will produce a computer printout with scores arranged in several different ways (high to low, alphabetical by last name, and so on), with such student information as file number or mailing address listed next to the scores. In addition, the printout can provide a statistical package with all kinds of useful numbers about the score distribution and correlations among parts of the test.

It is tempting to believe that an impressive list of numbers provides everything we need to know about the test. However, the printout only provides the raw material for what we need to know, and those responsible for the test still have a great deal of work to do after the production of the numbers. The unresolved problem that remains is to determine the meaning of those numbers and their appropriate use in the context of the measurement of writing ability.

For example, one number to be examined closely is the Standard Error of Measurement. This rarely discussed statistic is enormously important for the responsible use of a multiple-choice test score: It sets out the range of meaningful score difference. For example, the Standard Error of Measurement of the verbal portion of the SAT is thirty points. This means that if a student scoring, say, 500 on the test were to retake it, in two out of three instances that student would score between 470 and 530. It also means that one out of every three retests would be likely to produce a score outside of this sixty-point band. This set of numbers has important implications, although it is normally avoided or ignored by institutions despite the statements of responsible testing agencies. Even highly reliable multiple-choice tests, such as the SAT, yield approximations of student rankings, not absolute measurements, and the scores should be read as the center of a band of scores rather than as a single point. The Standard Error of Measurement describes the width of the band, and the possibility of greater error is always present.

It sometimes surprises those unfamiliar with multiple-choice test statistics to notice how wide the range of error is, even on the best of these tests. Everyone knows that essay test scores are approximate, but many people attribute an altogether unwarranted precision to what they like to call "objective tests." We ought to avoid that term *objective,* which is a judgment rather than a description, and remain aware that multiple-choice tests are a useful yet fallible method of testing some matters; they are no better than the questions they contain, which were themselves composed and evaluated by subjective human beings, just as essay tests are.

Anyone using multiple-choice test scores, then, needs to consider them as bands of scores, not simply as absolute points, and to consider them as approximations of the skills they measure, which are likely to have an undetermined relation to writing skill. For these reasons, as well as many others (such as their effects on writing programs), the best use of multiple-choice scores in the area of writing is as a portion of a test rather than as the test itself. The results of a careful multiple-choice test, when combined with the results of a careful essay test, will probably yield a more accurate and more fair measure of writing ability than will either test when used by itself (see Godshalk, Swineford, and Coffman, 1966, p. vi).

If a writing score is to be combined with a multiple-choice test score to produce a single total score, a statistician will need to perform a simple operation called scale matching. This ensures that the differences in numerical scale on different kinds of tests do not distort the weight each score should have in the total score. Scale matching puts different kinds of scores on the same scales so that they can be combined properly. However, someone still must decide if the different parts of the test are to have equal weight or some proportional weight. Should a twenty-minute multiple-choice portion weigh as much as a ninety-minute essay portion in determining the final score? Half as much? One sixth as much? As always, the numbers will serve those who understand how to use them.

Yet an additional burden falls on those receiving the numbers from multiple-choice tests: relating the numbers to decisions about the students. The numbers will not say who fails a proficiency requirement or who should be placed in a remedial class; only informed teaching faculty can make that decision after reviewing everything relevant to the test, including the numbers. It is tempting to imagine that the numbers, or those who report them, can make that decision, but such a reliance on numbers avoids responsibility. Test results, after all, are only data; the most important responsibility of those administering testing programs is to use well the data produced.

Evaluation and Use of Test Results

Reporting Test Results. There is a wide gulf between the message intended by most tests and the message received by those who use or hear about the test scores. This sad fact is true in classrooms, where students are ever ready to view grades and teacher comments on their work as judgments of their personality or of their relationship to the teacher. Many studies have documented the gap between what professors say or think they are saying in their commentaries on papers and what students actually perceive. Large-scale testing programs suffer the same distortions in score reporting, only, of course, on a much larger scale.

The desire to gain simple answers to complex questions leads to misunderstanding and distortion of test results. Schools receive test reports designed to help them assess their programs and use the information solely to argue that they are more (or less) effective than other schools and hence more deserving of funds. Writing tests at the upper-division college level, designed to warn juniors who are poor writers to develop their skills so that they will write better papers as seniors, turn into barriers for seniors who have met all other degree requirements. The full range of information provided by some national college entrance test results is always in danger of being read by students and admissions officers as a simple pass-fail cutoff score. Public school administrators in a few states, looking for an easy way to combine economy with the appearance of high standards, mandate particular scores on the National Teachers Examination (an entry-level test for credential candidates) for experienced classroom teachers looking for raises in salary. Multitest programs, such as the College Board Admission Testing Program or the College-Level Examination Program (CLEP), merge in many instances into a single conflated score or a hazily understood single test. For instance, some college administrators will talk about a student's "CLEP score," unaware that more than forty tests exist in that program—about half a dozen in English alone.

Since the principal pitfall in reporting test results, whether in individual classrooms or in schoolwide, statewide, or national settings, is the misunderstanding and misuse of scores, institutions and faculty must pay particular attention to the proper reading and interpretation of scores. Sometimes this means the development of graphs as well as numbers, presentation of several kinds of comparative or normative data, reminders of just what the examination is or is not testing, and other similar efforts. A number of writing tests with essay portions include the essay score in a total score and then, in addition, give the essay raw score, the sum, perhaps, of two readings on a given scale. This useful separate report for the essay portion allows those receiving the score to understand how that particular score was reached and to use it separately if they wish. But the danger here is that some audiences are so likely to misuse an essay score if they get one that it may be more responsible for test reports to bury that score in a composite score.

Finally, a testing program must provide some machinery for students who want to review the test and their performance on it. It would be irresponsible for a classroom teacher to give a test and then refuse to hold office hours afterward; it is just as irresponsible (as new legislation has made clear) for those who administer tests to refuse to allow students to challenge test questions or test results. Some large campus testing programs include in the test fee a charge for advising after the test, and even ETS has been persuaded to change some scores after students have had their say. Despite what those who see tests simply may think, tests are not devised solely for the purpose of failing students, and the best programs consider carefully how to make information from a test clear, meaningful, and useful.

Follow-Up Studies. Tests and testing programs must themselves be tested. If they do not pass the test, they should be failed and discontinued. Again, the classroom can serve as a model: If a test does not "work," it is abandoned and replaced by a better one. Many faculty never stop experimenting with their tests, so keenly do they feel the difference between their knowledge of their students, gained over a semester, and the final test grade. Large-scale tests require large-scale evaluations, but the same principle still holds.

The differing purposes of tests will require different kinds of evaluations. A college entrance test, for example, can be evaluated by discovering its predictive validity: Most of those passing the test should succeed in college. A college placement test, however, should be evaluated by discovering the accuracy of the placement, through such means as surveying the faculty to discover obvious misplacements. Predictive validity is a tempting but disastrous method of evaluating a placement test, since a placement test is designed to change predictions; weak students are placed in a program to help them succeed, and their success will lower the predictive validity of the test, whose prediction of failure the curriculum attempts to forestall. Thus anyone using predictive validity to evaluate a placement testing program is using the success of the writing program as a way to document the supposed failure of the test. A placement testing program has different goals from an admissions testing program and should be evaluated differently.

Proficiency testing and equivalency testing require follow-up studies, sometimes over many years, for evaluation. What happens, we may want to find out, to students who receive credit by examination for freshman English as they move through their college years? If the credit is too easily earned, we would expect these students to perform less well than similar students who had the benefit of the freshman English course. If the test is appropriately encouraging to the best students, we might expect to find them taking more English courses, at a higher level, than their counterparts—and doing better in them. The only way to know for sure is to design a follow-up study to trace the group through college and to compare it with a group of similar ability.

A proficiency test calls for a different kind of follow-up study. Those identified as not proficient on a writing test had better not be publishing articles and books or editing newspapers; proficient writers, according to the test, also should be proficient writers according to other measures, such as their grades in writing-related courses and their success in professions calling for writing skill. A recent court ruling in Florida has also required the public schools to show that they are in fact teaching the skills examined on their proficiency tests. Similar cases in relation to various professions have called attention to the appropriateness of tests for the job skills actually involved in the profession for which the test is given.

Committees and administrators evaluating tests and testing programs ought not to be those who devised the tests or who have demonstrable commitments to them. At the same time, evaluators who have little knowledge of the purpose or setting of the program will bring their own assumptions and biases to bear on programs they do not understand (despite the claims of objectivity made by "goal-free" evaluators). Among all the other pitfalls to avoid in the testing of writing, those responsible for such tests must seek out evaluators who are in fact neutral and uninvolved, as well as informed. Since no evaluation, insufficiently rigorous evaluation, or negative evaluation is likely to signal the end of the program, those responsible should not take lightly the selection of the evaluator and the evaluation design.

Political Pitfalls. Finally, it is important to remember that the teaching and testing of writing are, in a large sense, political acts. Those devising tests for the public schools are not likely to forget this fact, faced as they are with vocal parents, elected school boards, and public financing. College faculties, however, are more likely to imagine that the tests they choose or create deal only with academic matters. That may be so for an individual instructor, who often claims that academic freedom (which protects the scholar's right to speak freely without professional punishment) should extend to a right to grade students without interference from others. But testing programs are inevitably political, and college-level tests sometimes have high political stakes attending them.

These political matters exist at all phases of the testing program, from the planning of goals statements (which require general assent) to test development and scoring (which require funding and general participation) to evaluation (which is often prepared for the use of public funding agencies). Power over testing programs often resides with administrators or others controlling funds, and these people may well have goals that differ from those of the people who develop the tests. Sometimes, unfortunately, the political needs of these administrators—or even their personal career goals—lead them to assume control over testing programs and to change them radically. It is easy for administrators of successful testing programs to neglect these perennial issues and to find that power over dollars combined with personal ambition overwhelm academic concerns, academic due process, and even academic courtesy.

Finally, testing is power, and power is a root political issue. In our classrooms, we need to use that power with decency and humanity, and proper testing practice helps us to use that power wisely. In large programs, that power remains at our backs and over our shoulders, always to be reckoned with. Those who ignore the politics of testing may well find themselves replaced by better and smoother politicians, and even those alert to the power pressures and power drives of administrative and political figures or of the public may wind up defeated by forces with little concern for academic matters. No one should imagine a test to be above politics or a testing program to be outside the political arena.

The Pervasiveness of Pitfalls

Thus, in the long run, the pitfalls that await writing assessment programs do not differ significantly from those that await any major educational program. At every stage, from initial planning through reporting and evaluation, opportunities for confusion of purpose, improper action, and unprofessional influence offer themselves to the unwary. Fewer such dangers are open to classroom teachers, although it would be quite wrong to imagine that this difference in scope is a difference in kind. Classroom abuses of testing are no less to be condemned than public ones and, since they are usually less readily rectified, they may be even more heinous. As the extent of a program grows, so does the chance of encountering (or, more usually, failing to avoid) one of the many problems I have addressed in this chapter. The surprise is not that pitfalls occur in the testing of writing; the wonder is that, given the general lack of understanding of these issues and the general lack of communication among those involved in evaluation, so much testing goes on so competently and intelligently at large and small institutions throughout the country.

12

Continuing Issues in Teaching and Assessing Writing

The unresolved issues in the testing of writing reflect the uncertainty we find everywhere in the teaching of writing. Many of those teaching writing have little training in or knowledge of the field, and the training of composition teachers at all levels has remained a haphazard affair with little organization and even less scholarship. The small but increasing group with some professional background in composition is beginning to develop a body of standard references and a common language for dealing with instruction, measurement, and research; but here again it is hard to find much agreement even on such crucial matters as curriculum, textbooks, and proficiency standards. When Richard Braddock and his team surveyed composition research in the 1960s, they said that the field of composition was like chemistry as it was emerging from alchemy (Braddock, Lloyd-Jones, and Shoer, 1963, p. 5); Richard Young, more optimistically, argued recently that Thomas Kuhn's concept of the "paradigm shift" (during which a discipline redefines itself entirely, asking different questions, making different assumptions) applies to the field of composition in this generation (Cooper and Odell, 1978, pp. 29–47). But an emerging body of reference works and a few creative and concerned scholars do not, in themselves, create a field of study, and most of those trying to bring about changes in student writing remain closer to intuitive alchemists than to trained genetic engineers.

I think it unlikely that composition will emerge as a genuine scholarly discipline without improbable radical shifts in perception on the part of the university community. Those who specialize in composition now find themselves in the academic no-man's land of interdisciplinary studies; they need to read research done in psychology and education departments, cope with the medical and biological language of brain research, immerse themselves in pedagogy and psychometrics, all the while juggling their "real" work in (usually) the study of literature with their responsibilities of teaching and administering writing programs. Often their research is not respected and does not count toward professional advancement, while the graduate students they work with dare not devote too much time and energy to the teaching of composition that earns them small wages for fear that they will neglect the "serious" scholarship that in time will deliver them from freshman themes.

This situation, which shows no signs of changing, is not promising for research or even for pedagogical improvement. Even the foundations, caught up in the concern for writing of the late 1970s, have now backed away from investment in composition. Typical is the Sloan Foundation, which, after convening two meetings of composition specialists to advise it on how to spend its many millions, decided that writing, with its lack of consensus on so many issues, was insufficiently mature as a field to receive major funding. With perhaps unintentional irony, that foundation began supplying grants instead to a field known as "artificial intelligence."

When we look closely at the situation, the surprise is not that so little has been done but that so much has been accomplished in composition research; we ought not to be depressed by bad composition teaching so much as we should wonder at the very many teachers who are teaching writing well. We need to recognize that composition is probably going to remain the stepchild of rather unwilling English departments, that research in teaching and learning to write will continue to scrape by on the edges of several disciplines, and that few of those who will teach writing in American schools and universities will get much training or background as part of their regular education. At the same time, we also need to recognize that, as in the past, most of those who continue to teach writing will be those who are unusually interested in reading and writing themselves and who will bring much of that interest and pleasure to their work with students. From this large group of writing teachers will emerge the scholars who will pursue research questions of interest to them, whatever the lack of prestige or support.

When we refer to future issues in teaching and assessing writing, then, we must do it in the context I have been describing. We cannot look for the kind of sequential, well-funded, accumulative research that more prestigious and more established fields of study command, nor can we look for the grand designs that offer individual scholars small parts of a large fabric. The unresolved issues will emerge from the experience of teachers, and the efforts to deal with them will come from those with a pressing need to solve particular problems.

Thus, the measurement issues that are likely to receive the most attention in the near future are probably those most closely associated with problems in the teaching of writing. While we are unlikely to see systematic and orderly investigations into the following problems, I suggest this small list as a necessary agenda for immediate attention.

Process Issues in Measurement and Teaching

Almost all measurement of writing ability to date, whether direct or indirect, has focused on writing products, often such artificial products as testmaker prose on multiple-choice tests and first-draft student products for essay tests. The multiple-choice tests ask students to make editing decisions about sentences and paragraphs set out in isolation for the purpose of the test; the essay tests ask the students to produce quick products to be evaluated, usually by criteria that are unclear to the students. In both cases, the procedure seems to have considerable validity as demonstrated by the studies produced to support the tests: The measures, such as they are, correspond reasonably well to the assessments of the students' writing by teachers evaluating many writing samples over a considerable period of time.

This book argues that writing samples, a direct measure of writing ability, are preferable to the indirect measures produced by multiple-choice tests. But we need to be careful not to overstate the case. First-draft writing to a set topic is closer to the real writing students do than is an editing exercise, but it is by no means the thing itself. In fact, such a test contradicts directly one of the most important truisms of writing instruction—that first drafts are only the start of the writing process. Every teacher and writer knows, and writing process research is continuing to confirm, that revision is an essential part of writing. Every time we give an important grade for first-draft writing, we deny in practice what we say about revision.

While our most effective and practical tests of writing ability today ask students to produce and readers to score first-draft writing, we can hope that better tests will be developed that examine and emphasize the writing process. The few attempts to do so have not been notably successful, in large part because so few students know how to revise their work. The problem seems circular; until we stress the writing process more in our testing, students will continue to think of writing itself as essentially the first draft. And until effective ways of teaching the writing process become well known, there will be insufficient demand for process measures to assess that curriculum.

Rexford Brown, who directed much of the work in writing measurement for the National Assessment of Educational Progress, has told me of his frustrating attempt to develop a process measure during the 1970s. When students were given their first drafts and asked to revise them (using a different-colored pencil) in a second testing session, they were puzzled; they tended to recopy their first drafts in better penmanship, often so mindlessly that they would add numbers of spelling errors through inattention. A controlled experiment with college students has claimed better results with an extended essay taken home for revision (Sanders and Littlefield, 1975). Roberta Camp of the Educational Testing Service has reported on her project to develop a portfolio assessment procedure for writing; unfortunately, financial pressure seems to have brought that promising concept to a halt.

Many teachers have attended to various aspects of the writing process out of simple common sense. While those who are up on the latest fashion in composition teaching may now be asking their students to "cluster" ideas by drawing circles around random phrases on a page or to pre-write using functions they attribute to the right side of the brain, intuitive teachers have always spent time with their students helping them develop ideas. While relatively few teachers will use or know about such arcane heuristics as Young, Becker, and Pike's (1970) "particle-wave-field" theory (oddly adapted from quantum mechanics), many writing instructors spend class time developing ways of thinking about the subject assigned. Invention, after all, was a familiar concept to Aristotle, and revision is hardly a new concept.

Process theories of writing, then, serve mainly to reinforce what the best writing teachers have always done and to help make fashionable, even respectable, certain classroom activities that support the teaching of the writing process. The less capable teachers who confuse the teaching of writing with the mere grading of papers have much to learn from process theories, and every teacher needs to be reminded that students at all levels need help throughout the writing process, not merely a grade at the end of it. Despite the new name for an old idea, process research and the teaching ideas that follow from it must be welcomed by all who value student writing as an individualizing educational activity. But the lack of truly valid and reliable assessment of the writing process continues to hamper those who teach that the process is as important as the product.

It may be that the widespread use of personal computers and computer testing procedures at schools and colleges will provide the means to move into measurement of the writing process. As more and more students develop keyboard facility (a major stumbling block for the disadvantaged), word processing composition becomes more and more possible. As various institutions acquire computer writing laboratories, the advantages of word processing (clean copy, spelling checks, easy revision, and the like) will become more generally available; some privileged institutions already assume word processing as the standard mode of production for student papers.

The more advanced editing software, such as Bell Laboratory's *Writer's Workbench,* has led the way to even more advanced programs, such as UCLA's *WANDAH,* which is designed to help writers from planning to the end of the writing process. The editing programs help writers analyze their texts and so assist revision; the writing support programs add to an editing capacity a series of thought-generating and planning activities, as well as various reminders and other helps as the writing proceeds. It is not hard to imagine an assessment procedure that could evaluate the process the student has followed and that could prepare for a (human) product assessment at the end. Some such procedure could allow for both process and product evaluations, thus more accurately reflecting the teaching of writing than do present assessments.

Whether or not computer word processing allows for process assessment, it seems clear that the teaching of writing demands the development of some kind of process measures. Everyone concerned with better measurement of writing and better teaching of writing through better measurement will welcome such a development.

Mode of Discourse Issues

We know that assigned mode of discourse affects test score distribution in important ways; significant numbers of students who write well on personal topics, for example, write weak analytic papers, while numbers of those strong in analysis seem unable to write about themselves (White, 1973–1981). Writing teachers normally cope with this problem by varying assignments as the term proceeds so that students will have the chance to write in the modes they find most comfortable. Careful writing tests often will require two or even more kinds of writing for the same reason. But we do not know how to develop tests that will be fair to students who are skilled in the modes not usually tested. Every large holistic scoring is faced with a few odd pieces of writing that no one can handle wisely: the clever sonnet that satirizes the question, say, or the brilliant personal essay that either (no agreement is possible) avoids the analytic question or handles it by ingenious indirection. Less courageous students will sometimes be caught in forms of writing they obviously find contrary to their most comfortable expression. Sometimes, of course, the test in fact examines ability to write in a particular mode of discourse: Whatever their leanings, college graduates should be able to analyze and synthesize ideas. But tests of writing proficiency in general should give every student the chance to do his or her best work and should respect differences in modes of learning as well as expression.

The identification of modes of discourse is part of the subject matter of rhetoric, and rhetoricians have been working on the problem for several millennia. An exceedingly complex view of the subject appears in books by James Kinneavy (1971) and James Britton and others (1975), but, as Richard Lloyd-Jones has pointed out, this complexity of analysis has not helped testing to this point (Cooper and Odell, 1977). It now appears as if the rhetoricians will need to combine with those studying cognitive development before the rhetorical analysis of kinds of writing for different audiences can become more useful for measurement. Meanwhile, teachers who value and teach modes of writing not presently tested remain unhappy with the limitations such testing places on their teaching.

Cognitive Development and Curriculum Issues

Despite some of the basic work in this field by Piaget, Bruner, Vygotsky, Britton, Bereiter, Emig, and others, we do not understand the relationship between theories of writing instruction and theories of intellectual development. Hence, we do not know much about the most effective sequencing of composition instruction, nor do we even know if it is possible to develop such sequencing. At all levels of education, we find curricula that attempt to teach kinds of writing that seem inappropriate to the students at hand. We have little dependable information about appropriate tests at different levels of growth and education. We do not know much about why some good students write badly or are afraid to write at all. And, worst of all, most of those teaching writing in the schools do not know how little we know about these matters and believe that they have rather simple answers to these complex questions.

Subskill Definition

There are a considerable number of supposed subskills in writing, ranging from scribal and mechanical (punctuation) to profoundly intellectual (originality). Yet it is by no means clear that these subskills are in fact real, distinct, meaningful, or measurable. We are far from confident that even reading skill is separate and separately measurable from writing skill. This uncertainty is, of course, one of the principal arguments for holistic scoring, which refuses to evaluate subskills as isolated entities, and it is one of the principal arguments against analytic scoring, which assumes such subskills. Nonetheless, most writing tests, particularly those using multiple-choice items, supposedly measure and actually report all kinds of subskills.

Serious research in this area would be very valuable to all those who teach or assess writing. Much teaching, particularly but by no means exclusively in the lower grades, depends on a syllabus of subskills that supposedly lead to writing ability. Many teachers at all levels believe that systematic study of some grammatical system or some usage rules will improve student writing; the lack of agreement on which rules matter or on whether any of them in fact help students write seems not to diminish the dedication of such teachers to their favorite subskill. This teaching is supported by tests of subskills, obligingly constructed to meet the demand despite the lack of research support for the entire theory.

Equity Problems

As Chapter Four pointed out, the testing of writing ability shares with most other kinds of testing the problem of test bias. While many superficial means presently are pressed into service in an attempt to make tests fair to racial, ethnic, cultural, and economic minorities, the problem remains far more complex than its current solutions.

The problem of equity in American education and in American society goes far beyond the purview of this book. The problem is, of course, reflected in the assessment of writing and hence in most writing classes. It appears that holistic assessment of writing is the most equitable way to measure student writing ability at present, and thus it supports those teachers eager to open avenues of success to all their students. But no one should feel comfortable about the present situation or about the success of current efforts to value minority cultures and ways of expression. Many scholars register serious suspicions about possible bias in all current testing procedures (Whiteman, 1981).

Teacher Hostility Toward Measurement

Teachers of writing need to abandon the general hostility toward testing they have learned from bad and inappropriate tests in order to profit from the systematic thinking that has gone into recent measurement research and to understand the still more significant research to come. As this book attempts to show, test sophistication can reduce some of the major abuses of composition teaching: unclear, pointless, or casual writing assignments; overattention to editing to the detriment of invention and other parts of the writing process; quirky, personal, and arbitrary evaluation of student writing; useless or destructive commentary on student work; and failure to encourage and reward revision.

Since an understanding of the measurement of writing ability calls for attention to such matters as test criteria, question development, reliable scoring, and sensitive reporting, greater attention to issues in assessment during the preparation of teachers is crucial if these abuses are to be curtailed. Perhaps the clearest sign that such a change is taking place is the vast increase in the number of in-service training projects under the aegis of the Bay Area Writing Project, directed by James Gray of the University of California, Berkeley. Now called the National Writing Project and well established in most states, most of these summer institutes (with geometrically expanding sessions run throughout the year by those trained in the summer) include instruction and practice in holistic scoring as a routine part of their work.

In addition, a growing cadre of composition professionals is beginning to make its presence known nationally and is starting to direct more and more composition programs on university campuses. These informed faculty, with their knowledge of measurement, become extremely valuable to campuses requiring proficiency tests or program evaluation. Even when such requirements are not in place, these faculty tend to institute assessment programs as one way to bring consistency and accountability (and faculty development) to the programs they administer.

However, there is not much indication that pre-service training of school teachers includes the same kind of up-to-date experience that the in-service work of the National Writing Project provides. Furthermore, the professionalization of composition instruction at American colleges and universities is proceeding slowly, hampered by the fact that most of those teaching are still recruited from the ranks of literature students, many of whom tend to see composition as demeaning labor that pays the bills until promotion.

A major task ahead is to find ways to disseminate both knowledge of and experience in the measurement of writing ability throughout a profession made up, on the whole, of well-intentioned amateurs in the teaching of writing, who are often hostile to the very concept of assessment. An additional task is to develop a national research agenda to deal with the problems I have outlined in this chapter and others like them and to find the resources to allow this agenda to be carried out. Although we know much more now than we did ten years ago, that knowledge needs to be made much more widely known, and we must recognize that the measurement of writing ability is still in its infancy.

Our experience with writing assessment shows, however, that it cannot and should not be separated from writing instruction. As our understanding of the best ways to conduct that instruction grows, our assessment practice will improve; the best teachers of writing will continue to influence those who construct and score writing tests and demand that those tests support their teaching. And as more and more teachers understand the issues in assessment and the best assessment practice, the teaching of writing, in all disciplines and at all levels, is bound to improve.

13

Helping Students Improve Their Writing: Some Practical Approaches for the Classroom

Throughout this book, I have made every effort to connect assessment issues with classroom practice. But I am well aware of the real problems involved in applying theoretical knowledge to an individual teacher's day-to-day work. In my own case, it took five years for me to begin to apply what I had learned as a test director to my own composition classes. The purpose of this chapter is to help readers who teach composition not only see the connections between assessing and teaching writing but be ready to use what this book has to offer in their own classrooms.

I am not presumptuous enough to imagine that my own way of teaching composition should be set out as a model for the world to emulate. As John Barth says, "An excellent teacher is likely to teach well no matter what pedagogical theory he suffers from" (Barth, 1984, p. 200). There are many excellent approaches to the teaching of writing, each responsive to particular situations, student needs, and teacher personalities. Nonetheless, certain kinds of problems are common to composition teaching, whatever the approach, and most teachers are interested in ways of coping with these problems. I have thus chosen

251

to focus on three problems that will be familiar to every teacher of composition courses: helping students move from personal experience/expressive writing to expository/analytic writing, learn to use sources responsibly, and learn how to move from first to genuine revised drafts. In all three cases, I have found that incorporating what I have learned in assessment into my teaching practice has made these problems more manageable and my teaching more effective.

Helping Students Move from Personal Experience/Expressive Writing to Expository/Analytic Writing

Although, as Chapter Six points out, not every student finds personal experience or even descriptive writing easy, most students do write more successful papers in such modes than in the expository or analytic mode. Since I want my students to have a feeling of accomplishment at the start, I normally begin my writing courses by asking students to write to the following assignment:

> Describe as clearly as you can a person you knew well when you were a child. Your object is to use enough detail so that we as readers can picture him or her clearly from the child's perspective and, at the same time, to make us understand from the tone of your description the way you felt about the person you describe.

Discussion of the topic usually takes a full class hour. In the first place, we need to talk about the language of physical detail: concrete language such as "her crooked smile and her cigarette never left her lips" differs sharply from abstract or general language such as "she was a friendly person." Students need to notice in their reading and come to understand through discussion the importance of well-observed detail—and not only for this assignment. Concrete detail in a description is *evidence* for its meaning, and one important connection between the two modes of writing I am concerned about is the use of evidence to support conclusions.

Once we have established the importance of concrete detail in the assignment, we then discuss the differences in tone created by different kinds of language. The writing task has a special problem built into it: the description must convey feelings, but only indirectly, by way of the details selected by the writer and conveyed by the writer's language. I like to deal with the way particular words communicate different emotions by stressing the fact that writing is an act of human intercourse—the second definition of writing discussed in Chapter Nine. The concept of "tone," the relationship between writer and reader, emphasizes the fact, a fact sometimes easy for student writers to forget, that every act of communication sets up a relationship of one sort or another. So we speak of the different attitudes implied by various terms that describe roughly the same kinds of detail: "fat," "well-built," and "husky," for example, or "slim" and "skinny." The job, I want to make clear before the students go home to write, is to communicate an emotion about the person described by choosing exactly the right language for their audience.

Of course, one reason students have trouble with the concept of tone is that they often do not know just who their audience is supposed to be in school writing. Since we do so much small group work in class, that problem is easy to solve: we define the audience as a group of the most intelligent students in the class, an audience both knowable and accountable.

Finally, we talk about the role of the observer in this descriptive assignment. The writer as child needs to be present in the description somehow, without becoming the central subject. There is an important difference between "I loved her very much," which describes only the child's reaction, and "When she walked into the room, I always noticed first the unraveled hem of her dress." Many students think they are describing others when they are describing only their reactions to others. On the other hand, many students believe that it is simply wrong to use the pronoun "I" in an essay, although few of them know why they have been told a rule that most of their reading contradicts: many writing teachers enunciate that supposed rule in order to keep beginning writers from turning every assignment into a personal narrative. This assignment helps students control the "I" in their writing, without turning the writing from its purpose to simple subjectivism. It also helps introduce the concept that all writing has a voice of some sort.

I have gone into so much detail about this little assignment because it illustrates in classroom terms so many of the issues dealt with in this book. The assignment has a clear purpose: it is not only interesting and accessible to students beginning a college writing course but serves the curricular design as well—to help students move successfully from personal to analytic writing. The class discussion can be seen, in terms of assessment, as a clarification of both the writing task and the criteria for scoring the assignment. The students leave class well prepared to write to a specific assignment whose goals are clear. And I know, since I have given this assignment in various forms for many years, that it works; it has been fully pre-tested and will allow students to do their best work. The topic, in short, fulfills the requirements set out in Chapter Six.

My files are rich with wonderful little descriptions composed in response to this assignment. The demand for childhood memories is one that every writer can meet and that most writers find eminently satisfying for many and subtle reasons. Every writer can write something to the assignment, while the best writers will take up the challenge to convey complex emotions through subtle language.

When the students appear with their papers for the second class of the term, I hand out copies of a paper written by one of their predecessors and ask them to begin to compose a scoring guide to measure success in meeting the assignment. Perhaps they will receive this paper:

Looking back, practically the first thing I think of when I remember her is her behind. It was a ponderous specimen to the fourth grader that I was; always an impossible obstacle thrust out into the aisles of our desks as she leaned on her elbows, absorbed in the smudgy penciled work of one of her students. I would stand contemplating it, wrapping one white knee-socked leg around the other, waiting. It was not that she intimidated me—she that sat in the dirt of our playground as if she were one of us—I could have made my need to pass known, but where, where to poke or tap her? Her shoulders were bowed over the desk, her face beaming not two inches away from her pupil's.

Her face was an entirely different matter. The precision of her nose brought to mind the image of a pert little bird, a sparrow perhaps. Her eyes were a crisp blue, literally framed by scholarly brown glasses. Her hair might have reminded a student or two of the pictures of the thatched roofs in Norway that she enthusiastically waved at us during geography hour. (She once confided to me that she looked in the mirror but once a day, exclaiming, "God, you're gorgeous!" and then abandoned vanities for the rest of the day.)

Despite her decrepitude—she must have been over forty years old—she was a real Bohemian, complete with bean bag chairs and tie-dyed blouse. She had a deep affection for my father. She was widowed or divorced, I suppose, with three teenaged children, and when she asked me how my father was and told me that he had the most beautiful, happy eyes, I wanted to hug her and let her move into my room with me. She must have been very lonely.

She was generally a soft-spoken person, but was capable of an awesome bellow that would stop any taunting boy in his cruel tracks. How often I wanted to bury my head in her polyester lap, my friend, my protector, but she was my teacher. I respected her not only wholly, but voluntarily.

The discussion of this descriptive piece is always very lively. Some students, trained to expect negative examples in class and used to analytic scoring, immediately start finding fault; they find the punctuation error in the first paragraph, say, or the coherence problems in the last two paragraphs. They do not like the disrespectful beginning, and they point to the last sentence, which gives the game away in contradiction to the specific requirement of the assignment. I try to get past this phase of the discussion very quickly, by agreeing with these complaints (there is no reason to deny them) but suggesting that there are more important things to say about the piece of writing.

Eventually, someone ventures, usually timidly, that the piece is wonderful. I agree, with some enthusiasm, and ask what makes it effective. Well, comes a reply, you can *see* the fourth-grade teacher, and the child observer as well. As we discuss this example of writing as one that makes us see what the writer wants us to see, we wind up pointing to the precision of the detail: the teacher bending over the desk or sitting in the dirt or looking in the mirror and talking; the child on one "knee-socked" leg responding, in a child's way, to the teacher's loneliness. Someone may suggest that the child is described as much as the teacher and that the classroom setting seems real through the use of detail also.

As discussion proceeds, the class will begin to shape a scoring guide for the first assignment. I use the six-point scale discussed in Chapter Seven to score first submissions (reserving letter grades for revisions) and ask the class to begin by defining the characteristics of upper-half (score of five) and lower-half (score of two) papers. The following outline begins to take shape on the chalkboard:

Score of five: These papers give enough detail so that the reader can visualize the character. They also describe the narrator and give enough interaction between the two to allow the reader to understand an aspect of their relationship. Writing errors do not distract the reader.

Score of two: These papers give little or no detail, telling us about a person instead of describing one. The focus may be almost entirely upon the narrator or a situation, the language may be vague, and there may be more than an occasional spelling or grammatical error.

It is not hard to expand these statements or to fill in the scores on either side of them. For example, my classes will give the paper printed above a score of only five, not six, since it defines the attitude of the writer instead of allowing the tone of the description to convey that attitude. The writer could not resist the last sentence, which is not only unnecessary but too limited: what we have seen in the brief description is more than "respect." The score of four may be reserved for a paper that accomplishes the task without the vigor or style of the sample paper we discussed.

The brief reference to mechanical and grammatical matters at the end of the scoring descriptions is practical and necessary. As Chapter One argues, our function in a writing class is to combine somehow both the socializing and individualizing aspects of writing. We cannot ignore on our scoring guides matters of spelling and grammar that every reader will notice, though we can order priorities so that the more substantive matters come first.

Finally, the students group themselves into clusters of three or four to read and score each other's papers in accordance with the scoring guide in the front of the room. After quietly reading and scoring the papers written by their group, they compare scores and reconcile differences. The author of the paper will record the group score and the group reasons for that score on the paper. If there is time, I will ask the group to select its best paper to be read aloud.

If the class is capable and responsible in the group activity (I circulate from group to group during their discussions, so I have a good sense of what is going on), I do not need to collect and grade the papers. The students have received considered responses from three readers, using criteria for scoring developed publicly and by consensus. The group work tends to be constructive and useful (as simple subjective judgments—"I like it"—are not) because the scores must be justified by reference to the scoring guide. Most students find the expanded audience a major incentive to do good work, and most of them are ready to revise their work and submit it for a letter grade after the group discussion.

If the class is still tentative in its descriptive ability, I may follow this assignment with one that builds directly on it:

> This paper asks you to describe and analyze the relationship you had with someone you knew well as a child. The person may or may not be the one you described in the first paper. Your aim is to show the reader what things were like between the child you were and the person you describe, how you got along with each other, what the relationship meant to you then and means to you now.

This assignment allows the students further practice in the use of description as evidence, adds a requirement for some

analysis of the relationship, and further asks for management of
two separate perspectives in time on the meaning of the relationship. Usually, the scoring guide we develop will require that
upper-half papers (that is, scores of four, five, or six) make clear
the meaning of the relationship described both as it appeared in
the past and as it looks now upon more mature reflection.

However, the class may be ready for more speedy movement toward analytic writing. The following assignment still
asks for description but calls for increased attention to evaluation of meaning:

> This paper asks you to describe and analyze
> an institution of some sort that you knew well as a
> child. A school, a school group, a scout troop, a
> dancing class, a summer camp, a club, a Sunday
> School—any group with an internally consistent set
> of values you can see clearly will serve. You have
> two specific tasks to accomplish: clear description
> of what it was like to be a member of the group at
> the time, and an assessment from your mature per-
> spective of the meaning of the group's values.

This topic still asks the students to draw upon their personal experience but now makes clear that the purpose of the
paper is to understand the meaning of that experience and to
make that meaning clear to an outside audience. The assignment
not only requires that the students use what has been stressed
in the earlier papers but allows the inclusion of that earlier writing if it fits. (Each assignment is a bit longer than the one before.) As always, we spend the greater part of a class hour discussing the new assignment, considering its creative possibilities,
and drafting appropriate scoring procedures. We are also reading examples of professional writing on the same topic: Orwell,
Proust, Mill, Henry Adams, and so on. I use a textbook I edited
specifically for these assignments titled *The Writer's Control of
Tone* (White, 1970), but many composition anthologies offer
examples of this kind of personal evaluative writing, drawing on
the writer's experience of some group out of his or her past.

The quality of writing to this assignment, when the students are clear about what is needed, is generally very high. I

may distribute this paper from my files as an example of one that meets the requirements well:

I was brought up a sort of a Catholic and as such was required to take religious instruction in preparation for two solemn events: my First Communion, when I was six, and my Confirmation, when I was twelve. The two classes are intertwined in my memory, probably because I was as terrorized by them at twelve as I was at six. Most of the other children in my catechism class were Catholic school students and received daily religious instruction. My religious education came from my mother, who imbued her teachings with an inspired confusion of Catholic traditions, pantheism, and agnosticism, depending on how she felt at any given time. As a result, I wasn't sure who or what to believe, so I just generally felt guilty about everything. I didn't know it then, but this was the first step in becoming a good Catholic.

The purpose of the class was to convince an assemblage of formerly cheerful six-year-olds that they were sinners headed for eternal damnation. Since the preface to the First Communion was the First Confession, we had to find something to confess. This was much easier than we thought. Nearly everything, we soon found out, was a sin or a potential sin. There was original sin, venial sin, mortal sin, and endless variations of each. Even considering a sin was a sin.

The nuns who taught the classes were not a nurturing group. My earliest memories of them are hazy, blurred no doubt by my sheer fright. I remember how, with a sinking stomach, I had tightly gripped my mother's reassuring hand as I passed through the imposing black iron gates of the school for the first time. I was greeted (or rather, my mother was greeted; I was ignored) by a faceless, forbidding figure all in somber black and white with a huge black wooden rosary dangling from her ample waist. There I was abandoned. My stomach sank to my knees. Saturday, previously my favorite day, instantly became an occasion for dread.

In class, we were required to answer a series of questions from the Baltimore Catechism. It was simply rote memorization, and since I was a good student, this posed no problem. The problem was that I attended Mass only when I was coerced; and I soon learned that this was definitely a terrible sin. The dismal realization that I was a sinner was underscored by the feeling that the nuns just didn't like me. That they didn't seem to like *any* of us much didn't help to make me feel any better.

One time I successfully managed to fake a stomach ache on a Saturday (a previously unheard-of occurrence). When I returned to class the following week, they had already assigned places in line for the ceremonial procession to the church. I hesitated, waiting for someone to tell me where to stand (now I really did have a stomach ache). Soon I was roughly seized by a very cross nun who deposited me near the front of the line with a firm painful pinch to my upper arm. Tears came to my eyes. I had never been pinched by anyone over the age of eight before, and the shock and humiliation drove away any remaining possibility of religious curiosity. I didn't doubt that I had sinned: I had lied to avoid coming to class. Of course the nun had every right to pinch me so cruelly. Or did she? I knew someone was wrong. I suspected it must be me, but I wasn't quite sure. Angry guilt replaced my willingness to learn. I sullenly made a silent vow never to become conspicuous again.

I continued to attend Mass as seldom as possible for the next six years until, when I turned twelve, my mother was again overcome by the spirit of tradition and launched me into Confirmation classes. Back through those miserable black iron gates! Saturdays were ruined again. And again the nuns devoted themselves to cataloguing our infinite variety of sins. I remember identifying with one sad tale of a chubby girl who became so obsessed by vanity that she finally refused to eat at all. Not even the priest could force her. I was impressed. How I would have loved to have had the courage to defy a priest! Now *there* was an inspiring thought. The punch line to this story was delivered by an immense nun who had apparently read my mind. With a forbidding gaze directly at me she intoned sepulchrally, "She looked quite beautiful in her coffin." I flushed guiltily. Of course I knew where that immortal soul had gone!

The only other instruction that I can remember well concerned baptism. Anyone, we were told, can perform the sacrament of baptism if the un-baptised person's life is in immediate danger. This is accomplished by pouring a small amount of water on the forehead of the sinner and saying, "I baptise thee in the name of the Father, the Son, and the Holy Ghost." A big loud-mouthed boy who always sat near the back of the room, surrounded by admiring friends, waved his hand wildly:

"If you don't have water, but you've got orange juice, can you use that?"

"Yes," came the resigned answer, "you can use orange juice."

"How about milk?"

"Yes," a little less patiently this time, "you can use milk."

"Coffee?"
"Yes."
"Tea?"
"Yes."
"Seven-up?"
"Yes!"
"Coca-cola?"
By this time sister had had enough.
"NO! NO! Never! Absolutely not! You can't use Coca-cola!"
Roars of laughter from the back of the room.
End of discussion.
Yet I admired and envied those delinquents for their refusal to be intimidated. Obviously they were terrible sinners, much worse than I, but they were so dauntlessly self-assured; whereas I had elevated humble guilt to a fine art. Maybe the stern unforgiving tactics were necessary to keep in line the students who were immune to guilt after years of Catholic training, but they had devastated me. I have since learned that there *are* religions that do not rely on fear and guilt for salvation; that even the Catholic Church has miraculously eased up a bit, but it's much too late for me. Once I had confirmed my religious vows, I promptly abandoned them. For years the thought of entering a church, any church—even voluntarily—filled me with dread. I knew God saw right through me. He knew I had no business there.

The excellence of this paper illustrates the components for a scoring guide for the assignment. Three tasks are required: description of the group, including its people and its location; an evaluation of what it meant to the writer in the past, while a member of the group; and an evaluation of the group and its values from today's perspective. Papers scoring six or five need to accomplish all three tasks in a coherent or even dramatic way, whereas the paper with a score of four will be less well organized and less interesting. Scores of three or below will represent increasingly serious failures to meet one or more of the demands of the topic, lack of clarity in distinguishing past from present evaluations of the group, and distracting mechanical and grammatical problems.

Most students find this assignment challenging and interesting, but very difficult. They are not accustomed to organizing their personal experience or to developing it as evidence for an idea. But I am convinced that one valuable benefit of writing about personal experience is to gain an understanding of it— through the kind of organization and evaluation this assignment demands. While this is going on, the students are also learning the most important skills for writing expository papers: thinking systematically about aspects of their topic and relating careful description to a central controlling idea.

If the class needs another assignment with this same general purpose, I will assign the following topic, based on a reading passage:

> Write a short essay examining what the anthropologist Jules Henry means in the following passage and showing the extent to which the passage applies to your own schooling.
>
> "Another learning problem inherent in the human condition is the fact that we must conserve culture while changing it; that we must always be *more* sure of surviving than of adapting—*as we see it.* Whenever a new idea appears, our first concern as *animals* must be that it does not kill us; then, and only then, can we look at it from other points of view. . . . In general, primitive people solved this problem simply by walling their children off from new possibilities by educational methods that, largely by fear (including ridicule, beating and mutilation) so narrowed the perceptual sphere that other than traditional ways of viewing the world became unthinkable. . . .
>
> "The function of education has never been to free the mind and the spirit of man, but to bind them. . . . Schools have therefore never been places for the stimulation of young minds"[Henry, 1963].

This is a much more difficult writing task for students than it appears to be. Students generally have a difficult time understanding how anyone, even an anthropologist, can say such a wicked thing about the schools they have often come to love. So instead of noticing the complexity of Henry's idea that schools everywhere must conserve their culture before challenging it, they write essays defending school spirit and their prom committee's creative choice of colors to decorate the school gym.

The ability of the class determines how much pre-writing time I give to this assignment. If the class is very able, I may wait for submission of the first draft before discussing it, even though I know very well that only the best students will respond well to the assignment. Some of the first drafts will be good enough to illustrate the way to respond to a quotation that seems to attack values one treasures. They will both understand and discuss the Henry passage and will bring some experiences from their own schooling to demonstrate the degree to which the passage helps them understand those experiences. Such papers will allow us to construct a scoring guide. Small group evaluation of each other's papers, following that scoring guide, will provide enough useful comment for revision to take place.

A weaker class will need more help. I will ask such a class to read the chapter from which the passage derives and to write a summary of its argument. When these summaries are brought to class, we analyze the chapter as a group and construct on the chalkboard an outline of the principal assertions in it. From that outline, we develop a scoring guide for the summaries: upper-half papers must discuss at least three of these principal assertions, for example. Small group discussion and evaluation of each other's summaries follow, and students leave the class ready to revise their summaries and prepared to write the essay.

By the time we come to a straightforward expository paper, the students in this writing class find it no surprise. They have been analyzing their personal experiences, organizing complex materials, and learning to use evidence to demonstrate their assertions. In addition, they have been learning how to relate themselves to the material they discuss so that their writing remains interesting to themselves and their readers. They have also learned to look for the goal of a writing task, and to expect an audience beyond the teacher alone to assess it using a clear set of scoring criteria. Thus they take the following assignment as similar to what they have been doing, despite the fact that it no longer calls for personal experience.

Choose an advertisement from a popular magazine for careful analysis. An ad is, of course, designed to urge hasty readers to buy a product. Your concern, however, is not with the ad's selling power but with its concealed message. What does it assume and imply about its readers? What does it suggest about our needs, desires, motives, and so on? How does the ad define the self and the world for its readers?

The pre-writing discussion of this topic usually focuses on the problem of seeing below the surface, the difficulty of perceiving the concealed message most ads convey. Advertisements are particularly good material for this exercise because they are often designed to appeal to patterns of belief below the surface as a powerful way to sell products. I continue to be surprised at the innocence of even good students about this fact; exposed to selling techniques from their earliest days before a television screen, they tend merely to accept advertisements as a source of information (sometimes, amazingly, as a source of truth) without attending to the picture of their world and of themselves that advertising presents.

If the class is relatively inexperienced with the concept of seeing below the surface, I will spend at least one class hour discussing various advertisements that I project on the screen in front of the room. "How are the people dressed?" I will ask, or, more generally, "What is their social class?" We will talk about the ways the illustrations in advertisements sometimes send much more subtle messages than does the text, about the function of the design of the advertisement as art, or about the use of words to create a "world" sympathetic to the product.

We also attend to the problem of tone in responding to the assignment, since many students will assume that all advertisements are evil simply because they seek to manipulate an audience into buying something. It is no discovery, I need to remind the class, to point out that an advertisement is seeking to sell a product. The goal of the assignment is to discern the concealed, not the obvious, message and then to develop an attitude toward that concealed message. Is the world view of the advertisement wicked, or amusing, or sensible, or what? Analytic writing calls for clear and perceptive examination of detail, the use of that detail to develop generalizations of some sort, and the management of tone to convey a consistent attitude toward those generalizations.

When the students have written their papers, I bring, as usual, a good example from my files to begin developing a scoring guide. I often use this one:

Rick Ate the Whole Pot

I found an interesting, rather disturbing advertisement among the slick pages of *Good Housekeeping,* a magazine dedicated to mild fashion, conservatively good marital sex and white-teethed children. The ad, covering an entire page and appearing perfectly harmless at first glance, features an ecstatic, thirty-ish woman beaming out at us from her beautiful upper-middle class dining room that is both immaculate and crowded with food that would make Julia Child's mouth water. Everything in the decor of the room is color-coordinated and in its place; even her countertop gleams.

Yet we are still convinced that she is a real woman, for she is plump, rather plain and actually has a name: Darlene Hyrb. She even comes from a real place: Wixom, Michigan. She appears in one of the most widely read woman's magazines with her award-winning Brunswick Stew recipe, but most importantly, she has a husband. We learn this first and know that it is paramount because under Darlene's photo, in huge letters is her proclamation: "I knew Rick loved it. He finished the whole pot!" In finer print, we are told that because Rick "had polished off an entire pot of her Brunswick Stew," she knew it had to be a worthwhile, meaningful recipe, and consequently entered it in a recipe contest. Rick's overzealous and masculine appetite proved correct, of course, and the little missus received "French's Prize Recipe Award." To the right of the ad we see Darlene's recipe and underneath that are pictures of French's seasoning mixes that turn "ordinary chicken" and lowly hamburger into a meal fit for a husband.

French's advertisement is very shrewd. Placed in a magazine read by millions of middle class, married women, the ad's assumption hit the bull's eye of their target market. The ad assumes that its readers are average American women who strive to be the Ideal American Homemaker (who else would read *Good Housekeeping?*). We identify with Darlene at first glance.

In striking contrast to the cat-eyed, flawless panty hose model a few pages earlier, with legs from the neck down, Darlene is ordinary, like us. With her sparingly applied make-up, lenient waistline and short haircut that is a Xerox copy of millions of other housewives, she looks like a neighbor from whom we'd borrow the proverbial cup of sugar.

The advertisement assumes (and correctly so for all of us that call ourselves red-blooded American housewives), that all of us would like to have a house like Darlene's, that looks as though the interior decorator just deposited his check. Of course, we know, however, that it was Darlene who planned the decor, for the Ideal American Homemaker is naturally a talented designer.

French's ad also assumes that American society considers women admirable when they (1) keep an orderly, attractive household, (2) are interested in cooking, and (3) care about what their husbands think. These are not wicked assumptions and if they are true, they are certainly not things of which to be ashamed. Personally, I think keeping a nice home, cooking well and being sensitive to one's mate are wonderful qualities. What I find unsettling are the implications of these assumptions, for there is a catch in them, exemplified in French's motto "for cooking that could win a prize." The motto is not "for cooking you'll enjoy" or "for cooking you'll find personally satisfying." In short, the overall implication of the ad is that American women base their self-evaluations and esteem on external opinions, and I think, sadly, this is the case in our society. Darlene is not joyous because she knows she is a good cook or because she enjoyed her Brunswick Stew, but because "Rick loved it. He finished the whole pot!" (In passing, I'd just like to say that if someone had eaten *my* entire pot of stew, I would have called him a pig and gone out for steak and lobster.)

Darlene does not enter her recipe in French's contest because she is confident of her talents, but because Rick demonstrated his personal approval. She depends upon him to validate the expertise of her culinary skills, of her worth as a human being. In this so-called "liberated age," women in our society still define themselves not by who they are, but by who they are to other people: daughter, wife, mother. Certainly, today's "career woman" is not only widely accepted but admired—as long as she maintains top performance both on the job and at home. We still have that primal need to be a woman as defined by the role she has traditionally played in humankind. I think that all women, at varying depths of soul, believe that at the foundation of humankind are the inherent, biological and inescapable roles called "male" and "female." The French's advertisement plays upon this subconscious level by surrounding the Ideal Woman with the rudimentary appeal of food; real food on the table and in her hands and pictures of food hanging on the walls.

In spite of all our puffing away at Virginia Slims, keeping maiden names and running for office, we as the childbearing sex are forever as essential to human survival as food. It is only natural that we would—however subconsciously—cling to the self-denying traditions of our gender, to strive to fulfill all that a woman is "naturally supposed to be." What I feel is lacking in our society and made apparent in the seasoning mix ad is the complete acceptance of people, male and female, as individuals. Darlene should have had her recipe in *Good Housekeeping* because she liked it, not because Rick ate the whole pot.

While most students like this paper very much, as I do, those who are studying the social or natural sciences are quick to argue that such a personal tone would be inappropriate for analytic papers in their fields. I usually have on hand some paragraphs from the physician Lewis Thomas, the economist John Galbraith, and the sociologist David Riesman to demonstrate that (depending on audience and purpose) such a tone may well be appropriate whatever the field. A research report, however, or even a term paper in any field might require a much less personal approach to the analysis. The writer's job is to discover the appropriate tone to take for the topic and audience at hand.

As we begin to devise a scoring guide for essays written on this topic, the students begin to list the features of the sample essay that are most important. They see the precision of language and use of detail, the clarity of organization, and the arrangement of evidence to demonstrate an interesting conclusion. They admire the carefully balanced tone, amused and unfanatical about the advertisement's attitude toward women, yet absolutely serious about its concern for an inner-directed validation of individual worth. Although many students will be less than fully convinced that cooking—which is nothing much without the eating—is the right subject to make that case, most will agree that the argument is worth making. Certainly, no paper that merely describes an advertisement, or that has nothing to say beyond the fact that an advertisement seeks to sell a product, can be given a score of four or above.

After the scoring guide is drafted and the class divides into small groups to read each other's papers, they find that most papers fail to move much beyond description. They also discover that many of the best papers, including "Rick Ate the Whole Pot," seem to come to their topic only toward the end of the essay, and hence need considerable revision, particularly of the early paragraphs. Good writers, who may have been able to deal with the less complicated topics earlier in the term without serious revision, sometimes discover at this point that revision is not a matter reserved only for the incompetent. By this time, the small groups are accustomed to giving specific advice, usually in terms of the scoring guide: there are too few details to let us visualize the advertisement; your anger at the advertiser is not justified by the evidence in the paper; your attitude toward the advertiser is different at different places in the paper; the spelling and other mechanical errors make the paper hard to respect; you don't seem to have anything much to say. At the same time, the groups tend to be very determined to find good things to say, even about the weakest papers—something I know I should always do, although it is one of the most difficult for me.

I have said little so far about my response to the second drafts upon which I spend a great amount of time. I normally prepare and distribute a revised version of the scoring guide the class developed for group discussion, and I often direct my written comments to a forthcoming third draft, which may or may not be required. I find that the careful work in class with scoring criteria, and the extra commentary the writer has received from the small group, free me to spend time on the most substantive matters in each paper. If the writer seems to have little to say, I try to identify passages in the paper that indicate potential ideas for development; very often, an apparently empty paper will come to interesting concepts only at the very end, where they are easy to overlook. I try to be careful to link my comments and my grade to the original goals of the assignment, the criteria for writing established during the pre-writing class discussion, and the scoring guide. I also attempt to be consistent with the ideas expressed in Chapters Two and Five—that is, to respond to and evaluate the potential of the paper as well as its present form and to refrain from taking ownership of the paper from the writer.

The sequence of assignments I have just described brings students to analytic/expository writing through a series of rather gentle steps from the personal experience papers they are accustomed to in the schools. Each new assignment adds a new component and incorporates matters dealt with earlier. Although the writing tasks do not free the students to do anything they may want, the topics offer a wide range of choices within a specific and clear set of goals and criteria. By the time students have completed and revised these assignments, they are ready to handle such subsequent phases of the writing course as a research paper or literary analysis.

Helping Students Use Sources Responsibly

When we attempt to teach college students, usually in freshman-level courses, to use sources responsibly in their writing, we immediately encounter a series of misconceptions about the entire process. If we begin teaching something called "The Research Paper" or "The Source Paper," the problem is compounded, for most of our students already have an established idea of what such a paper involves. They begin by rummaging through the library taking random notes from books while seeking a topic; if they use periodical literature at all, they look in the *Reader's Guide* for popular magazines, since they tend to be quite unaware of scholarly journals; when they accumulate enough quotations and paraphrases from their work in the library, they string these selections together with some filler material and, if there are enough footnotes, hand in the paper expecting praise for their (sometimes very extensive) labor. The most diligent of these untrained students tend to be very worried about footnote form, since that technical matter has often been the principal or even the only concern of teachers responding to their "research." In the worst case, students will simply copy out what others have said and, in the sincere belief that such unintentional plagiarism *is* research, submit the work as their own, with a bibliography listing sources.

The assessment issues discussed in this book provide a way for the many teachers confronting this situation to change student attitudes toward the use of sources. In one sense, a source paper is no different from any argument or analysis paper, with the single exception that the evidence for the generalizations derives in part from library materials. But since the misconceptions students hold about the use of sources are so profound, we need to pay special attention to the connections between the writing of a source paper and the writing of the other papers we assign. That is, we need to be particularly straightforward and clear about the purpose of the assignment, the topic design, and the criteria to be used in evaluating the result in relation to the use of sources.

Purpose and Criteria for a Source Paper. One purpose of a source paper assignment is to help students learn to use reference material as evidence for their own conclusions, that is, to learn to find and use others' ideas and data in support of their own developed ideas. This means that a source paper begins not with sources but with student interest in a topic. The purpose is not merely to collect material in a general area but to collect evidence that allows discussion of a particular idea about a specific topic. A string of quotations from encyclopedias and other books will not fulfill the purpose of a source paper, since the paper (like all papers) requires that the writer have something to say.

Furthermore, until the writer knows what he or she has to say, it is very difficult to distinguish the ideas of the various sources from the ideas of the writer. This distinction between the ideas of others and those of the self lies at the very heart of the responsible use of sources; however, until the self has some ideas to call one's own, that distinction has no meaning. Students doing research are normally cowed by the weight and substance of the material they go through and become passive collectors instead of thinking researchers. They share the common view that whatever is printed is bound to be true and accurate, and sometimes cling to that view even in the face of contradictory evidence and opinions. Some students will claim that they have no right to form opinions, since they are not experts, and hence they cannot be expected to do more than accumulate the ideas of experts in their research.

Unless we can demonstrate the importance of understanding and developing one's topic as the principal purpose of a source paper, many students will have a hard time believing that we really expect them to evaluate and go beyond their sources. We cannot simply announce a research paper assignment without giving substantial attention to topic development, or without detailing the criteria by which we will evaluate the response. A primary component of the evaluation criteria needs to demand the active handling of sources, in particular the clear indication to the reader of what derives from sources and what does not.

Many teachers are reluctant to prescribe topics for research, since they believe that research depends upon the writer's individual curiosity about a subject. I tend to share that view, as long as the development of a clear and manageable topic becomes the joint responsibility of the student and the teacher, with early decision about a topic required. Inexperienced writers will confuse the identification of an area of inquiry with the selection of a writing topic, and they normally need help in seeing the difference. An area of inquiry is usually too large to manage: "What Is the Meaning of Love in Poetry?" A writing topic focuses and narrows that area of interest and poses a question that can be addressed in the time and space allowed: "Sexual Love Versus Spiritual Love in the Poetry of John Donne." It is important, as this book has stressed, that the student write on a topic whose demand is clear and that the assignment have goals that are clearly stated. For students with sufficient ability and teachers with sufficient time, the selection of a topic might well be part of the writing task and the writing process.

Some faculty, faced with this problem of clear topic definition but with insufficient time to spend with each student, will prefer to assign an area of inquiry for their students. The students' freedom of choice becomes restricted, but the advantages of economy of time, precision, and focus may well compensate. When I have faced such a situation, I have used such assignments as the following:

> The term *popular art* is loosely used to describe the kind of literature, music, painting, architecture, and so on, that is produced for unsophisticated mass consumption. Some popular art sometimes turns out to be very sophisticated indeed (Dickens's novels, for instance), but most popular art is designed to reaffirm and comfort, not challenge or examine, popular attitudes and tastes.
>
> Choose for this paper a relatively unsophisticated form of popular art for analysis. If you choose a type, or genre, be sure it is a coherent genre—not "popular music," but, say, "sentimental love songs of the 1950s"; not "comic books," but "Disney comics" or "monster comics" or "Superman-type comics." Popular art exists in almost all areas, for all kinds of specialized interests. Be sure to select a form of popular art in a field you find interesting to begin with.
>
> Your object will be to have something worth saying about the material you analyze, and then to demonstrate convincingly what you have to say. Evidence for your argument will probably come for the most part from analysis or descriptions of the popular art. But one requirement of the paper is that you consult relevant material about popular art and find a way to make use of at least three different sources on your subject in your paper. An incidental but required job is for you to learn and use standard ways of referring to these sources.

By stating in the directions, and discussing in class, the objectives of the assignment, I try to meet the requirements of topic development that are detailed in Chapter Six. Class time is spent discussing topic options and ways to use sources to develop ideas for papers.

Five Ways to (Mis)Use Sources. At the beginning of one class, I ask the students to suppose that they have decided to contrast two familiar comics—*Peanuts* and *Donald Duck.** I ask them to suppose that they feel, as most of them do, that there is an important difference between the quality of the two comics and that they are interested to discover if this difference is one between two forms of popular art or between popular art and art.

I then distribute the following passage from an essay on the subject by Abraham Kaplan and ask the students to imagine that they have copied it word for word on a note card for use in the paper.

> All art selects what is significant and sup-presses the trivial. But for popular art the criteria of significance are fixed by the needs of the stan-dardization, by the editor of the digest and not by the Author of the reality to be grasped. Popular art is never a discovery, only a reaffirmation. Both producer and consumer of popular art confine themselves to what fits into their own schemes, rather than omitting only what is unnecessary to the grasp of the scheme of things. The world of popular art is bounded by the limited horizons of what we think we know already; it is two-dimen-sional because we are determined to view it with-out budging a step from where we stand [Kaplan, 1966, p. 354].

We then go through a series of possible ways to use this material in a paper on the two comics. How, I ask the class, can this paragraph become part of a source paper? In the course of discussion, five different ways to incorporate the material emerge.

The first option, of course, is to copy it word for word and hand it in as part of one's own work. There is no point in hastening over this matter, since some of the students in any class will have done exactly that in the past without knowing that there was anything wrong with doing so. This is the place

*The following sections are indebted to an unpublished paper by my colleague Peter Schroeder and were printed in an early form in *The Pop Culture Tradition* (White, 1972, pp. 183-196).

to be explicit about the reasons for outrage over plagiarism: students are often quite unaware that the use of the words or even the ideas of others without acknowledgment is a sin akin to stealing. Like most of the issues in the teaching of writing, plagiarism is in one way an assessment issue; most universities mandate serious disciplinary action in response to plagiarized material. Students need to know what those penalties are. They are also likely to be keenly aware that any writing teacher would suspect plagiarism if the paragraph from Kaplan appeared in the middle of their normal writing. While it is useful to remind students of the likelihood of discovery and the penalties for detected plagiarism, the issue I prefer to stress has to do with the individuality of every writer. Plagiarism confesses a blurring of one's own integrity as a writer and a confusion of one's own identity with that of another. No one who respects his or her own uniqueness will deliberately plagiarize.

However, few students are deliberately dishonest and foolish enough to plan deliberate plagiarism. A more common problem afflicts honest and serious students who simply stumble into plagiarism because they do not clearly understand how to incorporate other people's ideas into their own work.

For instance, a second way to use Kaplan's material would be to copy what he has to say word for word into a paper and put a note at the end referring to page 354 of the *Journal of Aesthetics and Art Criticism* (Kaplan, 1966). Many students feel this is the right way to use a source, since the author is acknowledged by the note. They need to be shown that plagiarism is still going on, since Kaplan's words and ideas are being put forward as their own.

It is more honest, but only a little more responsible, to put the quotation in quotation marks; now there is no pretense. This third way of using the source is very common and is often rewarded by high grades. But a mere quotation, by itself, does not show that the source is being used as part of the writer's own thought about the topic—or that the writer has thought about the source—and the whole point of a paper using sources is to understand one's sources and to develop an argument. The quotation cannot simply substitute for an idea. Even if the student believes that the source says exactly what he or she would like to say, but more professionally, the quotation does not state the idea for the writer; it merely proves that Kaplan has stated an idea that the writer somehow finds important. The writer still needs to show why the idea is important for the paper and how it relates to the other ideas in the paper.

A fourth way to use the passage is to paraphrase it, that is, to look closely at it, to figure out what it is saying, and to put it into one's own words:

One important difference between popular art and art is that popular art is never new, never discovers anything out of the standard scheme of things. So popular art doesn't challenge people to think differently.

But the *idea* is still Kaplan's. Even if students recognize that a paraphrase requires a note and add that note as a caution against plagiarism, they still need to see that paraphrasing the ideas of others, however fully footnoted, does not fulfill their obligations. Readers will surely ask what such a footnote in fact means. How much of the paraphrased material, or the foot-noted paragraph, belongs to the source and how much to the writer of the paper? Or is there any difference? The overriding problem for a writer using sources is to become informed about the topic under discussion *and* about the sources; only then can the writer come to form opinions about both. The job is not only to understand Kaplan but to come to some personal under-standing of the material at hand (here, the two comics). This means regarding the passage from Kaplan critically. If the writer ends up agreeing with him, that agreement needs to be stated explicitly. If not, the writer should point out where and why differences occur.

So we finally come to the fifth way to use the quotation, the most difficult way, but the only responsible way. In order to read the source critically, the writer must come to an under-standing of his or her point of view toward the topic. This means returning to the two comics before deciding how to use the quotation.

The writer needs to consider questions about the two comics that will begin to provide answers to the issue of whether they embody different concepts of art. What is different about the way the characters are conceived, for instance? Why are there no "grown-ups" in *Peanuts*, while the Disney comic establishes a father and an uncle? What are typical story lines from each and how do they compare? What issues are central to these story lines and how do they relate to the "real" world? What kinds of responses do the two comics ask their readers to have? Do Kaplan's terms and distinctions apply wholly to these comics? Partially? Not at all?

To think this way is to come to terms with the problems of writing a paper using sources. Perhaps in the end the writer might produce something like the following paragraph:

The real art of *Peanuts* becomes clear when you put it next to the dreary stereotypes and stale plots that make up *Donald Duck*. *Peanuts* seems fresh and original, to have its own world with its own rules and systems of behavior, whereas the Disney comic, with its constant fussing about money and social class, seems a reduced and corrupted version of our own world. When Abraham Kaplan says, "popular art is never a discovery, only a reaffirmation" (1966, p. 354), he points to exactly this distinction. If we agree with Kaplan, as I do, that art is defined by the way it makes us see things from a new perspective, *Peanuts* appears to deserve the respect it has received from philosophers and theologians, not to speak of the general public. *Donald Duck* reveals to us what we believe when we are not thinking or seeing clearly; it reassures us. But *Peanuts* makes us expand our vision and so is a different kind of art.

The point I try to make with my classes is that in using sources we must not be simple sponges, soaking up uncritically everything we read. We must distinguish between the opinion of the author we are reading and the opinion we ourselves, after careful consideration, come to hold. Quotations or paraphrases cannot stand by themselves. Even if they seem to be opinions or conclusions with which we may agree, they are only facts, bits of data for the writer to integrate into a paper. The fact that a source has said something is only a piece of evidence for the writer to use in developing his or her own ideas.

The responsible use of sources, then, depends upon sorting out the ideas, opinions, interpretations of other people from those we hold ourselves. Each of us has our own intellectual identity, though most of our ideas inevitably come from sources outside ourselves, and we need to recognize that identity by distinguishing clearly between what we think and what our source thinks. It is no sin to accept wholly another person's idea: "If we agree with Kaplan, as I do. . . ." The sin is in not having sufficient respect for oneself as a thinking being, or as a writer, to interpose oneself between the source and one's own thinking and writing. Thus we need to show students that it is lazy and irresponsible to pass off anyone else's ideas as their own without first making those ideas their own through a process of critical scrutiny. Only then can the quotation from a source be part of the evidence a writer brings to support his or her own conclusions.

These five possible ways of using sources enter directly into my scoring guide for papers. I usually distribute this scoring guide to students shortly before their papers are due, since that is when they are actually integrating their sources into their work. No paper that leaves me wondering how much material is derived from a source or leaves me unclear about which parts of the paper are to be attributed to the writer will receive a high score. If I need to write in the margin a comment such as "Why is this quotation here? How does it relate to what you are saying?" the essay will not score above a four on the six-point scale. If a paper fails to comment on its sources or to distinguish among its sources, it cannot be scored higher than five. The best papers will use sources according to the fifth pattern I have described. My experience has shown that very few students can overcome their previous misconceptions about the use of sources, or their preoccupation with footnote form to the exclusion of the substantive issue, on their first drafts. The concepts I have been discussing in this section need to be reinforced by an explicit statement on the scoring guide for the paper, by small group discussion and evaluation of the use of sources in submitted papers, by class discussion of examples from papers the students have written, and by a requirement for repeated revision until each student gets it right. If we are absolutely clear that we are not dealing with footnote mechanics but with the basic issues of the integrity of the individual and the comprehension of the material, our students will respect our goals and learn what we have to teach.

Helping Students Move from First Drafts
to Genuine Revised Drafts

I have said repeatedly in this book that most students do not know how to revise their work and that attention to assessment will help them understand how to do so. My intention here is to demonstrate that concept by presenting a typical first draft, one I received in a freshman writing course some years ago, and tracing its improvement through two revisions. If a class has difficulty understanding the difference between editing and revision, I will duplicate the drafts of the paper that follow to help them understand the writing process. When I conduct workshops for teachers, I find that they are particularly interested in the teaching process that helps direct the student from one draft to the next. Following each draft of the paper, I give a summary of the assessment and response that led to the subsequent draft. The paper was written on the topic of popular art that I have been discussing.

The "Love Comics" View of Romance: First Draft.

One form of popular art that is present among pre-teen and young teenage girls is the romance or love comic books. They come in a variety of titles, including the four that I happened to pick up: *Young Romance, Falling in Love, Girls' Romances,* and *Secret Hearts.* These are aimed mainly at girls between the ages of about eight and fifteen, who have had little or no experience in love and romance and are still dreaming of the day they will fall in love. A typical cover says on it: "Thrill to the true-to-love story of Wendy Winthrop, television model, as she pursues her heart in and out of the loopholes of her romantic career."[1] Through these "true-to-love" stories, these comic books create a sort of temporary dream world for the young girl to live in. She can place herself in the position of a character such as Wendy Winthrop and dream of when the same experiences will happen to her. One little eight-year-old said, in the book, *Seduction of the Innocent,* "I like to read the comic books about love because when I go to sleep at night I love to dream about love."[2] Now this, in itself would not really be extremely bad except for the fact that the romantic experiences presented in these comic books are unrealistic and overly dramatic.

First of all, an unattractive or homely person is never seen in these comic books. The girls are all extremely pretty and shapely, and the men are extraordinarily handsome and masculine. Another thing never seen in these stories is a poor person. All of the characters seem to be either upper-middle or upper class in society. These two characteristics tend to make these stories even more ideal, while at the same time making them more unrealistic.

Most of the stories in these comic books fit into one basic style. That is, a girl thinks she is in love, or has been in love, with one boy, but through a series of actions and events, invariably including heartache and indecision, she meets her true love. However, another style that I found a few examples of is that of two friends, one who always gets the boy she wants while the other looks on. But in the end, the underdog finally gets the boy she wants, in spite of her friend. This second style of story would probably serve to give hope to the readers who are not very popular with boys, while the first, more prominent style, would meet every girl's dreams and hopes.

Every love comic story, despite all of the heartache and despair within it, ends happily. "The love comic formula demands that the story end with reconciliation."[3] The heroine always gets the man she wants and everything is summed up with a kiss.

However, nothing beyond a kiss is ever suggested in these stories. There is no hint of sexual relations. Everything is pure and innocent, and no one makes a move to make it otherwise. This helps to keep these stories within the realm of having dream-like qualities; anything less innocent would destroy a young girl's conception of love.

The covers of these various love comic books tend to be pictorial representations of the emotional appeal within. They always show a picture from one of the stories and, without fail, this picture is always the most romantic and emotionally appealing one the publishers could find. Every cover shows a heart-rending scene; out of the four comic books that I chose, all of them showed, among other characters, a girl with a pained expression on her face, and in three of them, she had a tear in her eye.

The titles of the stories within the comic books also have a definite emotional appeal. They include, "Love, Love Go Away!", "Reach for Happiness" (episode 24), "The Secret in My Past," "The Truth About Men," and "In the Name of Love." All of this is perfect bait for the young girl who is dreaming of when she'll fall in love.

Another interesting aspect of these comic books is the "Ann Landers"-type column found in the middle of each one. Under the title of "Counselor-at-Love" or "Romance Reporter," these big-sister type counselors answer questions from the lovelorn. Most of the letters tend to be from girls around the ages of thirteen to fifteen who are having problems with their love lives and think that the world is ending because of it. Or if this isn't their problem, then they are desperately in love with a boy and want advice as to how to make him notice them. The responses to these letters always seem to assume that these girls are perfectly mature enough to be in love and, thus, the answers proceed from there. Here again is the audience of young girls who really don't know what love is all about but want so desperately to find out. And they think they are finding the answers in these comic books.

The advertisements in these comic books are a little harder to figure out, for they are quite diverse. Quite a few of them have to do with bettering appearance, such as a Magic Nail Formula (which appeared in three of them), hairpieces (including a "Romantic-Exciting Fall!"),[4] a device for improving posture, and a hair-do tote bag. These ads seem to be aimed at the teenage readers while an ad for a "fully-furnished doll house with complete doll family"[5] is aimed at the younger readers. But the most interesting ad that I found in one of these comic books was for this type of comic book itself. It offers special rates for a two-year subscription to these magazines that contain "stories dedicated to those who love and are loved," and "stories dedicated to those who want to be loved."[6] Here again is just exactly what a young girl will fall for. The second part, especially, is a direct appeal to the inexperienced young girl.

Thus, it seems to me that all the parts of these magazines or "love" comics are in accord. Every aspect of them seems to be dedicated to the effort of creating a pseudo-lovelife and dream-world for the young girl.

---

[1] *Girls' Romances,* April, 1964.

[2] Fredric Wertham, *Seduction of the Innocent* (New York: Rinehart, 1954), p. 39.

³Wertham, p. 38.
⁴*Falling in Love,* Jan., 1969, and *Secret Hearts,* Jan., 1969, back covers.
⁵*Falling in Love,* inside back cover.
⁶*Girls' Romances,* inside back cover.

Assessment of the First Draft. This is a typical first draft of a source paper. It shows a good bit of thought about the topic (though it has not yet achieved a thesis about the topic), some attention to sources, and some care in the writing. The paper is most clearly a first draft in its emphasis on *description*; the thrust of the paper seems to be that the love comics *exist,* and the purpose of the paper seems to be to show just what they are like. The most important job for the writer now, at the point of serious revision, is to build upon this vivid description, to develop something to say about what is being described.

The draft without a thesis—that is, without something to say about its topic—is open to the most fatal of questions by the reader: "So what?" Notice how aimless this draft appears as you move from paragraph to paragraph. The eighth paragraph begins, "Another interesting aspect of these comic books is ..." (but *why* is it interesting?). The ninth paragraph begins, "The advertisements in these comic books are a little harder to figure out" (but *what* are we trying to figure out?).

Of course, the careful description is a necessary part of the paper, and the detailed clarity of the description suggests that the student is a perceptive writer on the way to a good paper. Something about these comics has seized the writer's imagination, and the description is waiting to be used as evidence for that something. The writer can find out what that missing thesis is by two kinds of reconsideration: returning to the material itself and then to both the old and possible new sources.

The paper suggests that the comics might be in some ways damaging to those who read them, but the idea is only an undeveloped hint in the draft. The first paragraph says the comics are "unrealistic and overly dramatic," although it is not clear why these traits should harm anyone. The last two paragraphs say the young readers will "fall for" the comics' view of love and thus enter a "dream-world"; again, it is not clear that such an exercise of the imagination should be bad, though the tone of the writing implies that *something* bothers the writer about the whole business.

When we turn to the use of the source, we find little help either for the writer or the reader. The writer has picked up a quotation from Fredric Wertham's book on comics and stuck it in the first paragraph; it is used there to demonstrate the power of the comics over children's dreams. Another quotation from Wertham appears in the fourth paragraph to support conclusions about the structure of the story lines in the comics. But what do such quotations mean? What is Wertham's point of view toward the subject, and how (if at all) does the essay writer differ? Where are the signs that the writer has understood and reacted to the source? It appears as if Wertham is used as a source of quotations, rather than as a particular point of view toward the material.

So the job for the writer is to rethink the topic, define the attitude to be taken toward the comics, and understand the source. One of the practical ways to do all three is to find some additional sources that offer some new perspectives on the topic and on the one source already used. Note that it is always a bad idea for a student to use only one source, since it is hard to evaluate that source, particularly if the student is not very familiar with the field.

The "Love Comics" View of Romance: Second Draft (First Paragraph).

In American society, children between the ages of about eight and fifteen are beginning to strive for an identity. They need something to relate to and to give them some sort of identity model to follow. "Adolescence is the age of the final establishment of a dominant positive ego identity. It is then that a future within reach becomes part of the conscious life plan." In establishing this ego identity, adolescents are influenced by such media as television, books, and comic books. Young girls in this age bracket are especially influenced by the "Love" comic books which can be found on the market under such titles as "Girls' Love," "Secret Hearts," "My Love," and others. These romance manuals create an exciting world for the young girl, one that she can put herself into and dream about. Thus, these magazines create a fantasy world, a pseudo love life for the reader. However, they try to convince the reader that they are realistic, true-to-life pictures of everyday occurrences. "Love comics . . . play up the angle that what they depict is real life. 'The girls are real people with real problems and real dramatic confessions,' says a typical issue. What do these 'real' girls want? 'More than anything in the world I wanted glamor, money, adventure. . . .' " The goals that these girls have are material and social; they want to be beautiful, rich and popular. What more could the young reader ask for? The heroine's goals become her goals.

Assessment of the Second Draft. Even though I present here only the first paragraph of this revision, two points are immediately obvious: the author has come up with an interesting idea about her topic, and the paper is at this point so jumbled that the writing is worse than the first draft. Let us consider each of these matters.

The writer, after a good deal of additional thought about the comics, decided that the topic she was really interested in had something to do with the development of a sense of identity in adolescents. Young girls, she had already seen, are apt to use the comics as one way of finding out who they are, most particularly, who they are sexually. The comics provide, as the first draft had made clear, a kind of dreamworld, a way of trying out a model of what it is to be adult and in love. Now, the writer's plan went, the description of the first draft would become the basis for a paper on the role of the comics in the ego development of young women. And the topic would in time lead to a thesis statement, a proposition about the comics, an idea, an attitude to be demonstrated in the paper.

At this point, it was time to return to the library for additional reading. After some discussion with a psychology professor, the writer read through some material on adolescent personality development, focusing finally on Erik Erikson's *Childhood and Society*. She filled several note cards with quotations from Erikson that dealt with exactly the concepts she was pursuing and then went back to the typewriter. All the problems of the first draft were solved: she had a fine and interesting topic, several valuable sources, a nicely detailed first draft for basic evidence, and a good idea of what the thesis statement about the topic would be. All that was left was the typing.

But alas! The new draft turned out to be terribly confused, actually worse than the original, which, though simple, was at least clear. The new material had to be merged not only with the old but with the writer's personal view of the topic. The paragraph of the second draft shows just how much new work is needed. The source is not properly used, not even footnoted properly. The quotation is once again stuck into the text with no indication of what it means. And the new, and substantial, idea of the opening sentence gets lost in the evidence that follows. As so often happens, the movement to a much higher level of complexity in the writing makes a whole new set of demands upon the writer. Yet another draft is necessary.

The "Love Comics" View of Romance: Final Revision.

Children between the ages of about eight and fifteen need something to relate to and to give them some sort of identity model to follow. Erik Erikson pointed this out in *Childhood and Society,* when he said, "Adolescence is the age of the final establishment of a dominant positive ego identity. It is then that a future within reach becomes part of the conscious life plan."[1] Children need to establish this ego identity for themselves before they can work out the rest of their lives. Once they decide who they are and what they want out of life, then they can work towards the accomplishment of this goal. In modern American society the adolescent is influenced in this task by many sources. Among these are parents, educational institutions, peer groups, and the mass media. The media are able to present a very glamorous and exciting picture of what life can be like, and this can be very influential, especially for an adolescent who is attempting to form an ego identity.

One of the mass media that is important to adolescents and pre-adolescents is the comic book. Through these magazines, the young person can find an exciting fantasy world. Young girls often turn to the "love" comic for an answer to what it means to be one of today's teenagers, which includes being beautiful, popular, and romantic. These comic books, which can be found on the market under such titles as "Secret Hearts," "Girls' Love," and "My Love," create a world that a young girl can put herself into and dream about. What's more, they try to convince the reader that they are realistic, true-to-life pictures of everyday occurrences. To do this, they present some common situations that almost anyone can identify with and use them to capture the readers' attention and confidence. For example, almost every issue of these comic books contains one or more heartbreak scenes within the stories. And since almost every young girl feels heartbreak at one time or another she can easily identify with this. Another common feature of the stories involves an argument between a teenager and her mother, who is constantly griping or meddling. Here again, since most adolescents experience parental problems, this is a situation that is easy to identify with. So these magazines lead the young reader to believe that what they represent is a realistic picture of life and love. The cover of *Girls' Romances* asks the reader to "Thrill to the true-to-love story of Wendy Winthrop, television model, as she pursues her heart in and out of the loopholes of her romantic career."[2] But "true-to-love" and true-to-life Wendy Winthrop is a beautiful, voluptuous redhead who always gets the man she wants. And this is not realistic, but yet it is apt to lead the young reader to believe that there is an easy solution to everything, including love and romance, and this, of course, would be a false conclusion. The comic books create a pseudo-love-life for the adolescent. She is urged to identify with the various heroines of the stories, and in doing this, she loses her own identity. She wants to follow the model set by the heroine, and achieve the same goals that she achieves because they would allow her to live a perfect, "happily-ever-after" life. In one issue of *Secret Hearts,* the heroine exclaims, "More than anything in the world I want glamor, money, adventure . . . !"[3] What exciting goals these are for the adolescent reader! She, too, wants to be beautiful, rich, and popular. In the world of these comics, there is nothing more to ask for. Those goals of the heroine are presented as being the only ones worth working for; intellectual or social responsibilities play no part here at all. The comics seem to be saying that if a teenage girl is rich and beautiful, she will therefore be popular, and this is all she needs to succeed in life. This, of course, is not always the case but it is what the reader is led to believe and would like to believe. Thus, she is presented with a false identity model to follow which urges her towards superficial goals.

The stories presented in these magazines further their unreality. First of all, the only unattractive or homely person that is ever seen is a parent or another unimportant figure. Every major character is good-looking and well-endowed. Special attention is given to physical, sexual characteristics. This seems to change the dreamworld into something that is not altogether innocent. Dr. Frederic Wertham, who has studied the effects of comic books on children, sees their sexual implication as distinctly unhealthy: "Comic books stimulate children sexually. That is an elementary fact of my research. In comic books over and over again, in pictures and text, . . . attention is drawn to sexual characteristics and sexual actions."[4] This is quite obvious, not only from all the attention given to physical characteristics and the many passionate love scenes, but also, as Dr. Wertham says, from the text itself. One heroine in *Secret Heart* speaks of being ". . . in his arms, powerless to resist";[5] another from *Girls' Love* says, ". . . his demanding kisses wanted me to really be a *woman* . . . for the first time . . ."[6] One heroine even reveals a dream she has had, saying, ". . . the stranger 'invaded' my bedroom . . . I imagined my lips throbbing with the sudden surge of blood as his hungry mouth came nearer . . . nearer . . . nearer. . . ."[7] Dr. Wertham implies that scenes and language of this kind are harmful to the adolescent mind. But it seems to me that this problem is not nearly as serious as the unreality of these magazines. Dr. Wertham does not seem to see that what these comic books represent is not realistic and in this lies their real harm.

Another version of ugliness, the poor person, is also rarely shown. Every major character is beautifully dressed and neatly groomed and drives a modern sports car. And it has to be this way. If the comic is going to be an idealistic dream world for the reader, then there can be no poor people in this world. That would destroy its perfection. So here again, the comics are portraying an unrealistic situation and passing it off as real.

The plots of the various "love" stories seem to be very much the same. For example, Beverly Bennett, a professional model, is torn between the two men in her life, Don Larrimer, her photographer, and Paul Kent, a male model. Through a series of adventures, conflicts, and indecisions, Beverly finally chooses Paul as her one and only love.[8] Very rarely is there an unhappy ending. In most cases the heroine gets the man she wants and everything is summed up with a kiss. This way, the reader can feel happy and fulfilled, as if she too has found the man she loves. An unhappy ending would probably leave her with feelings of discouragement and frustration and she would soon turn to some other means of supplying herself with a happy and successful "love life."

The world of the "love" comic book is an exciting and romantic one and, thus, sets up goals that are just what the adolescent female reader wants or, at least, thinks she wants. But these can be harmful goals because they are, in so many cases, unrealistic, unattainable, and what's more, unworthy. Not everyone can reach physical perfection and material and social success, but the comic leads the reader to believe that this is really possible. And when she finally realizes that this is not possible, she may be very disappointed. The impressionable adolescent girl wants desperately to find out what love is all about and in turning to one, easy source of information, she sets up an unrealistic, easily destroyed dreamworld for herself. And with the destruction of the dreamworld comes the destruction of the identity model and all of its exciting goals. And so the adolescent is left back where she started: in search of a positive ego identity. And so she will try a new source for her day dreams, perhaps turning to other, more sophisticated magazines as she grows older. But in all of them she can find an ideal dreamworld to put herself into in order to find, at last, happiness and satisfaction in her "love life."

---

[1] Erik H. Erikson, *Childhood and Society* (New York: W. W. Norton, 1963), p. 306.

[2] *Girls' Romances,* April, 1964.

[3] *Secret Hearts,* March, 1971.

[4] Fredric Wertham, *Seduction of the Innocent* (New York: Rinehart, 1954), p. 175.

[5] *Secret Hearts,* March, 1971.

[6] *Girls' Love,* April, 1971.

[7] *Ibid.*

[8] *My Love,* May, 1971.

Assessment of the Final Revision. The most important change in this much improved revision is in the thesis statement, the author's statement of her attitude toward and conclusions about the comics. Their "real harm," we are told, comes from the false identity models they contain and the "unrealistic, unattainable, and unworthy" goals they provide. Whereas the first draft gave interesting but pointless description, we now have a thoughtful assessment of the effects of the comics on adolescent girls; the description now helps the writer make her case. The essay is now not so much "about" the comics as it is about growing up, and the author seems clearheaded and mature about what it means to grow up.

The ten descriptive paragraphs of the first draft have become six analytic paragraphs in this third draft, even though the third draft is one and a half times longer. The six paragraphs are simply organized: after an introduction to the topic that focuses on the issue of adolescent ego formation and the role of the mass media in that formation, there are five paragraphs showing the "unreality" of the love comics (particularly the characters and the plot situations) and a conclusion demonstrating the harm the comics can do. The author stays cool— she, in fact, rebukes Dr. Wertham for a rather oversexed reading of the comics—and clearheaded. These are *comics,* after all, and hardly earthshaking; they are only interesting, in fact, because the writer has so much to say about the important subject of what it means to grow up. So no paragraph, no description, no quotation is in the essay only for its own sake; everything must contribute to the point being demonstrated.

The writer now takes seriously her obligation to *demonstrate* her ideas, rather than merely to assert them. The descriptions from the comics now serve as evidence for the "unreality" of the world they model. Furthermore, the characters and their glamorous activities are not shown to be a harmless fantasy but rather a damaging dreamworld for people at a critical stage of growth.

The sources here are more effectively used than we have seen in the earlier drafts, though some problems still remain. Dr. Wertham's book is now set in the context of this essay and his own perspective. We are told something about him and his work (he "has studied the effects of comic books on children"), we see where the writer agrees with him ("This is quite obvious . . . as Dr. Wertham says, from the text itself"), and where she disagrees ("Dr. Wertham does not seem to see . . ."). Although we might want to know even more about him (for instance, do his colleagues respect his opinion?), we at least can see how the writer is considering his ideas and where she shares, or does not share, his point of view. The quotation from Erik Erikson is less successfully integrated into the writing, even though his contribution to it is central. The first paragraph is not quite clear about who he is, even though the writer does seem to distinguish his ideas, in the quotation marks, from hers.

This third draft, then, represents good student work on a source paper, though more likely in the "B" than in the "A" range of grades. The research remains very thin indeed, with only the two books cited, and no periodicals reviewed at all. It would be very interesting to see what a few other (and more recent) psychological views of these comics might have to say. Do they have defenders, or at least are there some who find adolescent daydreaming a constructive activity? How do these comics relate to traditional myths or to the fairy tales that Bruno Bettelheim has recently analyzed and praised?

Despite its insufficiencies, the third draft remains well written and interesting, with a defined thesis about an important topic. It uses its sources with competence and presents evidence to demonstrate its ideas. While some writers would see this draft as only a beginning, on the way to a full-scale essay, many American college instructors would be very pleased to see their freshmen hand in work as good as this.

A student who has learned in a composition course to develop writing from the personal experience tasks that open this chapter to the analytic source paper we have just examined has learned a great deal indeed. If each step along the way is accompanied by small group discussion of early drafts, based upon scoring guides for assessing responses to the particular topics, the student has also learned enough about the writing process to keep improving. Assessing the quality of early drafts should become so much a part of the writing process that grading and revising lose much of their terror and uncertainty. When our teaching leads students to clear definitions of topics, well-stated criteria for assessment, and understandable procedures for revision, we can feel comfortable about our classroom teaching. The more we know, and the more we help our students know about assessing writing, the more effective our teaching will become.

References

Applebee, A. N. *Tradition and Reform in the Teaching of English: A History.* Urbana, Ill.: National Council of Teachers of English, 1974.

Applebee, A. N. "Teaching Conditions in Secondary School English: Highlights of a Survey." *English Journal,* 1978, *67* (3), 57–65.

Applebee, A. N. *Writing in the Secondary School English and the Content Areas.* Urbana, Ill.: National Council of Teachers of English, 1981.

Applebee, A. N. *Contexts for Learning to Write: Studies of Secondary School Instruction.* Norwood, N.J.: ABLEX, 1984.

Barth, J. *The Friday Book.* New York: Putnam's, 1984.

Bereiter, C., Scardamalia, M., and Bracewell, R. "An Applied Cognitive-Developmental Approach to Writing Research." Paper presented at annual meeting of the American Educational Research Association, San Francisco, April 1979.

Bettelheim, B. *The Uses of Enchantment: The Meaning and Importance of Fairy Tales.* New York: Knopf, 1977.

Braddock, R., Lloyd-Jones, R., and Schoer, L. *Research in Written Composition.* Urbana, Ill.: National Council of Teachers of English, 1963.

Breland, H. *Group Comparisons for the TSWE.* Research Bulletin RB-77-15. Princeton, N.J.: College Entrance Examination Board, 1977a.

Breland, H. *A Study of College English Placement and the Test of Standard Written English.* Research and Development Report RDR-76-77. Princeton, N.J.: College Entrance Examination Board, 1977b.

Breland, H., and Gaynor, J. "Comparison of Direct and Indirect Assessments of Writing Skill." *Journal of Educational Measurement,* 1979, *16* (2), 119-127.

Britton, J. *Language and Learning.* Coral Gables, Fla.: University of Miami Press, 1970.

Britton, J., and others. *The Development of Writing Abilities (11-18).* New York: Macmillan, 1975.

Bronowski, J. *The Common Sense of Science.* Cambridge, Mass.: Harvard University Press, 1966.

Bruner, J. *The Process of Education.* Cambridge, Mass.: Harvard University Press, 1960.

California State University English Tests. Long Beach: California State University, 1983.

Christensen, F. *Notes Toward a New Rhetoric.* New York: Harper & Row, 1967.

Conference on College Composition and Communication (CCCC) Committee on Teaching and Its Evaluation in Composition. "Evaluating Instruction in Writing: Approaches and Instruments." *College Composition and Communication,* 1982, *33* (2), 213-229.

Conlan, G. *How the Essay in the CEEB English Test Is Scored.* Princeton, N.J.: Educational Testing Service, 1976.

Cooper, C., and Odell, L. (Eds.). *Evaluating Writing: Describing, Measuring, Judging.* Urbana, Ill.: National Council of Teachers of English, 1977.

Cooper, C., and Odell, L. (Eds.). *Research on Composing: Points of Departure.* Urbana, Ill.: National Council of Teachers of English, 1978.

Corbett, E. P. J. *Classical Rhetoric for the Modern Student.* New York: Oxford University Press, 1965.

Daley, J., and Miller, M. "The Empirical Development of an Instrument to Measure Writing Apprehension." *Research in the Teaching of English,* 1975, *9,* 250–256.

Davis, B., Scriven, M., and Thomas, S. *The Evaluation of Composition Instruction.* Pt. Reyes, Calif.: Edgepress, 1981.

Derrida, J. *Of Grammatology.* (G. Spivak, Trans.) Baltimore, Md.: Johns Hopkins University Press, 1976. (Originally published 1967.)

Diederich, P. *Measuring Growth in English.* Urbana, Ill.: National Council of Teachers of English, 1974.

Emig, J. *The Composing Process of Twelfth Graders.* Urbana, Ill.: National Council of Teachers of English, 1971.

Fish, S. *Is There a Text in This Class? The Authority of Interpretive Communities.* Cambridge, Mass.: Harvard University Press, 1980.

Florio, S. "Learning to Write in the Classroom Community: A Case Study." Paper presented at annual meeting of the American Educational Research Association, San Francisco, April 1979. (Available from the Institute for Research on Teaching, College of Education, Michigan State University, East Lansing, Mich. 48824.)

Florio, S., and Clark, C. M. "The Functions of Writing in an Elementary Classroom." *Research in the Teaching of English,* 1982, *16* (2), 115–130.

Flower, L. "Writer-Based Prose: A Cognitive Basis for Problems in Writing." *College English,* 1979, *41,* 19–37.

Flower, L., and Hayes, J. "The Dynamics of Composing: Making Plans and Juggling Constraints." In L. Gregg and E. Sternberg (Eds.), *Cognitive Processes in Writing.* Hillsdale, N.J.: Erlbaum, 1980.

Flower, L., and Hayes, J. "Plans that Guide the Composing Process." In C. Frederiksen and J. Dominic (Eds.), *Writing: The Nature, Development, and Teaching of Written Communication.* Hillsdale, N.J.: Erlbaum, 1981.

Godshalk, F., Swineford, E., and Coffman, W. *The Measurement of Writing Ability.* New York: College Entrance Examination Board, 1966.

Gould, S. J. *The Mismeasure of Man.* New York: Norton, 1981.

Hayes, J., and Flower, L. "Protocol Analysis of Writing Processes." Paper presented at annual meeting of the American Educational Research Association, Toronto, April 1978.

Hayes, J., and Flower, L. "Writing as Problem-Solving." Paper presented at annual meeting of the American Educational Research Association, San Francisco, April 1979.

Henry, J. *Culture Against Man.* New York: Random House, 1963.

Holland, M. "Psychological Approaches to Issues in Writing: Writing Anxiety." Paper presented at conference on the State of the Art in the Teaching of Writing, California State College, San Bernardino, July 1979.

Holland, N. *Five Readers Reading.* New Haven: Yale University Press, 1975.

Hollingsworth, A. "Beyond Literacy." Paper presented at fall conference of the California State University English Council, Sausalito, October 1972.

Hunt, K. W. *Differences in Grammatical Structures Written at Three Grade Levels.* Cooperative Research Project No. 1998. Washington, D.C.: U.S. Office of Education, 1964.

Hunt, K. W. *Syntactic Maturity in School Children and Adults.* Monographs of the Society for Research in Child Development, No. 35. Chicago: University of Chicago Press, 1970.

Hunt, K. W. "Early Blooming and Late Blooming Syntactic Structures." In C. Cooper and L. Odell (Eds.), *Evaluating Writing: Describing, Measuring, Judging.* Urbana, Ill.: National Council of Teachers of English, 1977.

Iser, W. *The Implied Reader: Patterns of Communication in Prose Fiction from Bunyan to Beckett.* Baltimore, Md.: Johns Hopkins University Press, 1974.

Kaplan, A. "The Aesthetics of the Popular Arts." *Journal of Aesthetics and Art Criticism,* 1966, *24,* 351–364.

Kinneavy, J. *A Theory of Discourse.* Englewood Cliffs, N.J.: Prentice-Hall, 1971.

Kitzhaber, A. R. *Themes, Theories, and Therapy: The Teaching of Writing in College.* New York: McGraw-Hill, 1963.

Koch, K. *Wishes, Lies and Dreams: Teaching Children to Write Poetry.* New York: Chelsea House, 1970.

Kohlberg, L. *The Meaning and Measurement of Moral Development.* Worcester, Mass.: Clark University Press, 1981.

Krashen, S., Scarcella, R., and Long, M. (Eds.). *Child-Adult Differences in Second Language Acquisition.* Rowley, Mass.: Newbury House, 1982.

Kroll, B. "Cognitive Egocentrism and the Problem of Audience Awareness in Written Discourse." *Research in the Teaching of English,* 1978, *12,* 269-281.

Kuhn, T. *The Structure of Scientific Revolutions.* (2nd ed.) Chicago: University of Chicago Press, 1970.

Lederman, M. J., Ryzewic, S. R., and Ribaudo, M. *Assessment and Improvement of the Academic Skills of Entering Freshman Students: A National Survey.* New York: Instructional Resource Center, City University of New York, 1983.

Leitch, V. "Two Poststructuralist Modes of (Inter)Textuality." *Critical Texts,* 1982, *2,* 3-5.

Lloyd-Jones, R. "Primary Trait Scoring." In C. Cooper and L. Odell (Eds.), *Evaluating Writing: Describing, Measuring, Judging.* Urbana, Ill.: National Council of Teachers of English, 1977.

Mellon, J. C. *Transformational Sentence-Combining: A Method for Enhancing the Development of Syntactic Fluency in English Composition.* NCTE Research Report No. 10. Urbana, Ill.: National Council of Teachers of English, 1969.

Meyers, G. D. "The Phenomenology of Composition: Applications of Reader-Response Criticism to the Teaching of Writing." Paper presented at annual meeting of the Conference on College Composition and Communication, San Francisco, March 1982.

Moffett, J. *A Student-Centered Language Arts Curriculum, Grades K-13: A Handbook for Teachers.* Boston: Houghton Mifflin, 1968.

Myers, M. *A Procedure for Writing Assessment and Holistic Scoring.* Urbana, Ill.: National Council of Teachers of English, 1980.

Najimy, N. *Measure for Measure: A Guidebook for Evaluating Students' Expository Writing.* Urbana, Ill.: National Council of Teachers of English, 1981.

National Assessment of Educational Progress. *Writing Achievement, 1969-1979: Results from the Third National Writing*

Assessment. Vols. 1-3. Denver, Colo.: Education Commission of the States, 1980.

O'Hare, F. *Sentence Combining: Improving Student Writing Without Formal Grammar Instruction.* NCTE Research Report No. 15. Urbana, Ill.: National Council of Teachers of English, 1973.

Ohmann, R. *English in America: A Radical View of the Profession.* New York: Oxford University Press, 1976.

Ong, W. J. "The Writer's Audience Is Always a Fiction." *PMLA,* 1975, *90* (1), 9-21.

Palmer, D. J. *The Rise of English Studies.* New York: Oxford University Press, 1965.

Perl, S. "The Composing Process of Unskilled College Writers." *Research in the Teaching of English,* 1979, *13,* 317-336.

Perry, W. G. *Forms of Intellectual and Ethical Development in the College Years: A Scheme.* New York: Holt, Rinehart and Winston, 1968.

Piaget, J. *The Language and Thought of the Child.* (M. Gabain, Trans.) New York: New American Library, 1955. (Originally published 1926.)

Piaget, J. *Comments on Vygotsky's Critical Remarks Concerning "The Language and Thought of the Child" and "Judgment and Reasoning in the Child."* (A. Parsons, Trans.) Cambridge, Mass.: MIT Press, 1962.

Purnell, R. "A Survey of the Testing of Writing Proficiency in College: A Progress Report." *College Composition and Communication,* 1982, *33,* 407-410.

Rose, M. *Writer's Block: The Cognitive Dimension.* Carbondale: Southern Illinois University Press, 1983.

Sanders, S., and Littlefield, J. "Perhaps Test Essays Can Reflect Significant Improvement in Freshman Composition: Report on a Successful Attempt." *Research in the Teaching of English,* 1975, *9,* 145-153.

Schorer, M. "Technique as Discovery." *Hudson Review,* 1948, *1* (1), 67-87.

Scriven, M. "Goal-Free Evaluation." In E. R. House (Ed.), *School Evaluation.* Berkeley, Calif.: McCutchan, 1973.

Shaughnessy, M. *Errors and Expectations: A Guide for the*

Teacher of Basic Writing. New York: Oxford University Press, 1977.

Smith, M. *Reducing Writing Apprehension.* Urbana, Ill.: National Council of Teachers of English, 1984.

Sommers, N. "Responding to Student Writing." *College Composition and Communication,* 1982, *33,* 148–156.

Spandel, V., and Stiggins, R. *Direct Measures of Writing Skill: Issues and Applications.* Portland, Ore.: Northwest Regional Educational Laboratory, 1980.

Staton, J., and others. *Dialogue Journal Writing as a Communicative Event.* Vol. 2. Research Paper No. NIE-G-80-0122. Washington, D.C.: Center for Applied Linguistics, 1982.

"Teaching and Learning the Art of Composition: The Bay Area Writing Project." *Carnegie Quarterly,* 1979, *27* (2), 7.

Vygotsky, L. S. *Thought and Language.* (E. Hangmann and G. Vakar, Trans.) Cambridge, Mass.: MIT Press, 1962. (Originally published 1934.)

White, E. (Ed.). *The Writer's Control of Tone: Readings, with Analysis, for Thinking and Writing about Personal Experience.* New York: Norton, 1970.

White, E. (Ed.). *The Pop Culture Tradition: Readings with Analysis for Writing.* New York: Norton, 1972.

White, E. (Ed.). *Comparison and Contrast: The California State University Freshman English Equivalency Examination.* Vols. 1–8. Long Beach: California State University, 1973–1981. (Available through ERIC, 1111 Kenyon Road, Urbana, Ill. 61801.)

White, E. (Ed.). *The Best of 495: Selected Student Writing from the Upper-Division Expository Writing Program.* San Bernardino: California State College, 1983.

White, E. "Writing as a Paradigm for Thinking." *Selections,* 1984, *1,* 3–7.

White, E., and Polin, L. *Research in Effective Teaching of Writing: Final Report on Phase 1.* NIE-G-81-0011. Washington, D.C.: National Institute of Education, 1983. (Available through ERIC, 1111 Kenyon Road, Urbana, Ill. 61801.)

White, E., and Polin, L. *Research in Effective Teaching of Writ-

ing: Final Report. NIE-G-81-0011. Washington, D.C.: National Institute of Education, forthcoming.

White, E., and Thomas, L. "Racial Minorities and Writing Skills Assessment in The California State University and Colleges." *College English,* 1981, *42,* 276-283.

Whiteman, M. F. (Ed.). *Writing: The Nature, Development, and Teaching of Written Communication.* Vol. 1. *Variation in Writing: Functional and Linguistic-Cultural Differences.* Hillsdale, N.J.: Erlbaum, 1981.

Williams, J. "Defining Complexity." *College English,* 1979, *40* (6), 595-609.

Winterowd, W. R. *Rhetoric and Writing.* Boston: Allyn & Bacon, 1965.

Witte, S., and Faigley, L. *Evaluating College Writing Programs.* Carbondale: Southern Illinois University Press, 1983.

Witte, S., and others. *The Empirical Development of an Instrument for Reporting Course and Teacher Effectiveness in College Writing Classes.* Writing Program Assessment Project, Technical Report No. 3. Austin: University of Texas, 1981a.

Witte, S., and others. *A National Survey of College and University Writing Program Directors.* Writing Program Assessment Project, Technical Report No. 2. Austin: University of Texas, 1981b.

Young, R. E., Becker, A. L., and Pike, K. L. *Rhetoric: Discovery and Change.* New York: Harcourt Brace Jovanovich, 1970.

Index

A

Alloway, E., 149
Analytic scoring, 29-30; classroom problems and uses of, 121-123, 255; sample scale, 124
Anchor papers. *See* Sample papers
Applebee, A., 36
Aristotle, 116, 244
Audience, 253

B

Barth, J., 251
Barthes, R., 90
Basic skills in writing, 8, 10, 17
Bay Area Writing Project (National Writing Project), 5, 149, 248-249; evaluation of, 206
Becker, A., 176
Bereiter, C., 246
"Betterburg" research project, 183
Bettelheim, B., 289

Bias in writing tests, 71-83
Bleich, D., 90
Braddock, R., 175, 240
Bradley, R., 180
Britton, J., 57, 89, 116, 182, 246
Bronowski, J., 139
Brown, R., 243
Bruner, J., 117, 246

C

California State University, the, 5, 37, 40-41, 75, 208; English Equivalency Examination, 27, 63, 117, 149, 179; English Placement Test, 72-73, 149; San Bernardino, 138
California, University of, at Berkeley, 248
Camp, R., 243, 289
Carnegie Foundation, 206
Chief reader, 25, 154-155
Christensen, F., 145, 147, 176

Classroom activities. *See* Essay topics; Revision; Scoring guide

Coffman, W., 233

Cognitive development, and writing proficiency, 56-57, 246-247

College Entrance Examination Board, 20, 81, 235; Advanced Placement Program, 23, 63, 220; College-Level Examination Program, 63, 235; Scholastic Aptitude Test (SAT), 29, 38, 66, 80, 185, 198, 232; Test of Standard Written English (TSWE), 72-78; *The Measurement of Writing Ability*, 20, 82, 233

Combined scores, 233

Community Colleges, 38, 49

Comprehensive Test of Basic Skills, 36

Computers. *See* Word processing

Conference on College Composition and Communication, 19; Committee on Teaching and its Evaluation in Composition, 208

Conlan, G., 149

Cooper, C., 26, 124, 143-144, 240, 246

Corbett, E., 89

Costs of writing tests, 21, 166, 220-221, 224-225

Criterion referencing, and holistic scoring, 29, 125, 228-229

Criterion-referenced testing, 63-68

D

Dartmouth College, 196-197

Davis, B., 206, 209, 211

Derrida, J., 89, 94

Diederich, P., 22-23, 178, 185

Donald Duck, 273, 276

E

Edgepress, 206

Educational Testing Service, 19-22, 143-144, 149, 236, 243; Advanced Placement Program, 23, 63, 220; Berkeley readings, 161;

College-Level Examination Program, 63, 235; essay reader pay, 154; National Teachers Examination, 35; Test of Standard Written English, 72-78. *See also* College Entrance Examination Board

Emig, J., 89, 190-191, 246

English as a socializing discipline, 11-13

English as an individualizing discipline, 13-17

Erikson, E., 283-288

Error analysis, 175-176

Essay topics: as a form of writing, 119; characteristics of, 110; clarity problems with, 110-111; classroom development of, 114; correlation of different modes of, 117; development of, 108; freedom and choice in, 104-107; pre-testing of, 102-112, 114; sample, 53, 74, 106-107, 126, 133, 139, 252, 257-258, 262, 264, 271-272; samples with validity problems, 102, 111-114; types of, 116-119; validity problems in a single-mode test, 118

Evaluating College Writing Programs, 207-208, 211-212

Evaluating the teaching of composition, 208

Evaluation of Composition Instruction, 206-212

Evaluator, selection of, 210-211

F

Faculty development: by a common writing examination, 48, 166

Faigley, L., 207-213

Fish, S., 24, 89-90, 96-99, 163

Five-paragraph theme, 36

Flower, L., 56, 89, 191, 192-193

Fund for the Improvement of Postsecondary Education (FIPSE), 207

G

Galbraith, J., 267
General education: and upper-division writing requirements, 49
General Education Development Program (GED), 35
General impression scoring, 22
Georgia, University System of, 37, 40, 67
Godshalk, F., 20, 82, 233
Gould, S., 71, 185
Grading. *See* Scoring guide
Graduate Management Admissions Council, 50
Gray, J., 248

H

Hayes, J., 191
Hemisphericity, 171, 193, 244
Henry, J., 262
Heuristics, 176, 244
High School, 11
Holistic scoring, 18-33; abuses of, 30-31, 150, 163-164; and the interpretive community, 96-99; arrangement of test booklets for, 157; chief aide for, 156; costs of, 21, 166, 220-221, 224-225; distinguished from analytic and primary trait scoring, 23, 120, 148; distinguished from general impression scoring, 22-23; facilities for, 151-152; history of, 19-27; limitations of, 27-28; materials for, 157; organizing and managing, 149-169; pace of reading, 165-166; passing score decision at, 231; personnel for, 153-157; randomizing and batching test booklets for, 158; reliability of, 27, 177-180; selection of sample (anchor) papers for, 159-160; system for concealing first reading scores at, 160-161; test booklet design for, 158
Holistic scoring guide: classroom use of, 126, 139, 148, 251-289; for advanced college students, 140; for entering college students, 126-127; for students completing college composition, 133-136
Holland, M., 175, 192
Holland, N., 90
Hollingsworth, A., 10
Hunt, K., 173-174

I

Iser, W., 89, 94

K

Kaplan, A., 273-276
Keynes, J., 99
Kinneavy, J., 116, 143, 246
Kitzhaber, A., 197
Koch, K., 57
Kohlberg, L., 117
Krashen, S., 89
Kroll, B., 183
Kuhn, T., 240

L

Law School Admission Test (LSAT), 50
Lederman, M. J., 38
Leitch, V., 90-93
Literary theory, 84-99; new criticism (formalism), 85-88, 93-94; poststructuralism, 89-97; poststructuralism as resistance movement to formalism, 92-94
Littlefield, J., 243
Lloyd-Jones, R., 116-117, 143, 240, 246
London Schools Council, 182

M

Matrix testing, 218
Medical College Admission Test (MCAT), 50, 58
Mellon, J., 173
Meyers, G., 94

Miller, H., 90
Milton, J., 119
Multiple-choice testing, 20, 30, 34-
    35, 50, 61; in program evalua-
    tion, 198-199; sample item with
    validity problems, 65-66; score
    use and standard error of meas-
    urement of, 232-234; versus es-
    say testing of writing, 67-71

N

National Assessment of Educational
    Progress (NAEP), 19, 23, 116,
    143-144, 243
National Council of Teachers of
    English (NCTE), 175, 192, 208
National Institute of Education,
    208
National Teachers Examination, 35,
    235
National Writing Project. See Bay
    Area Writing Project
New criticism (formalism). See Lit-
    erary theory
New Jersey, Department of Higher
    Education, 5, 149
New York, the City University of,
    5, 37-38, 176
New York State Regents Examina-
    tions, 40
Norm-referenced testing, 63-68. See
    also Multiple-choice testing; Cri-
    terion-referenced testing

O

"Objective" testing. See Multiple-
    choice testing
Odell, L., 26, 143-144, 240, 246
O'Hare, F., 173-174
Ohmann, R., 10
Ong, W. J., 94
Orwell, G., 113

P

Palmer, D., 10
Peanuts, 273, 276

Peer evaluation of writing, 257,
    268
Perl, S., 89
Perry, W., 117
Piaget, J., 56, 117, 118, 246
Pike, K., 176
Plagiarism, 270, 274
Polin, L., 48, 132, 144, 208
Poststructuralism. See Literary the-
    ory
Pre-testing, 102, 112, 114. See also
    Essay topics
Primary trait scoring, 23, 142
Primary trait scoring guide, 145;
    classroom use of, 144-148
Process theories of writing, 170,
    190-193, 242-244
Program evaluation, 195-215; by
    experts, 201-202; pre-test/post-
    test model, 195-200; sources and
    references, 205-209; steps in,
    209-214; by surveys, 203; by
    varied measures, 203-205
Prompts. See Essay topics
Purnell, R., 19
Purposes of writing tests, 59-83; ad-
    mission, 50-56; course equiva-
    lency, 62; graduation, 40-50;
    placement, 62; proficiency, 34-
    58, 60-62

Q

Quarterly Review of Doublespeak,
    174
Question leader. See Chief reader

R

Randomizing and batching test
    booklets, 158
Range-finders. See Sample papers
Rankin, D., 132, 145
Reader drift, 25, 154, 164
Readers: calibration of, 25, 164;
    choice of, 156; qualifications
    for, 156
Reader's Guide, 269
Reliability, 22-29, 177-180; and

different scoring scales, 178; English Equivalency Examination study of, 179-180; need for independent scores for, 230-231
Reporting test results, 221-222, 234-236
Research in Effective Teaching of Writing. See White, E.
Response to student writing. *See* Scoring guide
Revision, 7, 243, 268, 278
Ribaudo, M., 38
Riesman, D., 267
Rose, M., 101, 175
Rubric. *See* Scoring guide
Ryzewic, S., 38

S

Sample papers, 24-25, 53-55, 254-255, 259-261, 265-267, 278-289; score of five (on six-point scale), 129; score of two (on six-point scale), 128; selection of, 159-160
Sampling problems in research, 192-193
Sanders, S., 243
Scale matching, 233
Scholastic Aptitude Test. *See* College Entrance Examination Board
Schorer, M., 85-87
Schroeder, P., 273n
Score reporting, 221-222, 234-236
Scoring guide, 24, 227-228, 261; all purpose, 228, 231; classroom samples of, 256, 261, 277; classroom use of, 130-147; and the interpretive community, 98; preparation of, 159; specifications for, 133-134. *See also* Analytic scoring; Holistic scoring guide; Primary trait scoring guide
Scoring scales, 125-126
Scriven, M., 206, 209-211
Seder, A., 149
Sentence combining, 173-174
Shaughnessy, M., 87, 176

Shoer, L., 240
Sloan Foundation, 241
Smith, M., 175, 192
Sommers, N., 93, 95, 97, 123
Sources, responsible use of, 269-278
Spandel, V., 35
Spelling, 12
Standard Error of Measurement, 29, 232
Staton, J., 183
Stiggens, R., 35
Subskills in writing, 247
Swineford, E., 233
Syntactic maturity, 173-174

T

Table Leader, 25, 152, 155
Tagmemics, 176
Teaching to the test, 59-60
Test development and classroom teaching, 114-115, 251-289
Test development committee, 108-110
Test officers, 226
Testing: and classroom teaching, 6-8, 248-250, 251-289; bias in, 71-83, 247-248; and cognitive development, 246; and computers, 244; costs of, 21, 166, 220-225; evaluation of, 222, 236-237; misused, 1, 234-236; and modes of discourse, 245-246, 291; political pitfalls in, 237-238; specifications for, 219. *See also* Educational Testing Service; Essay topics; Holistic scoring; Multiple-choice testing; Purposes of writing tests
Texas, University of, at Austin, 207, 211
Thomas, Leon, 72
Thomas, Lewis, 267
Thomas, S., 206, 209, 211
Time lines, 222
Tone, 253
T-unit. *See* Hunt, K.

V

Validity, 111, 184-189; concurrent,
185; construct, 188; content,
186-187; face, 186; predictive,
185-186, 236
Voice magazine, 173
Vygotsky, L., 246

W

WANDAH, 245
Wertham, F., 282, 288
White, E., 50; *Comparison and Con-
trast*, 27, 117, 180, 245; *Re-
search in Effective Teaching of
Writing*, 48, 132, 144, 208-209;
The Pop Culture Tradition,
273n; *The Writer's Control of
Tone*, 258
Whiteman, M., 248
Williams, J., 174
Wilson, W., 47
Winterowd, R., 89
Witte, S., 207-213
Word processing, 171, 244-245
Writer's Workbench, 245
Writing across the curriculum, 39,

46-50, 84, 141, 184, 204-205,
241; value of scoring guides in,
142
Writing apprehension, 101, 175,
192
Writing process research, 170, 190-
193, 242-244
Writing proficiency at the university level, 37-50; campus testing
programs, 41; course certification, 43; general faculty involvement, 46; multicampus testing,
39; test with course option, 45
Writing proficiency testing for admission to professional schools,
50-56
Writing Program Administrators,
Council of, 202
Writing research, 170-194; as communicative act, 181-184; as mental process, 189-192; problems
for teachers, 170; sampling problems in, 192-193; text based,
172-177

Y

Young, R., 89, 176